GEOPOLITICS OF
HIMALAYAN REGION

Cultural, Political and Strategic Dimensions

GEOPOLITICS OF HIMALAYAN REGION

Cultural, Political and Strategic Dimensions

Editors

Alok Bansal

Aayushi Ketkar

PENTAGON PRESS LLP

Geopolitics of Himalayan Region: Cultural, Political and Strategic Dimensions
Editors: Alok Bansal and Aayushi Ketkar

ISBN 978-93-86618-68-9

First Published in 2019

Disclaimer: The views expressed in this book are those of the authors and do not necessarily reflect those of India Foundation.

Published by
PENTAGON PRESS LLP
206, Peacock Lane, Shahpur Jat
New Delhi-110049
Phones: 011-64706243, 26491568
Telefax: 011-26490600
email: rajan@pentagonpress.in
website: www.pentagonpress.in

Printed at Aegean Offset Printers, Greater Noida, U.P.

Contents

Foreword

अस्त्युत्तरस्यां दिशि देवतात्मा हिमालयो नाम नगाधिराजः।
पूर्वापरौ तोयनिधी विगाह्य स्थितः पृथिव्या इव मानदण्डः॥ १-१

astyuttarasyāṁ diśi devatātmā himālayo nāma nagādhirājaḥ |
pūrvāparau toyanidhī vigāhya sthitaḥ pṛthivyā iva mānadaṇḍaḥ || 1-1

On the northern frontier of this country that forms the heartland of gods, intercalating himself into eastern and western oceans like a measuring stick of earth, there stands the sovereign of snowy mountains renowned as Mt. Himalaya.

This is how famous Sanskrit poet Kalidas described the great Himalayan mountains in his treatise 'Kumarasambhavam'. The mighty mountains to the north of India are not just geography; they are spirituality too. They are the very identity of Bharat – the provider, the protector and the liberator.

In its lap grew a mighty civilisation, spreading its perfumed aroma to the farthest corners of the world from Malaya to Mexico. In its embrace flourished gods and angels; saints and sages; philosophers and pilgrims. The divine energy that emanated from them meditating in the shadow of those mighty mountains has brought liberation, peace and glory to generations of humanity.

The Himalayas are the abode of spirituality, culture and religion. They are also home to unfathomable riches of nature. The rivers that take birth in the vast glaciers of the Himalayan mountains provide sustenance to more than 40 per cent of humanity. They manage ecological balance and protect in their bosom a huge biodiversity and animal kingdom.

But that is not all about the great mountains. They are today the world's most significant geo-strategic entity, the other being the mighty Indian Ocean. Between the two live the world's most ancient civilizational peoples, from China to India to Indonesia.

Mighty Himalayas have long been seen as nature's gift to the Indic civilization in terms of its protective value. However, a time has come for all the countries in the Himalayan region – Bharat, Nepal, Bhutan, Myanmar, Tibet, China etc – to look at the Himalayas as not just from the prism of security but as an opportunity as well. The Himalayas, instead of becoming barriers, can become a gateway for connectivity, commerce and confluence.

Thus, the modern scholarship needs to look at this great historical mountain range from the prism of opportunity as well. While appreciating the challenges that rise today in the world's most important geo-strategic region – security, strategic and environmental – it is important to keep in mind that overcoming those challenges is a Himalayan task, and requires all the nations in the region to go 'beyond' their peaks.

Alok Bansal and Aayushi Ketkar have brought together a thought-provoking compendium of articles by eminent scholars that deal with geo-strategic challenges of the Himalayan region. I am sure the authors have highlighted the need for 'going beyond', in search of answers to the challenges and opportunities for coming together of the peoples of the region.

Towards that end, constituting a Trans-Himalayan Authority, looking into ways of dealing with all the questions, conflicts and commons of the region, might be a worthwhile idea.

RAM MADHAV

Acknowledgements

This book is the result of an attempt by two Academic Institutions, India Foundation and Jammu and Kashmir Study Centre (JKSC) to initiate greater understanding of the Himalayan Region and its Geo-political complexities. The two institutions got together to organize a seminar on 'Geopolitics of Himalayan Region' at Leh, where such a seminar had never taken place. This activity was consciously undertaken in such a timeframe so as to coincide it with the Centenary Celebration of Rimpoche Kushak Bakula. As soft power has been an important component of the diplomacy and consequently, its usage has been a significant part of Geopolitics of this region; Kushak Bakula and his appointment as India's Ambassador to Mongolia was a good use of India's soft power. The seminar was supported by Nehru Memorial Museum and Library (NMML) and Ladakh International Centre.

This book therefore owes its existence to my colleagues in India Foundation, namely, Shri Ram Madhav, who has been the main guiding force behind this seminar and was magnanimous enough to pen the foreword; Maj General Dhruv Katoch, Shreya Challagalla, Siddharth Singh, Ngawang Gamtso Hardy and Thomas Jackson, who took great efforts to ensure that this project fructifies. I would also to acknowledge the great support that this book received from JKSC and its team, namely, its Director Shri Ashutosh Bhatnagar, Shakti Munshi, Abha Khanna and Ranjan Chauhan. I would also like to thank NMML and its Director Shri Shakti Sinha for extending unstinted support to make this project a success. It would not be out of place to acknowledge enormous efforts put in by Ladakh International Centre and its Director, Professor P Stobdan, without whose support, organising an event at a remote place like Leh, would have been a problem. He also helped us to get two valuable maps of Tibet Autonomous Region and Xinjiang Uyghur Autonomous Region, which have been unavailable in public domain. Our local needs were taken care of and our stay was made comfortable by the team of Ladakh International Centre. The project also received full support from the local administration at Leh.

The book would not have been possible without the timely contributions from its eminent contributors, who despite their extremely busy schedule submitted their valuable chapters on relatively lesser known subjects, quite expeditiously. I would especially like to thank my colleagues Shreya Challagalla and Shikha Aggarwal, who carried out research diligently to add academic contents to the chapters of two eminent practitioners. Dr Vivek Dhankhar of Institute for Defence Studies and Analyses helped to design two rare maps, which have added gravitas to the content of this book. I would be grossly failing in my duties, if I do not recognize the immense contribution of my coeditor Aayushi Ketkar, who literally burnt the midnight oil to correct numerous drafts and proofs. No words would suffice to express my gratitude to Shri Sandeep Dixit, Deputy Editor, The Tribune, who selflessly volunteered to go through the proofs, despite his own busy schedule. Finally, I would like to acknowledge the contribution of my publisher Shri Rajan Arya, the proprietor of Pentagon Press LLP, who went out of his way to accommodate our numerous editing requests and provided us repeated sets of proofs at possibly the fastest speed. I hope the readers find this book, which explores relatively lesser known regions of the world, useful and interesting.

ALOK BANSAL

List of Abbreviations

ADB	-	Asian Development Bank
AJK	-	Azad Jammu and Kashmir
ASEAN	-	Association of Southeast Asian Nations
BBIN	-	Bangladesh, Bhutan, India and Nepal
BRI	-	Belt and Road Initiative
BRICS	-	Brazil, Russia, India, China and South Africa
CAR	-	Central Asian Republics
CEDAW	-	Convention on the Elimination of all Forms of Discrimination against Women
CERD	-	Committee on the Elimination of Racial Discrimination
CIA	-	Central Intelligence Agency
CIS	-	Commonwealth of Independent States
CPC	-	Communist Party of China
CPEC	-	China-Pakistan Economic Corridor
CPN(UML)	-	Communist Party of Nepal (Unified Marxist–Leninist)
DoI	-	Department of Industry
EEAS	-	European External Action Service
ETIM	-	East Turkistan Islamic Movement
ETIP	-	East Turkistan Islamic Party
ETPFP	-	Eastern Turkistan Prairie Five Party
ETPRP	-	East Turkistan People's Revolutionary Party
EU	-	European Union

FATA	-	Federally Administered Tribal Area
FCR	-	Frontier Crimes Regulation
FDI	-	Foreign Direct Investment
FP	-	Foreign Policy
FTA	-	Free Trade Agreement
GB	-	Gilgit-Baltistan
GDP	-	Gross Domestic Product
IMU	-	Islamic Movement of Uzbekistan
ISI	-	Inter-Services Intelligence
ISIS	-	Islamic State of Iraq and Syria
ISRO	-	Indian Space Research Organization
JFS	-	Jabhat Fateh al Sham
JV	-	Joint Ventures
KGT	-	Katibat al Ghuraba al Turkistan
KP	-	Khyber Pakhtunkhwa
LAC	-	Line of Actual Control (demarcation line separating Indian controlled territory from Chinese-controlled territory in Jammu and Kashmir
LoC	-	Line of Control (military control line between India and Pakistan in Jammu and Kashmir)
MEA	-	Ministry of External Affairs (India)
MNC	-	Multinational Corporation
MoU	-	Memorandum of Understanding
NALC	-	Northern Areas Legislative Council
NATCG	-	National Anti- Terrorism Coordination Group
NDS	-	National Directorate of Security (of Afghanistan)
NEFA	-	North-East Frontier Agency
NHAR	-	Ningxia Hui Autonomous Region
NIC	-	National Intelligence Centre
NUG	-	National Unity Government (of Afghanistan)

OBOR	-	One Belt One Road
ODA	-	Overseas Development Assistance
PAP	-	People's Armed Police
PDR	-	People's Democratic Republic (Lao PDR - Laos).
PLA	-	People's Liberation Army (of China)
POJK	-	Pakistan Occupied Jammu and Kashmir
PRC	-	People's Republic of China
RCTS	-	Regional Counter Terrorism Structure
SCO	-	Shanghai Cooperation Organisation
SR	-	Special Representative
SRG	-	Special Representative Group
TAR	-	Tibet Autonomous Region
TGIE	-	Tibetan Government in Exile
TIM	-	Turkistan Islamic Movement
TIP	-	Turkistan Islamic Party
TTP	-	Tehrik-e-Taliban Pakistan
UNGA	-	United Nations General Assembly
UNHRC	-	United Nations Human Rights Council
UPR	-	Universal Periodic Review
WDP	-	Western Development Programme
WUC	-	World Uyghur Congress
XASS	-	Xinjiang Academy of Social Sciences
XPCC	-	Xinjiang Production and Construction Corps
XUAR	-	Xinjiang Uyghur Autonomous Region

Glossary of Terms

Azabliq	-	'Pain' in Uyghur Language
Azadliq	-	'Liberation' in Uyghur Language
Daraddesa	-	Land of Dards. Geographical territory corresponding to present Gilgit and adjoining areas
Daura Saruwal	-	National outfit of Nepalese men
Dhoti Kurta	-	Traditional dress worn by men in Indian Subcontinent. Dhoti is a loose piece of clothing wrapped around the lower half of the body while kurta is like a shirt that covers the upper half.
Islamiyat	-	Islamic studies (a subject taught in Pakistani schools).
Jihad	-	Literally means struggle. It is the only form of warfare prescribed in Islam. Although, it can be against rebels, robbers, apostates, non-believers and dissenters, it is usually used for struggle or fight against the enemies of Islam. There are passages in Holy Quran dealing with Jihad.
Lapchak	-	Mission carrying gifts to the Dalai Lama from Leh. Every three years a trade mission from Ladakh would visit Lhasa, carrying religious gifts. In return it would bring back merchandise from Tibet. Reciprocal trade mission from Tibet to Ladakh was called *Chaba*.
Madaris	-	Plural of *Madrassa*, which in Arabic means an educational institution. The word is generally used for institutions for the study of Islamic religion, though this may not be the only subject studied there.

Mehtar	-	Ruler, originated from Sanskrit word *Mehttar*, meaning King
Mujahideen	-	Plural of Mujahid, who is a participant in jihad
Polulo	-	Geographical area corresponding to present Baltistan
Serpon	-	Gold Superintendent in Tibetan
Shaoshu Minzu	-	Mandarin term for Ethnic Minority
Shung Tsong	-	Government Trader in Tibetan language
Swastika	-	It is a geometrical figure and an ancient religious icon in many cultures of Eurasia. It is used as a symbol of divinity and spirituality in Indian religions.
Terai	-	Lowland region in southern Nepal and northern India that lies south of the outer foothills of the Himalayas, the Siwalik Hills, and north of the Indo-Gangetic Plain.
Thanedar	-	Literally means in charge of a *thana* (Police Station). Used for an official responsible for maintaining Law and Order. In olden days, a *thana* in a remote region was both a military and a police post, and represented a sovereign's authority and *thanedar*, ipso facto, assumed powers of the local representative
Trishul	-	Trident. The weapon wielded by Lord 'Shiva'
Trulku	-	A reincarnate custodian of a specific lineage of teachings in Tibetan Buddhism who is given empowerments and trained from a young age by students of his or her predecessor
Vajradhara	-	Ruler of Vajra Beings (Vajrayan Buddhists)
Wazir-i-Wazarat	-	Governor (Responsible for a *Wazarat* or Governorate)
Yanda	-	Mandarin term meaning 'to crack down on' or 'to take severe measures against', usually mentioned as 'Hard Strike' or 'Stern Blows' campaign in western writings.

List of Contributors

Captain Alok Bansal is Director India Foundation. He is also an Adjunct Professor at New Delhi Institute of Management as well as the Secretary General of Asian Eurasian Human Rights Forum. He was the Founder Executive Director of the South Asian Institute for Strategic Affairs and the facilitator of India Policy Group on Afghanistan for Track II Dialogues by Friedrich Ebert Stiftung. He was a Visiting Professor under the Pakistan Studies Programme of Maulana Mohammed Ali Jauhar Academy of International Studies at Jamia Millia Islamia. He has been the Executive Director of the National Maritime Foundation, a Senior Fellow at the Centre for Land Warfare Studies and has worked with the Institute for Defence Studies and Analyses, for over five years.

Ms Aayushi Ketkar is a Senior Research Fellow with Asian Eurasian Human Rights Forum (AEHRF). She currently teaches International Relations at Gautam Buddha University, Greater Noida and is a core member of an ICSSR Project on Jammu and Kashmir. She has worked with the Jammu and Kashmir Study Centre (JKSC) as the Director (Research). She was the Ford Scholar with the Institute of Peace and Conflict Studies (IPCS) where she authored the Governance section of the Monograph on "Alternative Approaches to Security". She had secured the President's gold medal during her post-graduation at the University of Hyderabad.

Professor SD Muni superannuated from Jawaharlal Nehru University, in 2006 after 33 years of service. He has also been India's Ambassador to Lao PDR. In 2005, the Sri Lankan President bestowed on him 'Sri Lanka Ratna', the highest civilian honour for a non-national. A founder Editor of Indian Foreign Affairs Journal and South Asia Journal, he is also affiliated with the IDSA, and Monash Asia Institute, Melbourne, as Fellow. He also served Director of Research at the Observer Research Foundation, New Delhi. A founder Executive Member of the Regional Centre of Strategic Studies, Colombo, he was also part of India's first National Security Advisory Board

Professor Kulbhushan Warikoo did his MA and MPhil from University of Kashmir and Ph.D from School of International Studies, Jawaharlal Nehru University, New Delhi. Professor Warikoo joined the Central Asian Studies Programme in April 1987. His main research interests are Indo-Central Asian Relations, Geopolitics of Central Asia, Afghanistan, Xinjiang, Trans Himalayan Trade and Cultural Movements, Society, Culture and Politics in Kashmir. He has written over 20 books on these subjects. He is also the founding Editor of Himalayan and Central Asian Studies, a quarterly journal published regularly since 1997, dedicated to study of various issues pertaining to the Himalayan and Trans-Himalayan Region.

Shri Shakti Sinha is the Director of the Nehru Memorial Museum & Library, New Delhi. He is also a Distinguished Fellow at the Institute of National Security Studies Sri Lanka (INSSSL), Colombo. He has a master's in public policy from George Mason University, and a master in history from Delhi University. He was a member of the Indian Administrative Service from 1979 to 2013, and has worked in the Union government, different Union Territories, Afghanistan and at the World Bank. He has worked at various think tanks in India and Singapore, edited five books, written many chapters, working papers, policy briefs, columns etc.

Professor P. Stobdan is India's former Ambassador to Kyrgyzstan. A distinguished academician, diplomat, author and national security expert, he superannuated as a Senior Fellow from IDSA. He is a specialist on Asian affairs covering Central Asia and Inner Asia, including Xinjiang, Myanmar and the Himalayan region and has written extensively on a wide range of security-related subjects. He has also served as a Director in the Indian mission in Kazakhstan. He has also served as Joint Director in the Indian National Security Council. He was also the Director of the Centre for Strategic and Regional Studies at the University of Jammu.

Dr. Abanti Bhattacharya is an Associate Professor at the Department of East Asian Studies at the University of Delhi. Prior to this she was an Associate Fellow at Institute for Defence Studies and Analyses (IDSA), New Delhi. A post graduate in history from Jadavpur University, Kolkata; she has done her M Phil and PhD from Centre for Chinese Studies, at School for International Studies at Jawaharlal Nehru University, New Delhi. Her areas of interest include Chinese Nationalism, Chinese Ethnic Minorities, Chinese Foreign Policy, Tibet, Taiwan, Xinjiang, Hong Kong, India-China Relations and East Asian Order. She has published extensively on these subjects.

Dr. Mahesh Ranjan Debata is an Assistant Professor at the Centre for Inner Asian Studies, School of International Studies, at Jawaharlal Nehru University (JNU), New Delhi. He has done his Post Graduation from Centre for Political Studies and M. Phil and Ph. D from Central Asian Studies Programme, School of International Studies, JNU. His areas of research include Xinjiang and Central Asia. He has been a Guest Professor at the Centre of Business Anthropology, School of Continuing Education, Tianjin University of Finance and Economics, Tianjin, China He is the Sub-Editor of the quarterly journal Himalayan and Central Asian Studies, which is being published regularly since 1997.

Ms Prabha Rao is currently the Executive Director of South Asian Institute for Strategic Affairs (SAISA), a New Delhi based think tank. She was earlier a Senior Fellow at the Institute for Defence Studies and Analyses (IDSA), India's premier think tank dealing with security issues. A former officer of the Indian Police Service (IPS), she has served in the Cabinet secretariat for number of years. Her research areas include International Terrorism, with special focus on Al Qaeda and Islamic state; West Asia, Islamic Radicalism, India's Neighbours, Human trafficking and cybercrimes.

Shri Ranjit Rae, a former diplomat is currently an Independent Director of Bharat Heavy Electrical Limited (BHEL). An officer of the Indian Foreign Service (IFS) he has been India's Ambassador to Hungary, Vietnam and Nepal. He is a Post Graduate in Economics and has also taught in prestigious St Stephens College at Delhi, before joining the Foreign Service. He was Joint Secretary in the Ministry of External Affairs, looking after Nepal from 2002 to 2006, when Maoist insurgency was at its peak. He has served in the UN mission in Kosovo and Department of peace keeping operations of the UN at New York. He has also been the Press Secretary to the President of India.

Dr Medha Bisht is an Assistant Professor at the South Asian University. She was earlier an Associate Fellow at IDSA. She has a PhD from Diplomatic and Disarmament Studies Division of Jawaharlal Nehru University. In June 2008 she attended a graduate course on Peace Research, at University of Oslo, Norway. She has contributed to various reports commissioned by the United Nations, IDRC Canada and the Government of India including the Progress of Women in South Asia published and supported by UNIFEM. She has been one of the contributors (India section) to the Landmine Report published by the International Campaign to Ban Landmines, Canada.

Dr. Nihar R. Nayak is Research Fellow with IDSA, New Delhi. His areas of expertise are: political transition in the eastern Himalayan region, soft power diplomacy, left wing extremism, and cooperative security in South Asia. He has a PhD in International Politics from Jawaharlal Nehru University. He has been Visiting Fellow to the Peace Research Institute Oslo and did a special course on Peace Research at the International Summer School of Oslo University. He has been Visiting Faculty at the Centre for the Study of Nepal, Faculty of Social Science, Banaras Hindu University and at Lal Bahadur Shastri National Academy of Administration (LBSNAA), Mussoorie.

Professor Sunaina Singh is the Vice-Chancellor of Nalanda International University and amongst the most prominent leaders of higher education in the South Asian region. She was earlier the Vice Chancellor of The English and Foreign Languages University for five years. A distinguished academician and administrator, she currently also holds the position of the Vice President, Indian Council for Cultural Relations. She has the distinction of being the first Indian woman to head, as the President of the Shastri Indo-Canadian Institute, a bi-national Research Institution with headquarters in New Delhi and Calgary under the MHRD and Canadian Government.

Ms Shreya Challagalla is a Research Fellow at India Foundation, a think tank based in New Delhi. She was previously associated with the Observer Research Foundation where she authored a paper titled, "The Diaspora and India's Growth Story". Her fields of research and interest include India's soft power, the confluence of cultures and the Indian diaspora and indentured labour. She has graduated from FLAME University, Pune with a degree in International Studies and Journalism and New Media. She regularly writes for The Statesman, a leading English Newspaper of India.

Shri Anil Trigunayat is a former diplomat, who served as India's Ambassador to Jordan and Libya and High Commissioner to Malta. He also served in the Indian Missions in Cote d'Ivoire, Bangladesh, Mongolia, USA, Russia, Sweden and Nigeria. A Post Graduate in Physics, he also studied Russian History, Culture and Language at the Jawaharlal Nehru University. He has also conducted research work on "WTO and Regional Trading Blocs" at the Oxford University. He is a member of the All India Management Association, Oxford and Cambridge Society of India and the Association of Indian Diplomats. He is also the Honorary Member of the International Trade Council, Brussels.

Ms Shikha Aggarwal is a Senior Research Fellow at the India Foundation. She has previously been associated with the Centre for Air Power Studies and Vivekananda International Foundation. Ms Aggarwal has completed her Post-Graduate studies in International Relations and Politics, and holds a Graduate degree in Journalism (Honors) from the Delhi University. Her research focus includes India-China relations, China's Foreign Policy and Domestic Politics of China.

1

Introduction

Alok Bansal and Aayushi Ketkar

The Himalayas have traditionally defined India and the very identity of India is incomplete without the Himalayas. Consequently, Indic thought as well as Indian writings are replete with references to the Himalayas. Well before Jesus Christ was born, Bārhaspatyaśāstra, the foundational text of Charvaka School of Philosophy described Hindustan as

> हिमालयं समारभ्य यावत् इन्दु सरोवरम् ।
> तं देवनिर्मितं देशं हिन्दुस्थानं प्रचक्षते ।।
> "*Himalayam Samarabhya Yavadindu Sarovaram*
> *Tham Devanirmitham Desam Hindusthanam Prachakshathi*"
>
> The holy land, surrounded by Himalayas in the North and the Indian ocean in the south, created by the Gods themselves, is called Hindustan!![1]

Similarly, the salience of Himalayas is clearly established by the fact that Kalidasa, arguably the greatest Sanskrit poet, in his epic poem Kumarasambhava, considered the greatest long poem in classical Sanskrit, describes the Himalayas in its very first verse as

> अस्त्य् उत्तरस्यां दिशि देवतात्मा हिमालयो नाम नगाधिराजः ।
> पूर्वापरौ तोयनिधी विगाह्य स्थितः पृथिव्या इव मानदण्डः ।।
> *asty uttarasyāṃ diśi devatātmā himālayo nāma nagādhirājaḥ* ।
> *pūrvāparau toyanidhī vigāhya sthitaḥ pṛthivyā iva mānadaṇḍaḥ// Ks* 1.1 ।।

> On the northern frontier of this country that forms the heartland of Gods, intercalating himself into eastern and western oceans like a measuring stick of earth, there stands the sovereign of snowy mountains renowned as Mount Himalaya.[2]

The Vishnu Purana also describes Bharatavarsha as

> "*Uttaram yat samudrasya Himdreschaiva daksinam*
> *Varsham tat Bharatam nama Bharati yatra santati* "
>
> The region spanning in between the Himalayas in the north to the Indian ocean in the south is called Bharatavarsham and the natives of this region are called Bharatiyas (Indians).

All the above verses depict very clearly and categorically the centrality of the Himalayas in the Geo-Political consciousness of Bharat (modern day India). The reverence with which it is held is neither misplaced nor some kind of a passing fad but one that has held its sway since times immemorial. The Himalayas have been an integral part of Indian consciousness long before India emerged as a political entity post Westphalian nation-state system. Hence any strategic and national security discourse that fails to understand the gravity of its existence and the centrality of its cultural, political and strategic dimensions, will be hollow and bereft of the vital grassroot realities and will lack concrete substance and spirit.

The Himalayas are also an embodiment of divinity, of nature in its splendour, and of culture in the deepest sense of the word. The Himalayas are the highest and the most spectacular mountains in the world, separating the Indian sub-continent from the Tibetan plateau. The boundaries of South and Central Asian countries converge along the Himalayas, which lends unique geo-political and geo-strategic importance to the region. The mighty Himalayas, which are a natural frontier for India, have given this land a distinctive geographical, geological and climatic entity, with respect to the land masses on the other side of this mighty mountain range. This has resulted in the evolution of a unique ethno-cultural identity, which has defined India's spiritual and national consciousness.

The Himalayan region represents different terrain ranging from plateaus to high mountains and valleys, lower Himalayan ranges, each representing diverse ecology, resources and political identities. Consequently, the region itself displays wide diversity of cultural patterns, languages, ethnic identities and religious practices. The world's youngest mountain range, the Himalayas, is also home to two of the world's oldest civilizations that also happen to be contemporary Great Power aspirants – India and China. These two Asian Giants are not only the world's fastest growing economies, but also hold over one third of global population.

The Himalayan region stretching from Afghanistan to the mountains of Pakistan, India, Nepal, Bhutan and Myanmar is at the cusp of South Asia, Central Asia and China. The Himalayas have been seen as the protectors of the Indian subcontinent from invaders, as it prevented large armies from traversing it, but it did allow ideas to permeate as well as trade convoys to transcend the passes during fair weather. This unique permeability, despite its invincibility, not only facilitated movement of merchants and their merchandise, but also contributed towards confluence of cultures and ideas. Consequently, the region assimilated Hinduism and Buddhism along with indigenous cultures, languages, dialects and ethnicity, at the same time accepted Islam and Christianity on its Western and Eastern extremities. Indigenous people, as well as many from outside the region have emotional and cultural bonds with the Himalayas, especially Hindus, Jains and Buddhists, who venerate the entire mountain ranges with special reverence towards Mount Kailash and Manasarovar Lake, as well as numerous rivers emanating from there.

The region is rich in natural resources and consequently, there has been a scramble to control them to boost economic growth of a growing population in the region and its surroundings. This jostling for resources has not only disturbed the fragile ecology of this delicate region, but has also exacerbated geo-political tensions. The region contributes significantly to the water resources of Asia and ten of its largest and longest rivers (Amu Darya, Brahmaputra, Ganges, Indus, Irrawaddy, Mekong, Salween, Tarim, Yangtze, and Yellow) originate in the Himalayas. These rivers help provide water, food, and energy for nearly four billion people in India, China and across South and Southeast Asia—nearly half of the world's population. However, unbridled exploitation of these trans-border resources to meet growing industrial, agricultural and urban demands have the potential to disturb the delicate environmental equilibrium and exacerbate social, economic, and geo-political stress within the region.

Advancement of technology has resulted in breaching of various natural frontiers and consequently, Himalayas have no longer remained an impregnable wall, as was sadly realised by India in 1962. Trains run all the way to Lhasa and will very soon be crisscrossing the mighty Himalayas as Lhasa, Kathmandu and Gilgit are being brought on to the railway grid. New highways are being built and existing ones are being widened. Similarly, numerous new airstrips have been constructed and scores of aircraft are taking off from these remote airfields every day. With improving connectivity, the populace is being exposed to newer outside influences and existing paradigms may not be relevant in days to come. It is therefore essential to look *de novo* at the Geopolitics of this crucial region. This book is an attempt to look at the Geopolitics of the Himalayan Region from Cultural, Political and Strategic Dimensions.

K Warikoo in his chapter 'Himalayan Frontiers through the Ages' describes how the Himalayas have shaped India's identity and has found mention in ancient Sanskrit as well as Tamil texts. He highlights that although geographically Himalaya is often perceived to be defined by the River Indus and Brahamputra at its western and eastern extremities respectively, culturally, politically and strategically, it is impossible to separate it from the Hindu Kush, Karakoram and Pamir region, which are contiguous and interlocked with the great Himalayan mountain system. He has described the evolution of geopolitical frontiers within the region through centuries and has specifically focussed on Western Himalayas describing the evolution of Gilgit and Baltistan as well as highlighting the interface between Ladakh and Tibet, which eventually contributed to the evolution of modern boundaries of India.

SD Muni in his chapter 'India and the Unfolding Himalayan Geostrategic Context', has shown how Himalayas have always been integral to India and how the British colonialists understood it and strived to keep the outside influences away from this region. Independent India has tried to maintain this legacy, however, with some significant changes to cope up with the changing environment. According to him, changing Geo-strategic dimension poses three major challenges to India: namely the retreating glaciers, persisting socio-political turbulence in the Himalayas and the assertion of a rising China. India is conscious of these challenges and is using its soft power to counter China's hard power. However, according to him, India needs to expeditiously evolve a credible China policy, keeping in view India's strengths and Chinese vulnerabilities.

Shakti Sinha in his chapter 'The Himalayas: Bridge or Barrier?' states that

India's identity is closely linked with the Himalayas and is defined by a clear sense of geographical space and boundaries. Geologically, the rising of Himalayas is the consequence of Indian plate crashing into Eurasian landmass. The three parallel ranges that constitute the Himalayas also divide the region into three cultural sub-strands that run along its length. Tibet ideally showcases the Himalayan conundrum of simultaneously being both a bridge and a barrier. Although isolated for centuries, it maintained its links with India. Padmasambhava, the founder of Vajrayan Buddhism, introduced it to Tibet and traversed all over Himalayas. Tibetan monks were always present at Nalanda as long as it functioned as a monastery and a seat of learning. He perceives India-China border dispute to be driven by the Tibetan question and traces strong linkages between Tibet and India during the colonial period. He feels that changing Chinese stance makes it imperative for India to resolve its border dispute expeditiously. He also feels that India should not be in a great hurry to revive Trans-Himalayan trade till market access and border issues are resolved.

P Stobdan in the chapter, 'Developments in Tibet and their likely Impact on India's Himalayan Region', has analysed the issue of Himalayan geopolitics from the prism of Tibetan Buddhism. In the chapter, the author begins by explaining how the institution of 'Lamaism' was used by the Qing emperors to advance imperial claims all along China's peripheries. Later, this very institution was appropriated by Mao to extend claims over Nepal, Bhutan and the Indian territories of Arunachal and Sikkim. In addition to the Chinese expansionist approach, Himalayan geopolitics is becoming increasingly complex due to the rapid 'Tibetanisation' of the Himalayas, and the sectarian discords among various sects of Tibetan Buddhism. The author asserts that the increasing sectarian strife in the Buddhist Himalayas is being choreographed by China, and hence poses a security challenge for India. He has also explored the future of Tibetan cause by studying the relationship between the Dalai Lama and the Chinese leadership, and the revival of Buddhism in China in recent times.

Two factors make Tibet important for India. First is the religious and cultural factor. Tibet has an important place in the Indian imagination. The Hindu holy land of Kailash and Manasarovar is in Tibet. The second factor is ecological. The strategic importance of Tibet as an ecological buffer as it relates to ecological security is now well established through scientific research. Abanti Bhattacharya in the chapter 'The Tibet Conundrum' has brought out India's dilemma with respect to Tibet. It has the largest concentration of diasporic Tibetans, but its attitude towards Tibet is significantly determined by the dynamics of its relations with China. Therefore, while it granted asylum to the Tibetan refugees, its policies since 1954 are not geared towards an independent Tibet. India's policy is an outcome of its own concerns about its northern frontiers since the 1950s. In recognising Tibet as a part of China, New Delhi in 1954 had hoped to gain Beijing's recognition of India's border with Tibet and build peaceful and stable ties with China. It also hoped that its posture would facilitate Tibetan autonomy within China. This of course did not happen. Tibet has been China's Achilles Heel. Dalai Lama and the Tibetan movement have gained adequate international traction. The author contends that Tibetans have scaled down their demand from 'independence and self-determination' to 'genuine autonomy', but the Chinese consider the issue as not about the status of Tibet, but about the future of Dalai Lama. She asserts that Tibet conundrum is basically a Chinese creation and India's China policy should factor in Chinese insecurities and vulnerabilities in Tibet.

Mahesh Ranjan Debata in the chapter 'Xinjiang under the Shadow of Uyghur Nationalism and Islamic Radicalism' analyses developments in Xinjiang, the largest province of China. Occupying one sixth of the Chinese landmass, Xinjiang Autonomous Region has been an area of violent contention between its native ethnic group, the Uyghurs, and the rest of the Han Chinese population, ever since the People's Republic of China (PRC) was established by the Chinese Communist Party (CCP) and Mao Zedong in 1949. Policy changes throughout the history of the PRC have in turn resulted in differing attitudes toward the government, culminating in an uneasy relationship between Uyghurs, Han Chinese native to Xinjiang and the PRC representatives placed there by the government. The Turkistan Islamic Party (TIP) or Turkistan Islamic Movement (TIM), formerly known as the East Turkistan Islamic Party (ETIP) and other names, is an Islamic extremist separatist organization founded by Uyghur jihadists in western China. Its stated goal is the establishment of an independent state called "East Turkistan" in Xinjiang. The author contends that Beijing's repressive policies in Xinjiang have pushed some Uyghurs to move from nationalism into the arms of Islamic extremism. Demonstrated violence against the Uyghurs, violation of their human rights, and restrictions and prohibitions on Islamic practices have contributed to the evolution of this terrorist threat. Beijing, with its aggressive policies in Xinjiang during last few decades, has strengthened the position of the TIP which, in turn, has exacerbated the problem of Uyghur nationalism and separatism, which has joined ranks with global jihadi organisations. He sums up that situation in Xinjiang is grave, but the linkages of Uyghur militants with global jihadi organisations leave the international community, with no other choice, but to support the People's Republic of China.

Prabha Rao in the chapter, 'Uyghurs: China's Missing Minorities,' has studied the issue of Uyghur nationalism and China's tough measures against its Muslim minorities, which include interning a large number of Uyghurs in re-education camps. She tracks the historical trajectory of various Uyghur groups and presents a detailed analysis of the links between East Turkistan Independence Movement (ETIM) and international Islamic extremist groups like the Islamic State and the Al Qaeda. It is the presence of ETIM in the central Asian states of Tajikistan and Uzbekistan that is shaping China's proactive role in Afghanistan. The author asserts that China's assimilationist approach and cultural subjugation of the Uyghurs has added to the sense of alienation among the Muslim masses and fuelled their nationalist aspirations. China needs to learn from India to co-opt its minorities into the mainstream of national politics and society. She has also highlighted the linkages maintained by Pakistan's Inter-Services Intelligence (ISI) with various Uyghur militants.

India's relation with the two Himalayan countries of Nepal and Bhutan are formally founded on key treaties—the 1950 India-Nepal Treaty of Peace and Friendship and the 1949 Treaty of Friendship with Bhutan. Politically, India's bilateral ties with these two Himalayan neighbours have enormous significance as they serve as a buffer zone between India and China. The rise of an economically powerful and militarily assertive China imposes a constricting burden on smaller states like Nepal and Bhutan. Existential questions like how to continue resisting Chinese overtures loom large. In the Himalayan region, a powerful and assertive China wishes to see Nepal and Bhutan more connected with Tibet through roads, through trade, through cultural and people-to-people contact, and in the joint harnessing of water and other natural resources.

Ranjit Rae in his chapter 'Nepal and Bhutan: Changing Dynamics' describes how two countries with similar geography, culture and linkages with India, have taken quite dissimilar trajectories to development. While Bhutan has emerged as one of the most prosperous countries of South Asia, Nepal continues to languish at the bottom. Both the countries which were absolute monarchies at one stage have transformed themselves into a constitutional monarchy in the case of Bhutan and a republic in the case of Nepal. The chapter looks at recent internal developments in the two countries and different facets of India-Nepal and India-Bhutan bilateral cooperation, comprising issues related to trade-transit, customs and joint border management, legal framework of existing bilateral agreements, and energy cooperation. It also looks at Indian options in the face of growing Chinese influence in the region.

Medha Bisht in her chapter, 'The Making of "Space": Changing Geo-politics in Himalayas' has analysed Bhutan's evolution as a country constricted geographically by its two big neighbours. The author argues that the understanding of geographic space has a direct bearing upon the strategic choices made by nations. To illustrate her point, Medha has focussed upon the Doklam face-off of 2017. She insists that China has been following a two-pronged approach vis-a-vis its territorial dispute with Bhutan. While the physical aspect of the Chinese expansionist strategy is represented by the infrastructure being built in and around the disputed areas, the 'ideational' strand of this strategy is contained in the historical claims based upon the 1890 Anglo-China Convention. The author argues that the Chinese construction activities in Doklam were not directed towards changing the immediate status-quo in the region, but to create conditions for more incremental changes in near future. These changes will entail potent economic and military dimensions. However, the author insists that China will continue to pursue an 'ideational' strategy in the Himalayan region and not resort to any military action unless challenged overtly.

Nihar R Nayak in his chapter, 'New Nepal under Chinese Shadow and Indian Influence,' stresses that Nepal has been a significant theatre of Great Power rivalry, ever since a unified state emerged in 1769. He analyses recent changes in Nepal as well as China's growing profile in Nepal. China has been increasing its footprint in Nepal through the means of high-profile political visits, enhanced economic engagements, increased security cooperation, and growing people-to-people contacts. The author insists that China's approach towards Nepal has acquired a new dimension with the introduction of One Belt One Road (OBOR) in 2013. In spite of this multi-layered engagement policy towards Nepal, China recognises the leverage that India traditionally enjoys with the Himalayan nation. It is argued that China initially preferred

Indian influence in Nepal over any 'extra-regional' presence in the country. Now that China has been able to acquire a visible presence and influence in other continents like Africa and South America, it would not be very difficult for it to play a decisive role in Nepal as well. However, China would not like to disturb its relationship with India because of Nepal. According to the author, China wants to play a major role in South Asia without impacting the normal course of China-India relations.

Alok Bansal in his chapter 'Gilgit-Baltistan & Aksai Chin: Indian Territories under Foreign Occupation,' covers territories of Jammu and Kashmir, which are under the occupation of China and Pakistan, despite being constitutionally and legally an integral part of India. He primarily focusses on Aksai Chin and Gilgit-Baltistan, describing their unique geography and history, as these areas have virtually been out of peoples' consciousness in India specifically and South Asia in general. The author cites history to reinforce Indian claims to these territories and how Indian territorial claims over various enclaves and territories in Xinjiang and Tibet were never pursued by Indian government after independence. This chapter is more informatory than analytical and covers the current status of these territories, as well as unique cultural and linguistic identity of Gilgit-Baltistan. The author has tracked the changing administrative structures of Gilgit-Baltistan, since its occupation by Pakistan, and has also tried to demystify Aksai Chin.

Considering the fact that Himalayas allow permeation of ideas and trade, without allowing large body of troops to transcend it, soft power is always likely to have an enormous impact in this region. Sunaina Singh and Shreya Challagalla in their chapter, "Soft Power Diplomacy: A Legacy to Explore" contend that even though Joseph Nye may have given the term 'soft power diplomacy' to the academic world, India has included soft power diplomacy as a powerful tool since ancient times. Soft power has been an inherent part of Indian culture and permeated through all its forms—art, cuisine, dance, literature, music, folk traditions or even respect for elders and teachers. These have since become the defining canons of 'soft power diplomacy'. Indian Vedantic and Buddhist teachings have permeated across the length and breadth of Himalayan region and provide India a strong platform for soft power diplomacy. One of the finest examples of soft power that shines through the Himalayan region in independent India, is Kushok Bakula Rinpoche, a diplomat, widely acknowledged and admired for his wisdom and gentleness.

Kushok Bakula Rinpoche was declared a reincarnation of Bakula Arhat at the age of six, and was defined by his erudition, compassion and service to the growth and development of the Ladakh region. Under his vigilant and wise statesmanship, the region gained its identity and grew in stature. He not only revived Buddhism in the region, but also bound the neighbouring countries with the spread of Buddhist philosophy of 'Ananda Marga'. After the disintegration of Soviet Union, when Mongolia came out of the communist yoke, it experienced an enormous spiritual vacuum. It is at this juncture that Bakula Rinpoche, as a diplomat, revived Buddhism in Mongolia and ensured peace and harmony in the region. He also propagated the rich religious and cultural heritage of Buddhism in the communist stronghold of USSR and China. He encouraged and regularly provided visas to Mongolians to visit India to study Buddhism, and even gave monastic ordinance to women, a first in the history of modern Mongolia.

This book is a tribute to the great saint diplomat Kushok Bakula Rinpoche, whose grand centenary celebrations took place in 2018. He was hailed as a spiritual person with immaculate statesmanship, donning the twin role of a temporal guru and diplomatic ambassador. Kushok Bakula set new standards of excellence in soft power diplomacy and emphasised the primacy of ethics and spirituality in politics. Anil Trigunayat and Shikha Aggarwal in their chapter, 'Kushok Bakula Rinpoche: Exemplar of India's Soft Power Diplomacy', have described Anil Trigunayat's association with Kushok Bakula, when he was India's ambassador to Mongolia. They contend that Kushok Bakula was the real exemplar of soft power diplomacy with a lasting impact that continues to drive the Indo-Mongolian relations into the higher orbits. As a religious leader, politically astute negotiator and a fine diplomat, Kushok Bakula left an indelible imprint on the historical landscape of our relations with Mongolia and posterity will indeed benefit from this deep rooted synergy.

NOTES

1 Stephen Knapp, "About the Name 'Hindu'," from http://www.stephen-knapp.com/about_the_name_Hindu.htm (accessed on 15 February 2019).

2 Hank Heifetz, *The Origin of the Young God: Kalidas's Kumarasambhav.* Delhi: Motilal Banarasi Dass Publishers Pvt Ltd, 1990, pp. 1-21.

2

India and the Unfolding Himalayan Geostrategic Context

S.D. Muni

Himalayas have been integral to India's evolution as a civilisation and emergence as an independent Asian nation. Civilisationally, Himalayas have been the abode of Hindu gods and goddesses, particularly of Shaivism (Lord Shiva) sect as some of the most revered shrines, temples and pilgrimage centres like Mt. Kailash, Amaranth, Badrinath, Kedarnath, Vaishnu Devi etc. are located in the Himalayas. With the rise of Buddhism in India, the Himalayas, stretched to Hindu Kush ranges, also became a hub of Buddhism where it spread to Tibet, China, Afghanistan (Bamiyan Buddha statues) and Central Asia. The life sustaining river systems of the Indus, Ganges, Yamuna and Brahmaputra that have helped Indian civilisation flourish in all its richness and diversity, emanate from the Himalayas. The Himalayas have also proved to be a natural sentinel for India and South Asia due to its high peaks and inhospitable mountain ranges. And yet it would be a mistake to assume that this defence shield is a barrier for the movement of goods, people and ideas. The Himalayas are porous, punctuated by several mountain passes and river valleys. They have allowed habitation to grow and civilisations to prosper.

The Himalayas have also been known for some of India's important trading routes. Tibet was the hub of Himalayan economic activity. It linked India to China, Central Asia and further to Europe through trade routes. The products exchanged included musk, wool, Yak tails, gold, spices, perfumes and expensive textiles. With the cargoes went pilgrims, monks, missionaries and merchants. Thus culture and civilisation travelled through trade and trade was in turn promoted through cultural contacts and exchanges. Nepal, Tibet and Kashmir played a significant role in strengthening India's closer multidimensional engagement with the Himalayas. Two of the contributors in this volume have competently presented the evolution and consolidation of this engagement since the prehistoric (prior to the Christian era) period.

The strategic dimension of India's Himalayan engagement was systematically introduced and expanded during the British period. There were two important drivers of the British role in the Himalayas; to keep at bay all adversarial or unacceptable external influences, particularly the Russian/Soviet expansion, to keep the British Southern Asian colonies undisturbed; and protect and promote trade routes and links to extract wealth from the region for imperial benefits. The British competition with the Russians/Soviets in the Himalayas extending to Hindu Kush and the Pamir ranges took the form of what is now widely known as the "Great Games". To win these games, the British explored the glaciers, trade and strategic routes, waged wars and forged alliances and sought to firm up the borders and boundaries to keep their Indian empire secure and prosperous. Economic carrots and military sticks were ruthlessly employed by them in pursuance of their interests and objectives in the Himalayas. Territorial acquisitions, strategic assets and vulnerabilities and economic presence and influence claimed by the British were passed on to independent India in 1947 with the implied obligation to preserve the inheritance.

For independent India, however, preserving this inheritance in the Himalayas was not an easy task. More so in view of two major geo-strategic transformations that came with India's independence. One was India's partition and another Chinese military occupation of Tibet. While the first sapped India's access to Hindu Kush and Pamir ranges, the second pushed out Indian presence from Tibet, the hub of the Himalayas, and made a Communist China, India's new and immediate neighbour. The situation was further complicated as the unfolding Cold War intruded into South Asia, including the Himalayas, by way of West aligning with Pakistan and seeking ways to contain China. India, having decided to keep away from the Cold War had to bear the burden of this intrusion. Like the British India, independent India was neither integrated with the global power structure, nor was it as powerful and economically resourceful, in the aftermath of the partition and consequent domestic challenges.

Preserving the Inheritance

To preserve its inheritance, both in territorial and strategic sense in the Himalayas, India generally followed the British pattern, with some significant changes. In relation to the Himalayan Kingdoms of Nepal, Bhutan and the Sikkim protectorate, India renewed by re-writing, the treaties British had had with them. With Nepal, the bilateral arrangement of recruiting Gurkhas for the British Indian army now became a trilateral arrangement wherein both the United Kingdom and independent India had the privilege of recruiting Nepalese in their respective national armies. India extended the protective defence umbrella to Nepal under the Treaty of Peace and Friendship signed in July 1950. Under this Treaty India also respected Nepal's sovereignty which had not been explicitly mentioned in the Treaty of Perpetual Peace and Friendship, concluded in December 1923 between British India and Nepal. The 1923 Treaty, however, underlined that the two countries will "respect each other's internal and external independence" and it was recorded with the League of Nations. Bhutan also had a similar Treaty with India concluded in 1949. Independent India's relations with Sikkim were governed, until 1975, by their bilateral Treaty called India-Sikkim Peace Treaty signed in December 1950. While Bhutan gradually moved towards clearer recognition of its sovereign independence, Sikkim became an integral part of the Union of India in 1975.

The British had both befriended China periodically to ward of the growing Russian/Soviet influence in the Himalayas, while keeping China contained indirectly in different ways. Soon after the rise of Communist China, Nehru sent messages to the Tibetan leader Dalai Lama to prepare militarily for a possible Chinese intrusion. India was willing to help Tibet in this respect. Messages were also sent to encourage Tibet for seeking UN membership as an independent, sovereign entity, but that was not heeded in Lhasa.[1] The British records and advice, to Nehru was to accept Chinese 'suzerainty', not 'sovereignty', over Tibet. In his Asian Relations Conference, Nehru invited Tibet as an independent delegation, to which the Chinese had strongly protested. Subsequently, Nehru carried on with a vigorous 'forward' policy in the Himalayas to ensure that the territorial inheritance bequeathed by the British is preserved and consolidated, within the constraints of India's limited military capabilities. In the overall strategic context, Nehru pursued peaceful co-existence with China in view of the expanding Cold War in Asia and Asia's struggle for decolonisation and independence. That this approach did not succeed was due to various factors, most important of which were the breakdown of Sino-Indian understanding following Dalai Lama's flight in 1959 to India and China's unreliability and duplicitous behaviour.

The core of India's strategic defence structure in the Himalayas was constructed with mutual security arrangements and deep political understanding with Nepal, Bhutan, and Sikkim, bilaterally. As noted above, these arrangements were spelled out in their mutual Treaty relations. Besides the commitments made by India under these treaties for the defence of the Himalayan Kingdoms, India also undertook to modernise defences of these countries by placing Indian Military Missions there and building strategically important roads and air links with India. Unfortunately, the erosion of this structure started setting in by the end of the 1950s, and by the end of the century, there has been a radical transformation in India's strategic presence in the Himalayas, bringing under cloud its vital stakes and interests. For the past nearly two decades, India is struggling to redefine and restructure its Himalayan engagement.

There are many diverse factors that can be identified as being accountable for eroding India's Himalayan strategic presence. They include transport and communication technologies that have breached almost all the land barriers all over the world, obstructing movements of people. Among the factors that have strongly impinged on India's presence in the Himalayas, two stand out. To begin with, independent India's strategy deviated from the British in one critical way, regarding the stability of internal political orders in the Himalayas. The British approach refrained from disturbing feudal and archaic systems like that of the Ranas in Nepal and monarchies in Bhutan and Sikkim. India found this approach unsustainable in the context of rising and decolonising Asia. Accordingly, India sided with the forces of liberalisation in Nepal, beginning with the fall of the Ranas in 1951. It opted for the dominance of Wangchuks in Bhutan against the political aspirations of the Dorjis. The Wangchuks led monarchy in Bhutan came under pressure initially during 1950s, from the Nepalese population led democratic upsurge, but unlike in

Nepal, India helped the monarchy not the democratic forces. In Sikkim, it sided eventually with the democratic forces led by the Nepali population, against the ruling house of the Chogyals to facilitate Sikkim's integration in 1975.

The differentiated Indian approach reflected India's security interests. But as its consequence, India became an internally polarising force in these Kingdoms, especially Nepal, where the forces that were denied power, opposed India's strategic presence and security interests. A big jolt to India's stakes in Nepal was administered as a result of India's support for the democratic forces against King Mahendra who wanted to control the State in 1960. In reaction, the King brought in China as a countervailing factor in Nepal's relations with India and also got the Himalayan barrier breached by getting a connecting Highway laid down by the Chinese assistance to link Kathmandu with Kodari pass on Sino-Nepalese border. His successor King Birendra, following the same strategy to insulate his regime from India, supported democratic pressures, proposed that Nepal be declared as a "Zone of Peace" in 1975. India's inept diplomatic handling and overbearing diplomatic conduct further complicated the situation. Sikkim's integration into India in 1975 had also sent strong shock waves of fear and suspicion against India in Nepal and Bhutan, though both these kingdoms reacted differently towards India. In Sino-Indian relations also, India's role in Tibet's internal political turbulence became a key driver. In 1956, India had prevailed over the Dalai Lama to adjust with the Chinese suzerainty. But in 1959, India's decision to welcome the Tibetan revolt and house a Tibetan Government headed by Dalai Lama to operate from India in exile, contributed significantly to the deterioration in Sino-Indian relations. A key challenge for India has been the handling of internal political turbulence in the Himalayas, and it remains so even now. India's lapses in handling this challenge effectively impacted its Himalayan strategic presence adversely.

Related to the factor of internal turbulence within the Himalayan Kingdoms against India's strategic space was the second factor of external encouragement to this turbulence. The major external powers like the US and China facilitated, if not outright provoked and encouraged the counterbalancing tendencies in these Kingdoms. The US played this role rather assertively during the fifties in the wake of Cold War. India's resistance to the Cold War had been detested by the US, which sought to keep India contained somewhat in pursuance of its Cold War stakes in South Asia. The US was also simultaneously keeping China contained more resolutely. Recall the US surveillance missions against China with the help of its new found ally Pakistan, and support for a proxy war waged against the Chinese in Tibet through the Khampas of the Mustang region in Nepal. From the beginning of the 1960s, the tensions replacing the peaceful co-existence impulses between India and China, the latter replaced the US, and infact also joined the US during the 1970s and 1980s, to keep India in its place. China made itself available as a counterbalance to India when King Mahendra sought Chinese help. The territorial war inflicted by China on India in 1962 damaged India's credibility as a defender of the Himalayas. China started building strategic nexus with Pakistan. It gained about 5,180 square kilometres of territory in Kashmir region disputed between India and Pakistan, as a result of the 1963 boundary settlement between Pakistan and China. Pakistan's territorial link with China through the Karakoram Highway was secured and India's geo-strategic stakes in the Himalayas were dented. India tried to balance these disadvantages by the integration of Sikkim in 1975 that gave India a dominant position in the Tibetan-Chinese Chumbi Valley area. Integration of Sikkim had really been triggered to defeat the US machinations pushing Sikkim towards greater independence from India. In 1984, India's occupation of the Siachen Glacier was also a smart, though expensive, move to breach Sino-Pak geostrategic front in the Himalayas.[2] China's strategic assertion in the Himalayas, at the cost of India's stakes and critical security interests, has however remained unabated, gaining greater momentum with its economic rise and overall assertion in Asia.

Emerging Challenges

Changing geo-strategic dimensions of the Himalayas pose many challenges to India. Three of them need careful attention; namely the retreating glaciers, persisting socio-political turbulence in the Himalayas and the assertion of a rising China. Glacial retreat in the Himalayas has drawn serious attention from scholars and policy makers for more than two decades. Glaciers are retreating because of the climate change, rising temperatures and increasing dust and carbon particles in the air. Some studies have also underlined the contribution of military activities, like in Siachen Glacier, to the retreat phenomenon. Indian Space Research Organisation (ISRO) carried out a study in 2011 on the Himalayan glaciers as a whole. There are differences of opinions among scholars and institutions on the degree and extent of glacier retreats and their implications on socio-economic conditions. There is however consensus that glacier retreat is having damaging impact on water and food security and is affecting patterns of life and habitation. No wonder, the water issue in South Asia's major river systems like the Indus, Ganges and Brahmaputra is gradually gathering a strategic salience in regional relations. While Pakistan fears the eventuality of India disturbing the flow of Indus water to its plains, India and Bangladesh are worried about the reported plans of diversion of the Brahmaputra river by China. India needs to work out a thoughtful and long-term approach to Glacier retreat and its consequences.

A serious challenge to India's stakes in the Himalayas arises from the socio-political turbulence in the Himalayan states, especially Nepal, Bhutan and Tibet. There is a well-recognised explosion of identity and aspirations in all these societies, which is rejecting India's traditional approach to them. India can no longer protect its vital interests by conducting itself in a 'business as usual' style. Recent developments in Nepal regarding its 2015 Constitution resulted in a serious jolt to India's policy. Its coercive and intrusive diplomacy has harmed India's long-term strategic interests by consolidating the anti-India under-current in Nepal's nationalism and pushing it closer to China for seeking alternative transit and political support. The unity and reinforcement of pro-Chinese and Communist forces in Nepali politics has not come as a comforting development for India. The pressure on India's basic terms of engagement with Nepal laid down in the 1950 treaty of Peace and Friendship has increased many fold. India may have to revise and rewrite that treaty as it had to do so in case of Bhutan in 2007. Still fragile, unstable and evolving democracies in Nepal and Bhutan call upon India to revisit its policy towards these countries.

With the advancing age of the Dalai Lama and assertive management of its Tibetan affairs by China, India's approach to Tibet also calls for a careful revisit. India encouraged its Tibetan people to split the secular and temporal authorities that were merged in the Dalai Lama. One is however not certain if that alone would take care of a post-Dalai Lama situation. The confusion and contradiction that characterised New Delhi's approach to Tibetans' "Thank You India—2018" in March, did not bring any credit to India. The return of Karmapa Lama to India from the US may also prove to be an important piece in the post-Dalai Lama Tibetan puzzle.[3] Media reports that Prime Minister Modi discussed the Tibet question with the Chinese President Xi Jinping in his informal Wuhan summit have stirred the Tibetan pot in India's policy.[4] Voices are being raised from within India's strategic community that India should revise its Tibet policy and one China approach in view of China's assertion in the Himalayas. Foreign Minister Sushma Swaraj went to the extent of alerting China that India will maintain its 'One China Policy' as long as China also respects 'One India Policy'. It is also being argued that either India should seek to get a dialogue restarted between the Dalai Lama and the Chinese authorities or should raise the issue of human rights violations in Tibet in the United Nations and other international fora.

Since the beginning of this century, Asian geopolitics has been marked by China's rise and assertion and the Himalayan region has been no exception. During the 1960s and 1970s, China offered itself to be a balancing factor against India when lured and invited by the Himalayan states. In the present context however, China has been actively pursuing its objective of deepening its strategic presence. There are four major drivers behind Chinese moves in India's land and maritime neighbourhood. First, for stabilising and effectively controlling its vulnerable periphery in Tibet and Xinjiang, China finds it necessary to be present in the neighbouring South Asian states. Second, it cannot neglect South Asia if it has to sustain its own economic growth because this region, of nearly 1.5 billion people is growing at an annual average rate of around 6 per cent. This region, being still poor in infrastructure development offers promising prospects for China's over-saturated infra-sector. Third, China's presence in South Asia and the Bay of Bengal can cushion its 'Malacca dilemma' that accounts for more than 85 per cent of its trade flows. And lastly, this is the region where China must also counter the US influence if it has to ensure its primacy in Asia. China's Belt and Road Initiative (BRI) is a powerful economic and infra-structural construct to push its strategic presence in Asia and in India's neighbourhood.

There are three sectors of the Himalayan geo-strategic space where China's assertion is of critical significance to India; namely Pakistan and the Occupied Kashmir, the Himalayan States of Nepal and Bhutan and the bilateral boundary between India and China. China-Pakistan Economic Corridor (CPEC) project is an integral part of BRI and it covers the whole of Pakistan Occupied Jammu and Kashmir (POJK). China's presence in POJK helps it to secure the turbulent Xinjiang province and its important land link to Pakistan through Karakoram Highway. It may be borne in mind that Pakistan's radical Islamist forces had been active in Xinjiang and China has been repeatedly protesting to Pakistan in this respect. Rise of radical Islamist forces and political turbulence in Gilgit-Baltistan and Northern territories of the POJK can add to Chinese difficulties in Xinjiang. Joint patrolling of the POJK-Xinjiang border by the Chinese PLA and the Pakistani troops started in 2016, soon after the launching of BRI. Chinese military and economic presence in POJK is a clear violation of India's sovereign claims on POJK. That is one of the reasons for India's refusal to endorse the BRI, despite China's repeated appeals. There however, seems to be no way in which India can force China out of POJK. For decades, India seldom initiated any moves to gain control of the POJK except registering its notional claims. There have infact, been occasions when India appeared inclined to resolve the Kashmir issue with Pakistan along the Line of Control (earlier Ceasefire Line). Assertion of India's claims on POJK have become more audible under Prime Minister Modi's leadership, particularly after his mention of support for POJK and Gilgit people in Independence Day public address in August 2016. The contours of any concrete policy to back words with action on POJK are still awaited.

Besides Pakistan, China's South Asia thrust is also clearly evident in the Himalayan states of Nepal and Bhutan. Nepal, like Pakistan, is a part of China's BRI and China has offered an infrastructure aid package of $8.5 billion. Under the offered projects, Lhasa will be linked to Kathmandu through train and roads joining the two countries will also be laid down to improve movement of goods and people. China has also offered transit to Nepal for third country trade. It is printing Nepalese currency and held second military exercise to fight terrorism in Chengdu province of China in August 2018. The first of such joint exercise was initiated during 2004-2005, when King Gyanendra's regime was countering Maoist insurgency. China has been increasingly active in Nepal's political arena by showering its support and blessings to the consolidation of Communist forces following the adoption of Nepal's new Constitution that had led to the alienation of Nepal from India.[5] To balance its position against India's dominance over the Chumbi Valley, China is encroaching into Bhutan. The standoff between India and China in Doklam in June 2017 resulted from such encroachment and Chinese push to reach India's vulnerable and sensitive Siliguri corridor, generally referred to as 'Chicken's Neck'. Doklam is a disputed area between Bhutan and China. In the border talks between the two countries, China has been prepared to offer territorial concessions to Bhutan in its north-eastern sector in order to retain the Doklam area. Even after the resolution of the standoff, the Chinese troops' concentration continues in northern Doklam. Encroachment and standoff in Doklam could also be seen as Chinese pressure technique on Bhutan to secure a bilateral resolution of the border dispute and formalisation of diplomatic relations between the two countries. When that happens, China will invite Bhutan to join BRI, offering generous infrastructure projects and development assistance.

No less important than China's growing presence in Pakistan and the Himalayan region, is the careful shift in its position on the question of Himalayan border dispute with India. The process of bilateral relations initiated during Rajiv Gandhi's period in 1988-89 progressed well. The 1993 and 1996 agreements to maintain peace and tranquillity on the border have generally worked well, notwithstanding instances of incursions and encroachments. A major gain in this respect was the Agreement of 11 April 2005 which laid down political guidelines for the resolution of the border dispute. Under these guidelines, both sides agreed to "make meaningful and mutually acceptable adjustments...arrive at a package settlement...(offer) due consideration to each other's strategic and reasonable interests...(and) safeguard due interests of their settled populations in the border areas". Within these guidelines, there was an implicit acceptance by China, of India's claims on Arunachal Pradesh including Tawang monastery as they constitute "settled populations in the border areas". China has started challenging these claims for the past decade, and since 2005, there has been little forward movement towards settlement of the boundary issue. China has not been coming forward in defining the Line of Actual Control through exchange and acceptance of maps. China is accordingly, sharpening the new Great Game in the Himalayas with India. This is seen as China's response to the changing strategic equations in the Indo-Pacific region, particularly between India and the US and India and Japan. It may be kept in mind that these relations had started warming up after 2005-2006, with the gradual advance in the Indo-US nuclear equation and defence cooperation.

India is acutely conscious of the Chinese thrust in South Asia and the Himalayas. India's problem is that it does not have enough resources to match the Chinese initiatives and offers to its neighbours. Nor its diplomacy and delivery on promises are as efficient and assuring as that of China's. India's strength hopefully lies in its civilisational and cultural links, and accordingly,

India is emphasising on Hindu and Budhhist linkages in its diplomacy. But that cannot provide a befitting response to assertive hard power China is displaying. India is in fact groping for a viable response to China which needs to be carefully constructed keeping in mind, India's capabilities, China's vulnerabilities and the regional strategic flux precipitated by uncertainties in the US-China relationship. The longer India takes in evolving a credible China policy in the Himalayas, and elsewhere, the more harm will come to its vital stakes.

NOTES

1 Maharaja Krishna Rasgotra, *A Life in Diplomacy,* Penguin India, 2016. Prashant Jha, in his story, "With Beijing, does Delhi have a Tibet card?" writes: "But Gyalo Thondup, the brother of Tibet's spiritual head Dalai Lama, has written of how Nehru had sent him three separate messages, asking Tibetans to mobilise militarily and offering Indian assistance. Thondup did not hear back from his own government for six months. By then, it was too late", *The Hindustan Times,* 21 September 2016.

2 Colonel Narender 'Bull' Kumar and Prateek Joshi, "Siachen Glacier, the Fulcrum of the Great Game: Colonel 'Bull' Kumar's Perspectives", *Asian Affairs,* Vol. 49, No.1, 2018, pp. 103-117.

3 See P. Stobden's two articles on this theme; one in The Tribune (Chandigarh), 25 July 2018, and another in The Wire (Web Newspaper), 7 August 2018.

4 M.K. Bhadrakumar, "Modi won't play the Tiber card with Xi", *Rediff.com,* 9 August 2018, available at http://www.rediff.com/news/column/modi-wont-play-the-tibet-card-with-xi/20180809.htm

5 Sudha Ramachandran, "Sino-Nepali Relations: Scaling New heights", *China Brief,* Vol. 18, No. 6, 9 April 2018, Jamestown Foundation, available at https://jamestown.org/program/sino-nepali-relations-scaling-new-heights/ .

3

Himalayan Frontiers Through the Ages

K. Warikoo

The Himalaya is the embodiment of divinity, of nature in its splendour and of culture in the deepest sense of the word. The Himalaya has been inextricably interwoven with the life and culture of India since time immemorial. It has been the repository of rich biodiversity, source of main river systems and glaciers and the symbol of India's spiritual and national consciousness.[1] In the words of E B Havell, the Orientalist, "all Indian poetry and mythology point to the Himalayas as the centre of the world and as the throne of the great gods."[2] The geographical feature that dominates India most is the Himalayas, which has acted as a great natural frontier. Though geographically speaking Himalaya is embraced at its western and eastern extremities by the Indus and Brahamputra respectively, we can't isolate the Hindu Kush, Karakoram and Pamirs region, which is continuous and interlocked with the great Himalayan mountain system. Jawaharlal Nehru has described the Himalayas as being "closely connected with old myths and legends, which have influenced so much of our thought and literature. The mighty rivers of India flow from this great mountain barrier into the plains of India".[3] Rivers Sindhu (Indus), Jhelum, Ravi, Beas, Satlej, Yamuna, Ganga, Kali (Mahakali), Karnali (Ghagra or Saryu), Gandaki, Kosi, Brahamputra, Subansiri and the Siang flow through the Himalayas. Lofty peaks of K2 (8,611 m), Nanga Parbat (8,126 m), Nunkun (7,816 m), Dhaulagiri (8,172 m), Everest (8,850 m) and Namcha Barwa (7,756 m) stand magnificently on the Himalayas.

The importance of Himalaya as the natural frontier of India in the north is immersed in Indian history, ethos and psyche. In Puranic literature and religious invocations, India is described as part of *Jambudweep*, the Indian continent of which the Himalayan mountains form the northwestern, northern and northeastern border.[4] *Vishnu Puraan*, *Shiv Puraan*, *Matsya Puraan* and *Mahabharata* clearly state that "between the Himalaya in the north and the sea in the south lies *Bharatvarsh*".[5] According to *Vaman Puraan*, *Kurma Puraan*, *Matsya Puraan*, *Varah Puraan* and *Markandeya Puraan* the countries neighbouring *Bharatvarsh* across the Himalayas were *Ilavritvarsh* in the northeast (present day Tajikistan and Badakshan region), *Ketumalavarsh* in the west (present day Turkmenistan), *Harivarsh* in the southwest (present Afghanistan), *Bhadrashwavarsh* in the east (present Xinjiang), *Hiranyavarsh* in the northeast (present Kyrgyzstan), *Ramyakvash* in the northwest (present Uzbekistan) and *Kuruvarsh* in the north (present Kazakhstan).[6] The Puranas have also mentioned the rivers Oxus (Amu Darya) and Jaxartes (Syr Darya) as Suchakshu and Bhadra rivers respectively.[7]

Vishnu Puraan, one of the earliest Sanskrit texts makes it clear that the Himalayas formed the northern frontier of India. It states that the country south of the Himalayas and north of ocean is called Bharat and all born in it are called Bharatiyas.

> *Uttaram yat samudrasya himadres saiva dakshinam*
> *Varsam tad bharatam nama bharati yatra santatih*

Kalidasa in his *Kumara Sambhava* described the Himalaya as *devatma*—a divine personality, and as the measuring rod spanning the eastern and western oceans, thereby pinpointing the northern frontiers of India.

> *Astyutrasyam dishi devatma himalayo nam ngadhirajah*
> *urvaparo toynidhi vagaha sithati prathvya iv mandanda*

[In the north (of our country) stands the Lord of Mountains and the very embodiment of divinity—the Himalaya, like a measuring rod of the earth spanning the eastern and western oceans.]

Markandeya Purana states that "India is girdled on three sides by the sea and on the north by the Himalayan mountain range which stretches along on its north like the string of a bow".[8]

Early Tamil literature has described the Himalayas a *Devatta* (Divine).

Early Tamil poets "spoke and wrote highly of the Himalayas—its snow-clad peaks, its ever-lively rivers, its lovely valleys, its busy pilgrim centres and its beautiful flora and fauna. They not only pictured it as the 'abode of Lord Siva' and *Hemavati* (Parvati), but also of the 'house of snow' and the tapovans of saints and seers".[9] Early Tamils knew that the Himalayas formed the northern frontier of India and Kanyakumari was its southern tip. To the majority of Indians, Himalayas are mythical mountains referred to by the Vedas, Puranas and other scriptures. Himalaya is part of our history, tradition and cultural heritage. Most of our sacred shrines and places of pilgrimages are situated in the Himalayan heights. So much so, there is no fulfillment of life to an Indian without some sort of a Himalayan experience.

Ancient texts repeatedly refer to Kashmir *Mandala* which not only denotes its spatial and temporal locus in terms of a sacred geography but also has geo-political ramifications when one takes into consideration the extended sphere and influence of Kashmir outside its territorial frontiers. Kashmir has made lasting contribution in core areas of Indian cultural and intellectual endeavours from aesthetics, poetics, dramaturgy, historiography, linguistics, literature, folklore, transmission of the doctrines of Mahayana Buddhism, Kashmir Shaivism, mural, architectural and sculptural art etc. thus becoming an inalienable part of India's spiritual and national consciousness. Whereas some scholars have described Kashmir as the northernmost outpost of Indian culture, many prefer to call it as the fountainhead of Indian culture. Even as far as in south India, Hindus invoke *Sharda* as part of their popular rituals.

> *Namastase Sharda Devi Kashmirapuravasini*
> (We bow to Sharda Devi, resident of Kashmir)
>
> *Saraswati mahamaya Kashmirapuravasini*
> *Stadresamantat tam saraswata mahamunim*
>
> (We bow to Saraswati, who is the great *maya* and resident of Kashmir and also to the great Saraswata residing in the neighbourhood of *Satadri*)

Indian epics and the *Puranas* refer to ancient kingdoms of Pragjyotisha and Kamarupa in the eastern Himalayas. The *Ramayana* mentions the kingdom of Pragjyotisha which included the whole of modern Assam and North East Frontier Agency. Kalidasa in his *Raghuvamsa* (4th century AD) explicitly states that the kingdom of Pragjyotisha extended north of the Himalayas from

Hemakuta (Kailash) to Kamarupa (present day Assam). In course of time Pragjyotisha, Sonitpur (Tezpur) and other adjoining areas were all united under the rulers of Kamarupa. The *Vishnu Purana* states that Kamarupa extended for 100 yojanas in all directions from Kamakhya temple (situated near Gauhati). Prof. Suniti Kumar Pathak, well known authority on the tribes of the eastern Himalayas, refers to a document *Seryig* preserved in the Tawang monastery. The *Seryig* document was awarded to Mera Lama to exercise control on the Monpa area consisting of Tawang and adjoining villages, Tammaphu valley, Phutang, Tembang, Karit, But villages, Domkho, Duipla Ko river valleys etc. The Monpas of Tawang and Sherichokpas of Tammaphu and Phutang later accepted the British Indian authority.[10]

Stretching over a length of over 2,500 kms from Nanga Parbat in the west to Namcha Barwa in the east, the Himalayas have provided India with the natural and most formidable line of defence. However, the imposing geographical features and high daunting peaks of the Himalaya did not prevent this region from being a complex of cultural interaction, movement of races, overland trade and communication. Straddling the borders of the world's two major cultural areas—Central Asia and South Asia, the Himalaya is a contact zone between these two regions. To quote a well known anthropologist James F. Fisher, "Himalayas are not so much a boundary, border or buffer, as a zipper which stitches together these two densely textured cultural fabrics".[11] Abutting the borders of Afghanistan, China, Pakistan and India and being situated in close proximity to Central Asia, the Himalayan region has been an important constituent of India's trans-Himalayan communication network in the continent and beyond. The Himalayan region has been the cradle from where ancient Indian culture including Mahayana Buddhism spread to different countries in Central Asia, East Asia and Southeast Asia. Such cross-cultural contacts were not confined only to religious philosophy of Mahayana Buddhism, these also included art, architecture, literature etc. Such movements produced a harmonious blend of cultures, arts, science and literature. After the Chinese occupation of Tibet, Indian Himalayas became the last refuge of Buddhism. That explains the rationale behind the setting up of specialised Buddhist Studies Institutes in Ladakh, Gangtok and Arunachal Pradesh after late 1950s.

The very fact that boundaries of Tajikistan, Afghanistan, China, Pakistan, India and Myanmar converge along the Himalayas, lends a unique geostrategic importance to this region. Its potential for instability and conflict is furthered by the ethnic-religious jigsaw prevailing in the Himalayas and trans-Himalayas where people of Buddhist, Hindu and Islamic faiths are concentrated in various areas and are vulnerable to extraneous influences. Major international land frontier disputes pertain to this area. Whereas India and Pakistan have been locked in a conflict over Kashmir since 1947, the Sino-Indian border dispute remains to be settled. Any cross-border fraternisation of people of Xinjiang and Tibet in China, Uzbekistan, Tajikistan, Afghanistan, Pakistan, Indian Himalayas from Kashmir upto North East, Nepal, Bhutan, Bangladesh and Myanmar, on ethnic and religious lines is a potential source of conflict in the region and a threat to the security of concerned states. Active involvement of Islamist *Mujahideen* in cross-border terrorism and *jihad* (holy war), whether in the Indian state of Jammu and Kashmir, Tajikistan or some other Commonwealth of Independent States (CIS) countries, has adversely affected regional security, peace and stability in the Himalayan and adjoining Central Asian region. Western Himalayas have served as the Gateway to India for numerous invasions and influences from Central Asia and West Asia. Even in contemporary times, India has had to experience successive military aggressions from Pakistan in 1947, 1965, 1971, 1999 (in Kargil) and now in the form of proxy war in Kashmir that has been going on for more than three decades, besides the Chinese military offensive in 1962 from across the Himalayas.

Though the ancient history of the Karakoram-Himalayan region is shrouded in obscurity, the region is referred as *Daraddesa* (corresponding to present Gilgit and adjoining areas) and *Polulo* (corresponding to present Baltistan area) in several ancient sources. The entire region is also referred to as Bolor, Baloristan or Balawaristan. Whereas Gilgit was under the reign of *Palola* or *Patola* Shahis who practiced Buddhism during 6th to 8th centuries, Baltistan remained Buddhist upto 15th century. That this frontier area has been part of the Indian political and cultural system in ancient times, is corroborated by historical evidence. Thousands of rock carvings, inscriptions, petroglyphs etc. spanning the Karakoram-Himalayas provide clinching evidence of the prevalence of Hindu and Buddhist faith and rule since ancient times. Fourteen rock edicts of the Mauryan emperor Ashoka dating to mid-3rd century B.C. in Kharoshthi script and detailing both the moral teachings and administrative orders inscribed on huge boulders, have been found along the Karakoram Highway.[12] Ashoka is referred here by his titles of *Devana*

Priya Priyadasi Raja (The King, beloved of gods, of noble appearance)."[13] A number of inscriptions in Brahmi, Kharoshthi and Hindu temples with engravings of *Swastika*, *Trishul* (trident) and Buddhist figures found at Shatial, Thor, Hodur and Chilas point to the existence of Hindu faith and rule in the region in ancient times.[14] A Kharoshthi inscription near Chilas mentions *Uvimadasakesa* (a name referring to the second emperor Vima Kadphises).[15] Kharoshthi inscriptions belonging to Kushana period are concentrated at Alam Bridge, 25 miles west of Gilgit.[16] The Sacred Rock at Hunza also has Kushana inscriptions and carvings.[17]

It is thus established that Dardistan was a constituent unit of Kanishka's empire. Kalhana's *Rajatarangini* refers to the military exploits of King Lalitaditya of Kashmir (6-7th century) in Gilgit region. Similarly, Gilgit-Baltistan formed a part of medieval Kashmir Sultanate of Shahbuddin and Zain-ul-Abidin. Whenever the local chiefs asserted their independence, they continued to be influenced by Indian culture and way of life. Even in modern times, they have been known by their titles like *Raja* and *Mehtar*, which is the corrupt form of Sanskrit title *Mehattar*. Life-size images of Buddha carved out of rock, abundance of Buddhist inscriptions throughout this region, discovery of famous Gilgit Manuscripts there (in early 1930s) etc. are living testimony of the Indian cultural influence in this frontier area. Even as late as in nineteenth century, Muslims of Gilgit were found to be lax in their practicing of Islam. Major J. Biddulph, who joined as the Political Officer in Gilgit in 1877 is emphatic that "Buddhism was no doubt the religion of the country at the time of Shin invasion. There seem good grounds for supposing that the religion of the Shins was of the Brahminical type."[18] According to him, "till a very recent period burning the dead was practiced. The ashes were carefully collected and buried in rude wooden boxes, sometime carved out of a solid block, or in round earthen jars. The bones are neatly packed in the boxes, which have previously been lined with birch bark."[19] However, Biddhulph found that "the burning of the dead ceased to be practiced more than sixty years ago"[20] (i.e., around 1810 AD). Biddulph ascribes the "names of many of the rulers and of a number of places, not only in the Indus and Gilgit valleys, but also in the Chitral Valley," to a Brahminical origin.[21] It was actually the Sikh Commander, Nathu Shah who was Muslim by religion and Syed by caste and was functioning as Kashmir's governor at Gilgit for several years, who made his subjects follow Islam more strictly. According to Frederic Drew, who for several years was the British Joint Commissioner in Ladakh, the people of

Astor used to cremate their dead which practice was changed to that of burial after the arrival of Nathu Shah in 1842 AD.[22] Yet, they continued to light some fire near the grave.[23]

In ancient times Baltistan was under the sway of Kushans who introduced Buddhism here. However, in 7th century AD, Tibetans expanded their authority to this region, only to be expelled in early 8th century by Lalitaditya Muktapida of Kashmir. The presence of Buddhist inscriptions and rock carvings in Baltistan and the survival of Tibetan/Buddhist names, dialect and script to this day points to the prevalence of Buddhism and the existence of active socio-economic contacts between Baltistan and Ladakh. In 13th century, a Muslim adventurer Ibrahim Shah is reported to have come to Baltistan, married a local princess, assumed power and founded the Makpon dynasty.[24] A Muslim missionary Mir Shamsuddin Iraqi who came to Baltistan in 15th century, spread Islam and established Nurbakhshiya order here. Quite a large number of people in Baltistan continue to follow the Nurbakhshiya sect of Islam. Ali Sher Khan who ruled Baltistan from 1595 to 1633 AD, established matrimonial and friendly relations with the Mughal rulers.[25] However, following Ali Sher's, death, the internecine feuds among his sons and successors led the Mughal rulers Shah Jahan and Aurangzeb to extend their authority over Baltistan.[26] However, during the decline of Mughals, the Balti chiefs regained their authority, which lapsed again when the Afghan Governor of Kashmir Haji Karim Dad Khan sent a large force to Skardu in 1779 AD and brought Baltistan under Kashmir's control.[27] Whereas the Afghans were defeated in Kashmir by the Sikhs in 1819 AD, Baltistan witnessed internecine feuds amongst its chiefs. Ahmad Shah, the powerful chief of Skardu sought assistance of the Sikh rulers of Kashmir (1832-1834 AD) in his fight against the chief of Khaplu.[28] The internal feuds among the local chiefs facilitated the Dogra general Zorawar Singh's military campaign in the region which brought Baltistan under the control of Sikh/Dogra rulers of Kashmir. Zorawar Singh established a military post at Skardu in a newly built fort and appointed a *Thanedar* (Commander) to supervise the garrison.

Before Gulab Singh became the Maharaja of Jammu and Kashmir under the treaty of Amritsar (1846), he as the Raja of Jammu under the Sikhs had conquered the whole of Ladakh including Skardu (Baltistan), thanks to his trusted and dynamic military commander Zorawar Singh and Diwan Hari Chand. Maharaja Ranjit Singh—the Sikh potentate, who had long coveted

Ladakh (due to it being the transit route for shawl wool and a big revenue earner) recognised Gulab Singh's conquest of this frontier region. The area was thus brought under the full administrative control of Jammu and Kashmir State. When the Treaty of Amritsar was signed in 1846, the British not only recognised Gulab Singh as the Ruler of Jammu and Kashmir but also of Ladakh and Baltistan. In 1899, Baltistan, Ladakh and Gilgit were merged into one 'frontier district' and placed under *Wazir-i-Wazarat.*[29] Two years later in 1901, separate district of Ladakh was established which incorporated Skardu, Kargil and Ladakh tehsils.[30] The areas of Gultari and from Pari to Kharol were included in Kargil tehsil.[31] Now onwards Skardu became the winter headquarters of the Ladakh district. Amar Nath Pragal of Jammu was the last Wazir of Skardu, before he was brutally killed by Pakistan raiders when they occupied Skardu in August 1948.

Taking the case of Ladakh, it enjoys a unique geo-strategic location, being bounded by Xinjiang in the north, Tibet in the east, Kashmir and Baltistan in the west, and Lahoul, Spiti, Kulu, Bushahr and Chamba in the south. Ladakh has played an important role in the history and culture of this frontier region. Enjoying a central position in the network of overland caravan routes that were linked to the Silk Route, Ladakh acted as an important gateway in the Indo-Central Asian exchange of men, materials and ideas through the ages. Early history of Ladakh has been recorded by Ladakhi chronicles, which have been translated by A.H. Francke,[32] Luciano Petech[33] and Z.Ahmad.[34] *La-dwags rgyal rabs* (Royal Chronicles of Ladakh) written in Ladakhi language in the 17th century is an important source. A number of these chronicles have been edited and translated by Emil Schlagintweit (*Die Konige von Tibet.* Munich, 1866), Dr. Karl Marx (See his "Three Documents Relating to the History of Ladakh", *Journal of Asiatic Society of Bengal,* vol. 60, No. 3, 1891; vol. 63, No. 2, 1894; vol. 71, No. 1, 1902) and A.H. Francke (*Antiquities of Indian Tibet,* vol. II. Calcutta, 1926). A.H. Francke's *A History of Western Tibet* (London, 1907) is a standard work on the history of Ladakh, which Francke wrote after consulting various source materials available to him at that time. Francke provides an authentic account as was given by Basti Ram, a Dogra officer under General Zorawar Singh, of the Dogra conquest of Ladakh and Baltistan (1834-40) and subsequent campaign in Western Tibet during 1841.

Noted Ladakhi historian S.S. Gergan has also recorded the local views based on diaries/records maintained by Ladakhis in his book *Ladags Gyalrabs Chimed Ster*. Translation the account of Dogra war in Ladakh as reported by Basti Ram, who was the Thanedar of General Zorawar Singh, has been recorded both by Alexander Cunningham and Francke. Whereas Basti Ram's description of the Dogra campaign reflects the Dogra view-point, the local Ladakhi version of the Dogra war in Ladakh, which was recorded by a Lama (hiding in a cave in the mountains of lower Ladakh (Sham), and also by the secretaries of the last three kings of Ladakh-Tshespal, Chhog Sprul and Jigmed Namgyal in their private diaries has been brought out by S.S. Gergan in his book *Ladags r Gyalrabs Chimed Ster*.

Hashmatullah Khan's *Tarikh-i-Jammu, Kashmir, Ladakh aur Baltistan* (published in Urdu in Lucknow in 1939) is another contemporaneous account by the Dogra government official in Ladakh. *Gulab Nama* (in Persian) written by Diwan Kirpa Ram, Prime Minister of Maharaja Gulab Singh and Ranbir Singh and published in Jammu in 1875, provides the Dogra viewpoint of their rule in Ladakh. This book has since been translated into English.

In 1834, Ladakh came under Dogra control, and by 1840 the Dogra forces led by General Zorawar Singh had established their authority throughout Ladakh and Baltistan. In 1846, Ladakh became a part of the newly founded state of Jammu and Kashmir under the Dogra ruler Maharaja Gulab Singh and his successors. And after 1947, Ladakh including Kargil has been a province of Jammu and Kashmir state, with its borders abutting Xinjiang and Tibet regions of China to its north and east, and Baltistan in Pak-occupied Kashmir to its west.

The economy of Western Tibet was more closely linked to that of Ladakh and Kashmir than to Central Tibet. As the main manufactory of shawls, Kashmir provided a stable market for the fine wool produced in Western Tibet. Thus the demand for shawl-wool in Kashmir generated much of the trade that passed between Ladakh and Tibet. With the incorporation of Western Tibet within Ladakh under the kingship of Senge Namgyal (1595-1645)[35] these traditional trade contacts were cemented, But, around 1680, the fifth Dalai Lama (1617-82) after consolidating his authority in Tibet, began to challenge Ladakh's supremacy over Western Tibet.[36] What followed proved to be of far-reaching importance for the consolidation of the traditional economic contacts between Ladakh and Tibet on a regular treaty basis. In 1681 AD, the Tibeto-Mongol forces waged a war against Ladakh in which the latter suffered reverses. Ladakh which acknowledged Mughal suzerainty, now sought their aid. The Mughal Governor of Kashmir, Ibrahim Khan, was quick to realise that the Tibetan advance into Ladakh would have an adverse effect on the lucrative shawl trade of Kashmir. He, therefore, sent a Mughal army to assist the Ladakh forces. The combined Ladakhi-Mughal forces defeated the Tibeto-Mongol troops and pushed them back to the traditional Ladakh-West Tibet border at Tashigong. Eventually the two sides ceased hostilities and began negotiations for a final peace settlement. The Treaty of Tingmosgang was signed in 1684, which "fixed the border at Lhari stream, flowing into the Indus south-west of Demchok".[37] Ladakh was persuaded to cede to Lhasa the territory of West Tibet as "an offering to the religion of Buddha" and the revenue of this territory was to be used "to meet the expenses of the sacrificial lamps and the reading of prayers at Lhasa".[38] Notwithstanding this territorial concession to Lhasa, Ladakh acquired exclusive rights to the wool produced in West Tibet. The treaty also provided for the exchange of periodic missions between the two sides. Ladakh was to send a mission, which came to be known as *Lapchak*, to Lhasa carrying presents for the Dalai Lama and other spiritual authorities. Since the members of *Lapchak* mission were allowed to carry merchandise for sale inside Tibet, it soon acquired a commercial character. Likewise, Lhasa was to send each year a government trading mission known as *Chabha*, carrying brick-tea. The Tibetan government instituted two new posts-that of a Gold Superintendent (*Serpon*) and a Government Trader (*Shung Tsong*) in Nagari under the provisions of this treaty.[39] Both were non-civil list officers who held their appointments under the Dalai Lama's private treasury for only one year.[40] The *Shung Tsong's* duties included, among other things, the supply of two hundred loads of brick-tea to Ladakh.[41] This practice continued right upto the early twentieth century and regular visits of the official Government Trader at Gartok to Ladakh took place each year.[42] Simultaneous with the Ladakh-Tibet Treaty of 1684, Ladakh entered into an agreement with the Mughals under which all the fine wool imported from Tibet was to be sent only to Kashmir. The Ladakhi authorities were guaranteed the right to act as intermediaries in the lucrative wool trade between Tibet and Kashmir. Four Kashmiri merchants who were to reside at Spitak, were to supply the wool to Kashmir. No other Kashmiris were to go to the Tibetan highlands to purchase wool.[43] In this manner, the Treaty of Tingmosgang regulated the trade traffic between Ladakh and Tibet.

Shawl-wool being the most important article of trade between Ladakh and Tibet was a lucrative source of income for the ruling class in Ladakh and the Kashmiri and Arghun traders who had privileged access to Tibet through their agents who spent most of their time purchasing wool in the wool raising areas of Chang Thang, Rudok, Gartok and other highlands of Tibet.[44] The Arghun traders brought the wool to Ladakh each year during the autumn months. They also received money from the Ladakhi authorities to take back merchandise for sale in Tibet, the proceeds of which were used for the purchase of wool and tea. These traders were granted the concession of carrying on their own trade between Tibet and Leh on which no taxes were levied.[45] On their part the Gartok authorities strictly observed the 1684 treaty stipulations with regard to Ladakh's monopoly over wool till the early nineteenth century. Any attempt to export this item to areas other than Ladakh was severely punished by the Tibetan authorities. The importance of this trade to Kashmir can be gauged by the following observations made by William Moorcroft during his stay in Leh: "Ladakh can deprive Raja Ranjit Singh of an annual revenue of 11 lakhs of rupees merely by withholding her supply of shawl-wool, from Kashmir. Ladakh can raise a disturbance almost amounting to an insurrection amongst the seditious and discontented Kashmiris merely by stopping the supply of tea".[46] Thus, any dislocation in the flow of Pashm from the established route, i.e., West Tibet-Ladakh-Kashmir, was bound to affect adversely the economies of both Ladakh and Kashmir.

In the early nineteenth century, the British Indian authorities made several attempts to divert this traffic to the newly acquired British territory of Bushahr. In 1810, a British trader, Mr Gillman of Bareilly, purchased a small quantity of shawl-wool in Gartok through his agents. When the Ladakhi authorities came to know about it they promptly protested to the Garpon or the Tibetan Governor at Gartok, who issued an edict forbidding the sale of wool to anyone other than the Ladakhis on pain of death.[47] Two years later in 1812, another such attempt was made, when Moorcroft undertook a journey to Gartok with the object of opening "to Great Britain, means of obtaining the materials of the finest woollen fabric".[48] He succeeded in purchasing a small quantity of shawl-wool. At about the same time, a number of Kashmiri artisans migrated to Amritsar, Ludhiana, Nurpur and the adjoining hill areas, to escape the heavy exactions levied by the Afghan Governors in Kashmir. The settlement of Kashmiri weavers in the hill areas of Punjab created a new demand for shawl-wool. Rampur, the capital of Bushahr, also began to develop into another whole-wool trading center. According to Moorcroft, who was at Leh during 1821, some 150 horse loads of wool were smuggled over various passes to British India.[49] The 1830s saw a rapid rise in the export of shawl-wool to Rampur, a fall-out of the political unrest in Ladakh. According to J.D. Cunningham, who spent a year in Kinnaur in the year 1842, the value of wool sold at Rampur rose from 35,630 rupees in 1837 to 94,807 rupees in 1840.[50] Thus with the arrival of the British in the Western Himalayas, the value of shawl-wool imports from Tibet into Ladakh and Kashmir started to decrease causing anxiety to the authorities in Ladakh and Kashmir. By 1840, Dogras had firmly established their authority over Ladakh and Baltistan. Gulab Singh's main object in this new conquest, was to encircle the Kashmir valley and to gain access to the lucrative wool trade which was the key to Kashmir's prosperity. With Ladakh in his hands, Gulab Singh now attempted to stop the direct trade between Tibet and British territory, and the wool imports to Rampur dropped to 17, 766 rupees in 1841.[51] Gulab Singh desired to establish total control over the coveted wool trade by conquering the wool producing areas in West Tibet. In early 1841 Zorawar Singh, the Dogra military Governor of Ladakh and a trusted lieutenant of Gulab Singh, wrote to the Garpon of Gartok not to supply Pashm wool to any other area except Ladakh. He also demanded a tribute from him thereby seeking to enforce Ladakh's old territorial claim to West Tibet.[52] Zorawar Singh, not satisfied with the response from Gartok, marched his forces towards West Tibet in the summer of 1841. After initial successes in conquering Tibetan territory up to Taklakot, Zorawar Singh's army suffered a crushing defeat in December 1841 mainly because of heavy snowfall. Eventually, with the arrival of Dogra reinforcements, the Tibetans were defeated and a peace treaty was concluded between the Tibetans and the Dogras at Leh on 17 September 1842. Under the terms of this treaty, the Tibetans accepted the Dogras as the legitimate authority in Ladakh and the 'old established frontiers' were reaffirmed. The Ladakhi king was allowed to continue sending gifts (*Lapchak*) to the Dalai Lama and his ministers. The Tibetans, in turn, undertook 'to carry on the trade in shawl-wool and tea in accordance with old customs via Ladakh year by year'.[53] In short, the *Lapchak* and *Chabha* missions were to be continued as earlier. The Ladakhi traders were entitled to free transport and accommodation during their travel and stay in Tibet, while the official trading caravan from Tibet would enjoy similar facilities during their annual trip to Ladakh. In this manner the 1842 treaty not only reiterated the traditional frontier but also reinforced the traditional trade ties between Ladakh and Tibet, with one major difference. The *Lpachak* mission lost its earlier religious character and became a purely commercial affair managed by the professional traders mainly Kashmiri Muslims settled at Leh, who earned large profits in the transactions.

The British Indian government sent two commissioners Alexander Cunningham and Vans Agnew to Ladakh in August 1846 to "ascertain the ancient boundaries between Ladakh and Tibet and to lay down the boundary between the newly acquired British possessions in the Hills and Gulab Singh's territory".[54] Though the British sought cooperation of the Tibetan and Chinese officials to the joint demarcation of the Ladakh-Tibet border, both the Chinese and Tibetans evaded the issue, as they did not want to give access to the British for trade in Tibet. When the British commissioners arrived at the border at the end of August 1846, there were no Chinese officials. They were also met with the hostility of Tibetans. In fact the Chinese Viceroy at Canton, Key-ing wrote to the British Plenipotentiary at Hong Kong clearly stating that "a liberalised Chinese trade policy in Tibet would violate the Treaties of Nanking, which gave the British special rights on five Chinese ports."[55] As regards the border issue, Key-ing stated that "the borders of these territories have been sufficiently and distinctly fixed so that it will be best to adhere to this ancient arrangement".[56] Cunningham confirms that "with Rudok on the east there has been a long peace. The boundary is well defined by piles of stones, which were set up after the last expulsion of the Skopo or Mongol hordes in 1687 AD."[57] Cunningham adds that "a large stone was then set up as a permanent boundary between the two countries, the line of demarcation being drawn from the village of Dechong (Demchok) to the hill of Karbones."[58]

Old established frontiers on the Tibet-Ladakh border were reaffirmed by the Peace Treaty signed between the Dogras and Tibetans in September 1842. The Tibetans also accepted the Dogras as the legitimate authority in Ladakh, and trade in shawl-wool and tea was continued in accordance with old customs via Ladakh. Similarly, Baltistan (Skardo) which was later occupied by Pak forces in 1947-48 and has ever since been part of Pak-occupied Kashmir/ Northern Areas, remained part and parcel of Ladakh division of Jammu and Kashmir State under the Dogras. However, Lahoul and Spiti which were part of Raja Gulab Singh's territory of Ladakh, were taken away by the British in 1846-47 and merged with the British possessions of Kangra in the Western

Himalayas. This ensured that the trade route between Gartok and Rampur remained under the British control.

Since a sizeable portion of Ladakh territory (Baltistan, Raskam, Aksai Chin) has been under the occupation of Pakistan and China after 1947-48, this remains an important issue of study and research by Indian scholars. Similarly, Baltistan (Skardo) which was later occupied by Pak forces in 1947-48, has ever since been part of Pak-occupied Kashmir/Northern Areas. Ladakh's distinct geo-cultural identity was consolidated by the Dogras who maintained a separate *Wazarat* for Ladakh and Baltistan. Ladakh maintained social, cultural and economic linkages with Western Tibet and also with the neighbouring principalities of Lahoul, Spiti, Kulu and Bushahr. The history of Ladakh's control over Gartok and Rudok in Western Tibet is a matter of importance. Minsar—an enclave of Dogras within western Tibet, used to pay revenue to the Dogras till early twentieth century. The British used Ladakh and adjoining areas in Gilgit, Skardo, Hunza and Chitral as 'frontier listening posts' to monitor the developments in Central Asia and Xinjiang throughout the Dogra period.

In early twentieth century, Lord Curzon who had explored the Pamirs and the Karakoram, observed that "the holders of the mountains had an immense advantage against the occupants of the plains. He advocated a scientific frontier uniting the natural and strategic strength which would place both the entrance and the exit of the passes in the hands of the defending power".[59] Lord Curzon had visualised the Himalayan regions of Ladakh, Sikkim, Bhutan and North East frontier as an "inner defence line for India protected by a Tibetan buffer region." Curzon was convinced that protection of the British colonial state in India required dominance of the strategic Himalayan neighbourhood to stem any incursions by other interested regional state actors like Russia and China. The idea of developing 'buffer states' formed an integral part of this strategic philosophy and formed the crux of efforts to develop an integrated external policy paradigm during his term in India.

Thomas Holdich, the Surveyor General of India, described the Himalayas as the natural and accepted frontier. He opined that "it is the finest natural combination of boundary and barrier that exists in the world...a God-given boundary set to such a vast, impressive and stupendous frontier".[60] Later China viewed Himalaya as its outer line of defence necessary for the protection of Chinese interests in Tibet. Some analysts felt that Communist China considered the high plateau of Tibet to be palm of the hand with Ladakh, Nepal, Bhutan,

Sikkim and North East Frontier Agency as five fingers.[61] China has the palm under its control and now it seeks influence over the strategic five fingers.

The importance of the Himalayas as the protective barrier of India is enhanced by the vast expanse of the Tibetan plateau, whose elevation is above that of ordinary mountain ranges. In the words of K.M. Pannikar, "the plateau of Tibet has Kunlun mountains as its boundary in the north, the Karakoram in the west and south, and the east is equally mountain-bound. The mountainous area to the north of India has to be considered strategically as one—a great quadrilateral, the middle of which is an elevated plateau of 15,000 feet above sea level, and the southern ramparts, an invulnerable range of an average height of 20,000 feet. The area enclosed is 500,000 square miles, frightening and formidable in its geographical features, an arid waste, wind-swept and waterless where trees do not grow."[62] So in spite of the new and sophisticated advancements of weapon and communication technologies, the traditional importance of Himalayas as the land frontier and natural barrier has not been diminished. As Pannikar emphasised, "the essential point about the Himalayas is not their width of 150 miles, but the plateau behind it, which in itself is an elevation of about 15,000 feet and is guarded on all four sides by high mountains. In fact, the vast barrier upland behind the Himalayas provides the most magnificent defence in depth imaginable."[63]

Here it would be relevant to recall what Prof. Leo Rose, Margaret W. Fisher and Robert A Huttenback wrote soon after the Sino-Indian war of 1962, about the security challenges posed by "a united and dynamic China controlled Sinkiang and Tibet linked together to the arid wastes of northeastern Ladakh into an all-weather communication system routes". They believed that West Tibet and Ladakh together formed a natural geographic unit, which if joined together under the control of an aggressive power based south of the Himalaya could under conditions of conventional warfare, provide a vital and perhaps decisive key to Central Asia".[64]

NOTES

1 K. Warikoo, Editor, *Himalayan Frontiers of India*, London and New York: Routledge, 2009, p. viii.

2 E.B. Havell, *The Himalayas in Indian Art*, London: Jouhn Murray, 1924, p. 2.

3 Jawaharlal Nehru, *The Discovery of India*, Oxford University Press, 1946, p. 51.

4 K.S. Valdiya, *Geography, Peoples and Geodynamics of India in Puranas and Epics*, New Delhi: Aryan Books, 2012, p. 13.

5 Ibid., p. 33.
6 Ibid., pp. 36-43.
7 Ibid., p. 41.
8 See Binod S. Das, "The Himalaya Frontier from the Sanskrit Sources", in N.R. Ray, Editor, *Himalayan Frontier in Historical Perspective,* Calcutta, Institute of Historical Studies, 1986, p. 2.
9 See K. Sadeswin, "The Himalayas in early Tamil Literature", in N.R. Ray, Editor, *Himalayan Frontier in Historical Perspective,* Calcutta, 1986, p. 8.
See also Puliyar Kesikan, *Commentary of Manimekhalai,* 4th edition. Madras, 1967, p. 12.
10 See S.K. Pathak, "The Last Three Centuries of the Bhotias of the Himalayas", in K.Warikoo, Editor, *Society and Culture in the Himalayas,* New Delhi: Har Anand, 1995, p. 166.
11 James F. Fisher (Ed.), *Himalayan Anthropology: The Indo-Tibetan Interface,* Hague: Mouton Publishers, 1978, p. 2.
12 Ahmad Hasan Dani, *Human Record on Karakoram Highway,* Islamabad, p. 18.
13 *Ibid.,* For full text of these rock edits see pp. 20-22.
14 *Ibid.,* pp. 30.34.
15 *Ibid.,* p. 35.
16 Ahmad Hasan Dani, *History of Northern Areas of Pakistan,* Islamabad, 1989.
17 *Ibid.,* p. 122.
18 J. Biddulph, *Tribes of the Hindoo Koosh,* Reprint by Delhi, Bhavana Books, 2001, pp. 112-113.
19 *Ibid.,* p.113.
20 *Ibid.,* p.114.
21 *Ibid.,* p.115.
22 Frederic Drew, *The Jummoo and Kashmir Territories: A Geographical Account,* London, 1875. (Reprint by Delhi, Oriental Publishers, 1971), p.429.
23 *Ibid.*
24 Ahmad Hasan Dani, *History of Northern Areas of Pakistan,* p. 215.
25 *Ibid.,* p.222.
26 *Ibid.,* p.223.
27 *Ibid.,* p.224.
28. *Ibid.,* p.225.
29 *Ibid.,* p.320.
30 *Ibid.*
31 *Ibid.*
32 A.H. Francke, *Antiquities of Indian Tibet,* 2 Volumes, Calcutta, 1915, 1926.
33 Luciano Petech, *A Study on the Chronicles of Ladakh,* Calcutta, 1939.
34 Zahiruddin Ahmad, 'New Light on the Tibet-Ladakh-Mughal war of 1679-84'. *East and West,* Vol. 18, 1969, pp. 340-361.
35 C.L. Data, *Ladakh and Western Himalayan Politics,* Delhi, 1973, p. 61. M.W. Fisher, Leo E. Rose and R.A. Huttenback, *Himalayan Battleground,* New York, 1963, pp. 35-36.
36 M.W. Fisher, *ibid.,* p. 37.
37 Dorothy Woodman, *Himalayan Frontiers,* London" Barrie & Rockliffe, 1969, p. 20.
38 A.H. Francke, *Ladakh: The Mysterious Land,* Reprint, Delhi, 1978, p. 113.
39 Ram Rahul, *The Government and Politics of Tibet,* Delhi: Vikas, 1969, pp. 34-38.
40 *Ibid.*

41 Ram Rahul, "The structure of the Government of Tibet, 1644-1911", *International Studies,* Vol. 3, January 1962, pp. 282, 285. A.H. Franke, *op cit.*, p. 113.
42 See Charles A. Sheering, *Western Tibet and the Indian Borderland,* London, 1916, pp. 158, 300-1.
43 A.H. Francke, *op. cit.*, p. 111.
44 *Foreign, Political,* 10 October 1823, 27.
45 *Ibid.*
46 W. Moorcroft to C.J. Metcalf Secretary, Political Department, Government of India, 15 August 1821, See *Foreign, Political,* 20 September 1822, 63.
47 *Asiatic Researches*, Vol. 12, 1816, p. 451.
48 *Ibid.*, p. 456.
49 *Foreign, Political,* 10 October 1823, 27.
50 J.D. Cunningham, "Notes on Moorcroft's Travels in Ladakh", *Journal of Asiatic Society of Bengal,* Vol. 13, 1844, p. 210.
51 Cited in Alasair Lamb, *Britain and Chinese Central Asia,* London, 1960, p.66.
52 *Foreign, Secret* C., 21 June 1841, 15.
53 M.W. Fisher, *op.cit.*, p. 56.
54 *Ibid.* p 62.
55 *Ibid.*
56 *Ibid.*
57 Alexander Cunningham, *Ladakh*, London, 1854, p. 261.
58 *Ibid.* pp 328-29.
59 Curzon, *The Romanes Lecture 1907,* London: Clarendon Press, 1907, p 7.
60 Thomas Holdich, *Political Frontiers and Boundary Making,* Macmillan, 1956, pp. 280-81.
61 W.M. Jenkins and P.P. Karan, *The Himalayan Kingdoms,* New Jersey: Nostrand, 1963.
62 K.M. Pannikar, "The Himalaya and Indian Defence", *India Quarterly,* Vol. 3, Nos. 2-3, April-June/July-September 1947.
63 *Ibid.*
64 Margaret W. Fisher, Leo E Rose and Robert A Huttenback, *Himalayan Battleground: Sino-Indian Rivalry in Ladakh,* New York, 1963, p. 10.

4

The Himalayas: Bridge or Barrier?

Shakti Sinha

India's identity is very closely linked to the Himalayas. The early Indians imagined India to be an island, Jambudvipa, the southern end of a four lotus-leaf formation, each pointing in a different cardinal direction. Every description of India, or Bharatdesha, has the Himalayas at the north with major rivers, streams and rivulets watering the broad plains; then two converging sides surrounded by seas. This is the standard description across millennia and genre. This imagined homeland was accompanied by a very strong sense of geographical space and borders. The Himalayas, as the northern borders of the Indian Plate, is not coincidental. It arose, and continues to grow, as the Indian landmass crashed into the Eurasian landmass causing the latter to push upwards in response to this massive northward movement. The Himalayas and the rise of the Tibetan plateau is the result. While the waters flowing down the Himalayas is the key to the rise of flourishing human societies in the landmass south of the hills, the entire monsoon system which helped create conditions for this to happen would not have developed but for the critical role of the Himalayas. It has a decisive role in setting in place the wind systems that make the south-east and north-west monsoons and, in that sense, limiting precipitation in the trans-Himalayan region. It would not be wrong to say that the broad contours of what physically constitutes India are a direct outcome of this. The reverence that Indians hold the Himalayas in is therefore not surprising.

While the actual length of the Himalayas is around 2,400 kilometres, its influence is much greater because it joins up with other major mountain ranges, the Pamirs, Hindu Kush, Karakoram, Kunlun and Tian Shan, in what is known as the Pamir knot. At its eastern end, it tapers into the relatively lower hills separating India from Myanmar. With its three parallel ranges running across its length, the width of the Himalayas at 150 kilometres makes its extremely unusual, preventing heavy flows of men and material but porous enough to allow for their movement in limited numbers. In fact, the net effect of the combined Himalaya—Karakoram-Hindu Kush ranges allowed the development of the unique Indo-Iranian cultural space that produced the Vedic system as well as the two major, early challenges to it led by Zarathustra and Buddha that burst upon the regional scene in the sixth century BCE, coincidentally, though not in close proximity geographically and chronologically. Though there were other great spiritual movements in this region, the impact of these three philosophic systems has been well beyond those directly influenced by them.

Like the three ranges that constitute the Himalayas, there are three cultural sub-strands across its length with the Tibetan and the Indic at the northern and southern ends. The upper middle Himalayas running through Ladakh, Spiti, Kinnaur, the Bhotia-dominated areas of Uttarakhand, Mustang and other Buddhist areas of Nepal, Upper Sikkim, Bhutan, the Monpa area of Siang and further east through to the tri-junction of India, Myanmar and Tibet are home to heterogeneous sub-cultures that are a mix of the Indic and Tibetan cultures.[1] Their individuality must be respected and celebrated, while accepting that these areas are changing and will continue to do so.

The Himalayas, narrowly defined, links India, Pakistan, Tibet (part of the People's Republic of China), Nepal, Bhutan and Myanmar, though the last named is not often seen as a Himalayan country. Other than India and, to a lesser extent Bhutan, there is continuing political contestation in all these countries; Bhutan 'solved' its ethnic, linguistic, religious and political challenges with the mass migration, forced or voluntary, of the Lhotshampa community over two decades ago. It is inconceivable if Bhutan could, or would, have moved towards democratisation if this Nepali-origin community that constituted almost 40 per cent of Bhutan's population at one time was still in that country in large numbers.

Tibet is the best example that showcases the Himalayan conundrum of simultaneously being both a bridge and a barrier. Its isolation for centuries was well-known and it took the British considerable efforts to open it to the world. But what is less known and less acknowledged is that, for over a thousand years, it has always kept its links with India open. Tibetan Buddhism in its present form can be traced to the monk Padmasambhava, who travelled all over the Himalayas, from Ladakh to Bhutan and Tibet. He is accepted as the founder of Vajrayana Buddhism. Similarly, the role of Nalanda University and monk-scholars known as the Nalanda masters on Tibetan Buddhism is immeasurable. The regular presence of Tibetan monks at Nalanda, Vikramshila and other Indian universities and the reciprocal visits to Tibet by Indian monks strengthened the links considerably. What is even more important is that the Tibetan alphabet, grammar and vocabulary are based on Sanskrit. At the same time, geographical obstacles, lack of resources and low population meant that trading relations were limited but not non-existent. Tibetan traders not only went to the Himalayan regions but had settlements in the plains, as did Indian traders in Yatung, Gyantse and Lhasa. Indian traders were not limited to those from Ladakh who had spiritual links with Lhasa. The Lhasa-Gyantse-Yatung-Jelep La was the best access that Lhasa had to the world, a point that would come back later in this chapter.

This is why the British missions to Tibet took along Indian guides and translators like Nain Singh. When Heinrich Harrer, the Austrian prisoner-of-war in India during the Second World War escaped from Dehra Dun and finally reached Lhasa, he saw a car there. On enquiry, he was told that it had been brought over the mountain passes in a knocked-down condition from India. Similarly, he met Tibetans who had studied in India. Indians were running the Tibetan postal and wireless communications systems. Chinese control over Tibet has waxed and waned in history ever since the Mongol rulers brought it into their (Chinese) empire. Earlier, after a prolonged period of conflict, China and Tibet had demarcated their border. The relationship has been a complicated one varying from acceptance of suzerainty to more direct control by China. The key to trying to understand it is by referring to the Chinese world order, which is best expressed in the word 'Tianxia' (all under Heaven). This implies an emperor (Tianzi or Son of Heaven) in respect of the empire, a father/husband at home and a middle country (Zhongguo) internationally. There is a web of concentric circles around Zhongguo paying tribute to it. The Tianxia system is based on strong notions of superiority and hierarchy and one could, in the modern context, point towards suzerainty rather than sovereignty. In effect, there is the existence of a Sino-centric system, which was very different from Pax Britannia or Pax Americana, or even Westphalia.

Under this system, the Chinese emperor would provide assistance and protection in return for periodic tribute, which were often more symbolic than substantial. This was however a flexible system that depended on how strong the emperor was in enforcing his writ. Those on the edges could move out and come in depending on relative strength; for example, Mongolia stopped paying tribute at time of the Ming dynasty but was still part of the Sino-centric system insofar as China was concerned. In their own eyes, even when its system was weak, China acted as a moral role model. Tibet and Japan were outliers often but that did not alter their notional positions in the system. The Sino-centric system's limitations become obvious when it is seen that the famous British mission to Beijing in 1803 led by McCartney is recorded in Chinese documents as tribute from the King of Britain to the Emperor of China (Tianzi).

The India-China border dispute is driven by the Tibet question, a question that arose primarily out of the Great Game of the 19th century, but which actually began earlier and did not ever end. The rapid expanse of the Russian Empire, particularly as it swallowed the Khanates of Central Asia, nibbled at Iran and threatened Afghanistan. The British saw this as not only an expression of Russian desire for access to the warm waters of the Indian Ocean but as a threat to India itself, the jewel in the crown. The frontlines where the Russians had to be stopped were obviously Iran, Afghanistan and Tibet, somewhat matching Mackinder's delineation of the southern borders of Eurasia's Heartland. The story of Afghanistan is well-known even if completely misunderstood; the British were successful in stopping the Russians at the Amu Darya, an outcome achieved at the Pamir Conference between the two where Afghanistan's northern borders were decided upon, even if the Afghan Amir was not invited to it. Iran should not bother us here. But a brief outline of Tibet would be in order.

The British saw Tibet as a weak spot since it lacked a credible government that could defend itself securely against any potential Russian threat. British spies had reported the presence of Russians in East Turkistan (now Xinjiang), another area relatively ungoverned and proceeding towards Tibet. Xinjiang and Ladakh had regular trade. Aksai Chin is also the most favourable route from Tibet to Xinjiang, over which is what the People's Republic was ready to go to war with India; their simultaneous attack on the eastern frontier was only to use it as a bargaining chip. In late 19th century and early parts of the 20th century, contrary to conventional wisdom, it was the British who encouraged greater involvement of Manchu China in Tibet. British missions to Tibet persistently were to try and ward off potential Russian influence and realising the costs and impracticality of directly controlling Tibet, they turned to China. If there was a figure similar to Afghanistan's Amir Abdul Rahman, the British would have been happy to subsidise him so that a functioning security apparatus in Tibet would act to dissuade Russia from proceeding with their perceived plans. It is extremely likely that Tibet, like Afghanistan, could have emerged as a regular buffer State in this alternative scenario. In this context, the Chinese refusal to sign the final agreement at Simla (Shimla) must be seen.[2] The Chinese delegate had initialled the draft but the contentious border between Inner Tibet and Outer Tibet came in the way. Like Inner Mongolia, the Chinese were exercising much more direct control over parts of Tibet bordering Sichuan and Qinghai provinces, which have since been incorporated in these provinces; Outer Tibet based out of Lhasa exercised almost complete independence. Harrer's book, *Seven Years in Tibet*, refers to jostling in Lhasa between the Nationalist Chinese Government (Goumindang) representative who wanted to assert his authority and the refusal of the Tibetan government to accept this claim. This view is contested by some on the ground that during his seven years in Tibet, Harrer had become a tutor to the young XIVth Dalai Lama and so was biased but there is no proof that the Chinese had any meaningful role in Tibetan matters in this period.

The incorporation of Tibet into the People's Republic of China, the withdrawal of Indian technicians who ran Tibet's telecommunications system and later surrender of India's trading privileges changed the ground scenario quite considerably. As the PLA moved into Tibet and the Chinese started exercising greater control, Tibetans rose in regular revolts and uprisings. The Chinese refusal to accept the borders agreed to at Shimla, the McMahon line, meant that the two countries, China and India, that had now become neighbours, moved towards confrontation. Tibet, which historically acted as a buffer, was now the battleground. As mentioned earlier, India had certain traditional rights in Tibet. Besides, Mount Kailash and Manasarovar Lake, sacred to the Hindus and Jains in addition to the Bon and the Buddhist, lay in

Tibet. All access to Tibet ran through India. In fact, after the PLA moved into Tibet by defeating the miniscule, under-equipped Tibetan army, the Political Commissar sent by Beijing flew to Kolkata (Calcutta), took a train to Siliguri and then proceeded via Kalimpong before crossing over to Tibet through Jelep La.

What does the future hold for the Himalayas? Can, or should, India live with the status quo? Does the Chinese argument hold that the border is a colonial legacy and best left to the next generation? And is the time right for re-looking at the Himalayas, identify the traditional trading routes and open them up, hoping that increased economic inter-dependence would facilitate conditions for settlement of the border dispute? Can Nepal act as a bridge between the two big Asian economies?

International relations theory as exemplified by John Mearsheimer (*The Great Delusion*) teaches us that while one can assess a country's capabilities, one cannot assess its intentions. Even if one were to somewhat arrive at its present intentions, it is obviously not possible to predict its future intentions. A proxy approach would be to critically review its behaviour in similar circumstances.

President Xi Jinping has warned Taiwan that China would forcefully reunite it if Taiwan does not do so peacefully and that the Chinese people would not wait for the next generation. It must be remembered that mainland China has ruled Taiwan for only four years (1945-49) since it passed into Japanese hands in 1895. Taiwan has emerged as a robust democracy with a strong rule of law. The back-sliding of the rule of law in Hong Kong in recent years and the reneging of the Sino-British agreement which underpinned the reversion of Hong Kong to the mainland and under which China promised to allow direct elections of Chief Executive, has not gone unnoticed in Taiwan. Therefore, to expect them to easily give up their de facto independence and the democratic rights of its citizens is not going to be easy. But this problem, which is far more intractable than the Sino-Indian dispute and which has its origins in colonial rule, cannot be left to the next generation. Obviously what is sauce for the goose is not sauce for the gander!

What is one to make of the increased violations and brazenness, of the border/line of actual control by the PLA? China's actions in the South China Sea and the gradual firming of its claims under the so-called nine-dash line are instructive.[3] China has very gradually changed the facts on the ground, actually sea, by first preventing other countries from fishing in these waters or prospecting for hydrocarbons. Even as it went along with ASEAN to try and arrive at a Code of Conduct to prevent disputes degenerating into confrontations, it actually stalled for time and did two things. One, it created islands on rocks, shoals and coral beds but then denied that it would use them for military purposes. Two, simultaneously, it broke ASEAN solidarity by winning over Cambodia and Lao PDR to begin with. It ignored the ruling of the Permanent Court of Arbitration that its claims of sovereignty in the South China Sea had no basis and bullied the winner of the case, Philippines, to come over to its side. Lastly, in open violation of its own commitments, it has militarised the created islands. The PLA's actions in Doklam, Depsang (Daulat Beg Oldi), Demchok, Pangong Tso, etc., must be seen in this light.

Doklam actually deserves a proper study for it comes closest to the South China Sea island-building exercise. The Chinese are in occupation of parts of northern Bhutan. Doklam in the west is actually more strategic for them since control over the disputed portion would give them an advantageous position overlooking the Chumbi Valley. Chicken's Neck is actually very far away but the control of Chumbi Valley would be like a dagger plunged into India. The PLA's attempted control over the disputed portion of Doklam did make a few Bhutanese to openly question why the Chinese could not be accommodated in the west so that they could give back the occupied parts of north Bhutan, little realising that Bhutan would lose both. However, it served the purpose by making a few Bhutanese question their alliance with India, a stand that could become more pronounced if similar events take place in future.

China has also changed its stance on two key positions on the negotiating front with India. It did make offers in 1959-60 and again in 1984 to settle the border issue by accepting India's position in Arunachal in return for India accepting the status quo in Ladakh. That is a forgotten chapter now. Much more significantly, during the negotiations between the two Special Representatives, they agreed that settled areas would not be disturbed. However, for the last decade plus, not only have they raised the temperature over their claims to Tawang and the rest of Arunachal Pradesh, they object vehemently whenever an India VVIP like the President and Prime Minister visit that state. Perceptively, the Indian government felt the heat and reduced such visits for some time.

It is obvious that it is not in India's interest to agree to delay the resolution of the border dispute and leave it to the next generation. Nor should India move ahead to open up trans-Himalayan trade. China's exports to Nepal travel via Kolkata and other Indian ports and this should not be allowed to change. Nepal cannot become the bridge to unite the Indian and Chinese markets till market access and border issues are sorted out. If Lipu Lekh cannot handle the Kailash-Manasarovar traffic, the alternative should be to travel via Ladakh, not Nathu La.

These problems should not mean that India should not be active in the Himalayas. The road system is finally getting attention but it still needs more focus. All forms of connectivity promote economic growth and from Ladakh to Arunachal, access should be made far more efficient and comprehensive by road, air, rail and telecom. Similarly, even the smallest hamlets, which are far from power grids, should have electricity 24x7. Mini-grids with a mix of solar, micro-hydel and diesel generation can provide the answer. The villagers of Demchok should not see how the conditions of life of the Tibetans across have changed so dramatically while they suffer from under-development. Indian development assistance to Nepal and Myanmar should offer to build a few hydro-electricity projects on generous terms, as India did in Bhutan in the early years. This would develop the market so that later the private sector could crowd in.

In times to come, the Himalayas can once again become the bridge between countries, cultures and economies. For that to happen, countries would have to pro-actively try and settle disputes in an open spirit that would benefit all. India as the country that hosts the largest part of the Himalayan chain has much to gain from the development of the territory under its control and to help the smaller countries grow. Mutual respect with prosperity can lead the Himalayan states to move forward and make this the next growth hub. In doing so, sustainable environmental practice would be necessary so that the Gangetic plains continue to benefit from the presence of the Himalayas as they have since human beings made their first appearance in this part of the world.

NOTES

1 Though Tibet has borrowed a considerable part of its cosmology from India, the former was never part of the Indic imagination, Kailash-Manasarovar apart. Interestingly, though three major rivers, the Brahmaputra (Yarlung Tsangpo), Indus and Sutlej emerge in near-proximity from the Kailash-Manasarovar area, there is a belief that the Ganga too rises from here and not from the Gangotri glacier. This could very well have been the case before the Himalayas rose to the point when this route was cut-off, with paleo-channels substantiating this belief.

2 In 1914, the representatives of the Republic of China, Tibet and the United Kingdom met at Simla to define the boundary between Tibet and British India (which later became known as the McMahon Line).

3 Nine Dash Line is vaguely located demarcation line used by People's Republic of China to claim major part of South China Sea.

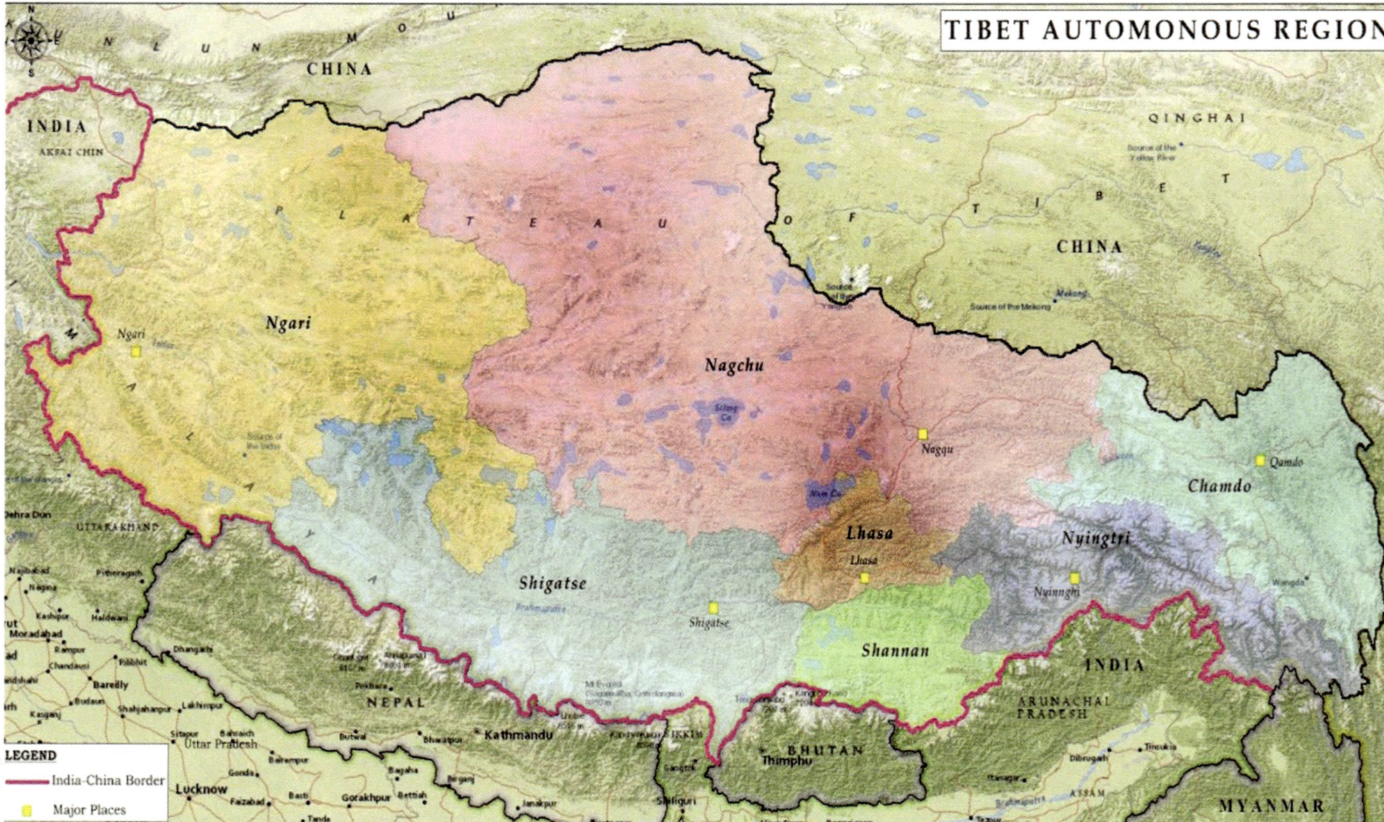

isclaimer: This map is not to scale and should not be used for navigation or legal purposes, depiction of boundaries is not authoritative. It is intended for general reference use only

Courtesy: Prof. P. Stobdan

Designed by: Dr. Vivek Dhankar

New Delhi, GIS Lab.

5

Developments in Tibet and their Likely Impact on India's Himalayan Region

P. Stobdan

The developments in Tibet since 1959 and escape of the Dalai Lama along with some 80,000 of his followers from Tibet to India have changed the complexity of the Indian Himalayan geopolitics. In fact, the share power and influence of the Dalai Lama and his efforts at drawing attention to the Tibetan political cause, combined with the power of publicity in the West, ensured that the Himalayas were projected as a kind of cultural and geopolitical exotica to the world outside.

A plethora of books have brought to light the grandeur of the Buddhist Himalayas, mostly by tapping into various aspects of Tibetan Buddhism that were found to be appealing and even exotic especially in the Western world.

It was largely due to the phenomenal role played by the 14th Dalai Lama and his skilful compassionate encounter with the West that the esoteric practices of Tibetan Buddhism got disseminated to interested Western audiences in the second-half of the twentieth century.

Tibetan Buddhism even became the subject of pop and rock songs in the 1960s and 1970s. Fictional novels like '*Lost Horizon*' by James Hilton[1] inspired many myths, such as the one about the legendary Shambhala – a sort of Shangri La located in the Himalayas. It is also noteworthy that the myth-making process ran parallel to China's reckless destruction of Tibetan Lamaist culture since 1960.

Yet, the myth of Shambhala and its profundity had grossly overshadowed the reality of Himalayan complexity, intricacy and the urgency of its political and social situation. While the traditional perception about the Buddhist Himalayas as an instrument of political and cultural interest in the West will linger on but the degree of interest in the subject appears to be dwindling in the face of the rising power of China.

The article aims to deal with Tibet, Buddhism and the Indian Himalayan region within the framework of power contestation between India and China.

Myth and History

The genesis of the Himalaya's linkages with Tibet is rooted in their geographic continuum located in High Asia between the Indian Plate and the Asian landmass. *But more importantly, it is the mythical and historical perspective of the Himalayas as* the earthly manifestation of the cosmic Mount Meru or the epicentre of Indian mythical world order *Mandala* that integrates the two regions in terms of their spiritual disposition.

Further, during the reign of Tibetan King Songtsen Gampo (629-49) the ties between the Himalayan region, Tibet and China got cemented through matrimonial arrangements. The King Songtsen Gampo obtained a Nepalese princess Bhrikuti as his wife and later got a Chinese princess Wencheng as his wife. These two wives are regarded as having played great role in spreading Buddhism in Tibet and shaping the political history of Tibet.

Later, Tibet fell politically into the 'Sino-centric' political order of '*Middle-Kingdom*'[2] that functioned on the imperial tributary system of China dominating the peripheries through economic, trade and spiritual relationships. As a result, the Himalayan region too came into the Chinese sphere of influence.

The linkages were particularly formed ever since the Chinese emperors started to patronise Tibetan Buddhism—starting from the *Mongol period* (1206–1368) when the Yuan dynasty court patronised Tibetan Buddhism under the tutelage of Tibetan spiritual leader *Sakya Pandita* Kunga Gyeltsen.[3] The period was also the beginning of a spiritual bonding between the Chinese, Tibetans and the Mongols that got strengthened during the Ming period (1368–1644) as well.

But more critically, it was under the Manchu period (1644–1912) when the Qing Emperors formally adopted Tibetan Buddhism as China's official religion that the bond among the trio was formalised through a celestial and devotional order. The Dalai Lamas and Panchen Lamas of Tibet were quick to confer the Qing rulers as the emanations of the Great Celestial *Manjushri* King, thus accepting them as the protectors of the *Tibetan Buddhism, particularly of* the Yellow Hat Gelugpa sect. In return the Dalai Lama of Tibet was christened as *Avalokiteshvara* Incarnate (Bodhisattva of compassion) and the Mongol Kings were considered as the 'Ruler of Vajra Beings' or *Vajradhara* (Bearer of the Thunderbolt).

As a consequence of the *Qing* emperors officially adopting the Buddhist faith—the Buddhist Himalayas probably fell in the peripheral circle of Chinese imperial tributary influence albeit circuitously, through tribute or homage paid by Tibetan Lamas to the court of Peking.

Trülku System: The Sino-Tibetan Institution of the Dalai Lama

Indian strategic thinkers should study in depth the Tibetan history, especially the evolution of Tibetan Buddhism's *trülku* (reincarnation) tradition from the seventeenth to the nineteenth centuries. Enough literature is available on the history of relationship between the Dalai Lama and the emperors of China both from spiritual and political perspective.[4]

It is particularly important to understand how Peking court controlled the political aspects of *trülku* institutions that shaped the dynamics of relationship between Tibet-China (core) and the Himalayas (periphery) for centuries.

Although, the modern nation-states today conform to linear line, fixed boundary and bureaucratic apparatus that still guides contemporary conduct of foreign affairs and policy prescriptions – call it geopolitics. However, the unique Tibetan system of rule by reincarnation and acceptance of Lama as object of devotion among the people in Inner and High Asia holds the Buddhist Himalayas in a state of flux even in the current context of India-China relations.

Sino-Tibetan Game in the Buddhist Himalayas

Although, from Chinese perspective, the old Qing era order has long been demolished both structurally and politically; but Chinese were aware of the fact that the traditional celestial allegiance between China, Mongolia and Tibet (the Himalayas inclusive) can never be severed formally. Notwithstanding the political developments, the Chinese, Mongols, Manchus, Monpas and Tibetans continued to revere the Dalai Lama and other Tibetan high lamas as objects of fidelity.

For this reason, China, even after the Communist Party of China came to power, continued to view the Himalayas as a bridge and Tibetan Buddhism as a useful vehicle of influence. Of course, as mentioned earlier, this has underpinnings in the past strategic policy of patronising institution of Lamaism as a means of advancing Chinese imperial expansion all along China's peripheries. That is why, Chinese scholars consider the Himalayas, along with Mongolia and Tibet, to be within the pale of Manchu influence, or, in layman's terms, fair game for inclusion into the modern Chinese state.

It appeared that China was prompted to play the Himalayan Buddhist game as early as in 1950s. Mao Zedong talked about Tibet and the Himalayas in the 1930s saying: "Xizang (Tibet) is China's right hand's palm, which is detached from its five fingers[5]—of Ladakh, Nepal, Sikkim, Bhutan and Arunachal (formerly NEFA). As all of these five are either occupied by, or under the influence of India, it is China's responsibility to 'liberate' the five to be rejoined with Xizang (Tibet)."

In fact, Mao Zedong wasn't alone and this is something less known in the public domain is the most striking incident of Prime Minister Nehru having received, barely two months after India's independence, two telegrams from Tibetan Government in Lhasa asking India to return the (lost) territories' of Tibet.

The telegram (dated 16 October 1947) forwarded through Indian Mission in Lhasa sought the return of territories "such as Sayul and Walong and in direction of Pemakoe, Lonag, Lapa, Mon, Bhutan, Sikkim, Darjeeling and others on this side of river Ganges and Lowo, Ladakh etc. up to boundary of Yarkhim."[6]

Nehru was stunned over the Tibetan demands but concealed the Lhasa Notes from Indian Parliament and chose not to bring it out for purposes of discussion also. Nehru seemingly rejected the Tibetan claim unequivocally and instead advised Lhasa to maintain the status quo until new agreements can be reached out.

From India's perspective, right from 1950, it favoured a position of accepting China's suzerainty over Tibet. India's position became clearer after the Dalai Lama's representatives signed the 17-point agreement with Chinese authorities on 23 May 1951 affirming Chinese sovereignty over Tibet. And, it was only after Tibetans themselves accepted Chinese sovereignty that India signed the Peace Treaty with China on 29 April 1954 – which explicitly recognised Tibet as part of China.

But, it was not later than 5 years after the 1954 Panchsheel Treaty was signed that Nehru received a lengthy letter from Premier Zhou Enlai's letter dated 8 September 1959[7] that described the McMahon Line as a product of the British policy of aggression on a weak Tibet. Among others, Zhou Enlai claimed additional 40,000 square miles of Indian Territory; raised the issue of China's non-ratification of 1842 Tibet-Ladakh border; reminded Nehru of Lhasa's 1947 correspondence relating to the return of Tibetan owned areas by India; claiming the frontier east of Bhutan as traditional frontier; repudiating that Sikkim and Bhutan boundary issues fall within the scope of India-China discussion; asserting China having 2,000 kilometres long boundary instead of 3,530 claimed by India etc.

Did the Chinese Purposely Allow the *Dalai Lama* to Escape?

The Tibetan Revolt in 1959 and the subsequent escape of Dalai Lama from Tibet have been viewed not without advantage for the Chinese, as observed by many commentators. Important facts coming out on the surface show that China's military showdown was perhaps pre-planned and well calibrated. For example, Mao was said to have been least concerned about the possibility of the Dalai Lama leaving Tibet, for he may have considered the Dalai Lama an impediment to Chinese plans for Tibet.

There are references about Mao's conversation with Soviet premier Nikita Khrushchev[8] on 3 October 1959, wherein Mao admitted that China was waiting for an opportunity to crush resistance in Tibet: "We could not launch an offensive without a pretext. And this time we had a good excuse and we struck." When Khrushchev charged that letting the Dalai Lama escape was a mistake, Mao said: "We could not keep the Dalai Lama, for the border with India is very extended and he could cross it at any point."

While the world outside was quick to decry Mao's 1959 actions in Tibet, but the Chinese may have felt relieved and would have considered it as an opportunity to promote internal dissension and at the same time consolidate their hold in Tibet.

Externally, as it appears, in hindsight that instead of containing the Tibetan political standoff within its borders, Beijing may have calculatingly approved the Tibetan dynamics to spill over into the Indian side of Buddhist Himalayas. This could have served the Chinese objective of implementing their frontier assimilation policies by leveraging the Qing era network of Lamaist institutions beyond proper Tibet into India.

Hence, since the 14th Dalai Lama fled from Tibet in 1959, the enormity of China's game plan for Buddhist Himalayas seemed to have only increased. Of course, there have been other narratives as far as the Dalai Lama's flight is concerned. Here, the American key motive (well documented) was to use Lamaism as a geopolitical weapon against Communist China, just as the Afghan Mujahedeen were used against the Soviets during the Cold War.

How the Americans then may have convinced the Indians to play the 'Tibet Card' is another story, but the Indians too actually rejoiced in harbouring the Dalai Lama since 1959. It is a hitherto undisclosed fact that this might have actually suited Beijing perfectly. A former Indian diplomat has told this author that Chairman Mao Zedong conveyed a message to Prime Minister Jawaharlal Nehru through a visiting Indian Communist leader in late 1959, that "he should keep the Dalai Lama in India".

Undoubtedly, China hasn't failed to exploit the presence of the Dalai Lama in the Indian Himalayas to the utmost. The Dalai Lama's departure from Tibet was followed by escape of other Tibetan high Lamas to India—willingly and also perhaps in connivance with Chinese authorities—to set up their parallel sectarian institutions in India and Nepal. For example, the escape of Karmapa, Ugyen Trinley Dorje, who was living under house arrest in Tibet, was suspected to have been masterminded either by Chinese authorities or by Tibetan leaders in India. Consequently, myriad Tibetan Lamas have set up their parallel sectarian institutions and also restored their traditional monastic network across India and Nepal—mostly concentrated in the Southern Himalayas.

Fall outs in the Indian Himalayan Region

Over the decades, the Buddhist Himalayas has assumed a serious political, strategic and cultural dynamics and this should be a matter of concern particularly for India.

Tibetanisation of the Himalayas

First, the excessive Tibetanisation of Indian Buddhist Himalayas has been a cause of worry and this came about via a gradual process of the taking over by Tibetan Lamas of Indian monasteries which continues to be the focus of society and polity in the region.[9] If one were to map the Tibetan Lamas controlling India's key monasteries today, the picture might be hair-raising. A major case in point is the struggle over Rumtek monastery in Sikkim. The takeover of almost all the monasteries in Ladakh has been rather hassle-free despite Article 370 impeding even the Indian citizens from owning properties in J&K.

In fact, Tibetan issue is becoming less about 'freeing Tibet from China' but more about creating Tibet in India. It may be reflecting how the Indian Government is perhaps weighing heavily on the minds of the Tibetans – something that requires more in-depth investigation.

Sectarian Discord

Second is the growing inter-Tibetan sectarian strife which becomes an influence of instability factor for Buddhist Himalayas. The sectarian suitors of all sorts with foreign funding are seen creeping in, over the years, to toy with their interests in the region. This include, in particular, the powerful Tibetan masters of all sects setting up their parallel sectarian network as they also built mega religious infrastructure along the region from Ladakh to Arunachal Pradesh. The sectarian divide is already creating confusion and discord among people hitherto devoid of any differences.

For example, in the Western Himalayas, externally-driven contests have already threatened to divide the society. The situation took a critical turn in 2015 when the Dalai Lama issued a virtual gag order against the people in Ladakh facilitating the visit of a rival Karmapa, Thaye Trinley Dorje who has not been recognised as the true 17th Karmapa by the Dalai Lama.

While majority public followed the Dalai Lama's directive, but barring the Gelugpa sect other sectarian groups i.e. Druk-pa Kagyu, Drikung Kagyu, Ning-ma and even the Sakya sect chose to defy his gag and formally accorded religious reception to Thaye Trinley Dorje. The incident in Ladakh in 2015, however, led to split in the All-Ladakh Gompa Association (an equivalent of a local *Sangha*).

Clearly, majority sects of Tibetan Buddhism do not question the spiritual authenticity of Thaye Trinley Dorje unlike the Dalai Lama who recognises Ugyen Trinley Dorje as the authentic 17th Karmapa. Ugyen is also recognised by Beijing. The issue of dual Karmapa do impact the Himalayan Buddhist world. This also indicates that the Dalai Lama is no longer able to hold his religious flock together. In fact, inter and intra sectarian and leadership rifts would be undermining the authority of Dalai Lama.

A rift has, in fact, widened in the Dalai Lama's own Gelug ranks after he banned worshiping of the sect's protector deity Dorje Shugden in 1996. He has a good political reason to outlaw deity Shugden, but his opponents, mostly Western converts, have been trumpeting the iniquity of the Dalai Lama, calling him a "Muslim" and "the worst dictator" in modern times.

Schisms and differences within and among sects could not be without instigation by the Chinese. China's hand was suspected in many such cases including the unrest in Tawang in May 2016 over a dispute to build dams for hydroelectric projects. Two persons including a monk were killed in the incident.

Similarly, Sikkim has been on the boil for decades over contesting sectarian parties claiming rights to Rumtek's ownership. In Nepal, the Chinese have been trying to fund Buddhist projects. In May 2016, China had sent a Tibetan monk Drukhang Thubten Khedrup Rinpoche, Vice Chairman of the Buddhist Association of China to oversee the Buddha Jayanti celebration in Lumbini. In Bhutan too, Chinese have been using the Tibetans to influence the trend of Buddhism there.

These developments make situation in the Indian Buddhist Himalayas rather perilous and whose ends are not in sight. This would inevitably spark a string of pent-up sectarian strife and inter-ethnic tensions—possibly making the Himalayas a bigger tinderbox in the longer run. Moreover, India's own Buddhist profile in Tawang, Sikkim, Ladakh and the local institutions of Kushok Stag-sang Raspa, Kushok Bakula, Kushok Thiksy, Kushok Togdan, Kushok Stag-na, Sona Rinpoche and others are speedily undermined to the detriment of India's interest. This is where China could win both Tibetan and the Himalayan Buddhist game.

To be sure, power struggle among various Tibetan sects will get heightened especially in the post-Dalai Lama scenario, for the issue will remain linked to Gelugpa sect retaining its present supremacy over the Tibetan order.

Future of the Dalai Lama

Third and linked to it is the critical issue of finding the next Dalai Lama. It is clear that Tibetans would certainly need a Dalai Lama to lead them, and Beijing too understands the need to find the next Dalai Lama either of its own choice or otherwise.

As for the Dalai Lama himself, the whole idea of searching for his next incarnation seems an absurd idea and he probably wants to put an end to the politics of reincarnation—can't be feasible in the 21st century politics though he has spelled out several ideas for his successor.

What has really complicated the case is the Dalai Lama not sticking to a definite position on succession issue. He has been making numerous and conflicting statements i.e. he will not be re-borne; he will only reincarnate in a free country; the reincarnate might be a female; he could "emanate" in someone else during his own lifetime, so on and so forth.[10]

The Dalai Lama has also made an unseemly remark about a woman could succeed him and she would have to be "very attractive" otherwise she would be "not much use". The statement sparked outrage from women world over who expressed shock to hear such a "retrograde opinion" coming from a man of compassion.

It is hard to figure whether his ambiguous and inconsistent position is directed against China or an expression of his unhappiness over lack of unity amongst his clergy.

It was also widely believed that the Dalai Lama would prefer to install his chosen Karmapa, Ugyen Trinley Dorje as the next Tibetan leader—at least in the interim. But since then the Karmapa has fled to the United States possibly due to differences with the Dharamsala authority. Making Ugyen Trinley Dorje as the next leader will be contested by other Lamas such as Druk-chen Rinpoche of Druk-pa Kagyu sect as well as by others. And, here the critical issue also linked to whether the Gelug sect could retain its supreme role over the Dalai Lama's selection process in future if Karmapa becomes the interim head. A recent media report highlighted communication between the Dalai Lama's aide (from the Gelug Monastic Council) and Chinese authority about a joint 'project' to decide the 15th Dalai Lama.

Nonetheless, internal crisis would intensify over the Dalai Lama's succession. The crisis period would start within the immediate gestation period, normally the immediate five years to locate and authenticate the reincarnate boy. Creating the Regency Council itself would not be without a controversy given the problems with Beijing, besides deep divide among major Tibetan sects, feudal elite, family clans and coteries that impact the process.

The conflict would intensify if there will be a dual Dalai Lama. In such a case, the exiles would surely reject any Beijing chosen candidate, and it needs to be seen which candidate gets more international legitimacy. Here again, from what it seems, the world powers are going to be locked into a major contestation over the next Dalai Lama. As Beijing prepares to select the 15th Dalai Lama, the US, India and others too seem to be gearing up to play a counter game. But, Beijing is bound to deploy its political prowess, economic arsenal and media skill to get global endorsement for its chosen Dalai Lama. The practicing *Vajrayana* states like Bhutan, Mongolia and even India are unlikely to directly interfere in the selection process.

While considering the resetting of ties with China, Modi and Xi would have discussed the issue of the Dalai Lama's future. New Delhi may have considered the pros and cons of playing with the next Dalai Lama—whether the Indian government will allow reincarnation of the next Dalai Lama to take place in India or not. Should India opt in favour of using the next soul as a political tool, then the possibility of current hostile relations lasting for another century will become real.

Meanwhile major Tibetan head Lamas have successfully built their own persona with their foreign supporters. For them to accept a central authority especially a contested one, would remain a problem. Such a scenario is also inevitable after Dalai Lama's abdication of his power. No doubt, China will exploit all of these to its advantage.

The Tibet Question

Fourth and the most critical aspect to the Himalayan stability is the key issue of solving the Tibet question. And of late, there has been speculation about an imminent Sino-Tibetan rapprochement, especially after a recent statement made by the Dalai Lama that "we are not seeking independence, want to stay with China" to pursue "development" and "if China agrees, he would return to Tibet at once".[11]

The signs of a thaw particularly came after the 19th Party Congress and the affirmation of President Xi Jinping as the 'most powerful' Chinese leader in 45 years. Speculation in this regard has heightened after one of the Dalai Lama's newly appointed envoys, Samdhong Rinpoche, making a 'discreet' visit to Tibet[12]—possibly facilitated by Chinese officials.

It is not clear as yet how seriously the thaw is progressing and whether it would actually lead anywhere. In the past, China has quashed talk of a rapprochement with the Dalai Lama, insisting that he must drop his demand for 'greater autonomy' for Tibet and stop his "splittist" activities – hence his desire to return to Tibet, even for a short while, could never materialise.

How, then, might we assume that the efforts to arrive at a rapprochement will succeed this time? It is because Xi is known to have a soft spot for Tibet, and he may have played his cards close to his chest so far fearing stiff resistance from hardliners in the Party.

Xi also possibly believes that an opportunity for solving the problem would peter out once the current Dalai Lama's life comes to an end.

After becoming the second most powerful leader in China's modern history, Xi finds himself in a perfect position to resolve the Tibet issue – perhaps the biggest ever opportunity which no other Chinese leader thus far has enjoyed. For Xi has also more to gain both politically and in moral terms to become China's strongest leader ever in history. In Dalai Lama's return to China, Xi hopes to elevate his own international image as a statesman and a global leader.

The Dalai Lama too has been hopeful about Xi adopting a different tack on Tibet than his predecessors. Clearly, informal talks were taking place with Chinese officials over a possible return to Tibet, even if for a short while, and the Dalai Lama has hailed Xi Jinping as a "realist" and more "open-minded" than his predecessor, Hu Jintao.

Media reports have suggested that moderate elements within the Chinese leadership might have been exploring the possibility of a rapprochement with the Tibetans. The Dalai Lama admitted to having received some encouraging signs from top Chinese officials, including a large number of Han Chinese who visited him in the last five years during the Xi Presidency. The Tibetan leader also seemingly received advice directly from Tibetans living inside Tibet to settle for a mutually satisfying, win-win solution during Xi's second term, before the window for a deal closes 2-3 years from now when his influence of power will begin to wane. It is quite possible that President Xi may have conveyed the Dalai Lama to help him assuage the situation.

Xi Jinping may be contemplating a solution for Tibet keeping in mind his larger dream of realising the Belt and Road Initiative (BRI), for Tibet's borders with Nepal, Bhutan, Myanmar and India, and the plateau is also the source of all the 10 major river system of Asia.

For China, the closure of the Tibet chapter is seemingly easier now than ever before, if they want it. Time is running out, however. The danger of fossilizing intractable stances – radicalising the Tibet issue by not solving it – should worry China the most.

The Dalai Lama can be anything but hopeful, as the time for him has been fast running out too. He has been steadily losing international support in the face of China's rise as a world power. No longer does any country dare receive the Dalai Lama in any official or state visit.

Apart from the fact of his own age, the Tibetan leader faces the challenge of keeping his flock together. For example, the delay in a solution might cause anxiety, uncertainty, and division among his people.

Should there be a possible Sino-Tibetan spiritual pacification or political reconciliation, the entire political and social landscape of the Buddhist Himalayas, in terms of people's spiritual allegiance, would undergo profound changes. Moreover, in the current context, and more so given the Chinese propensity to reflect on the past in their strategic overview, there should be no doubt that the probability of returning to the old 'Sino-centric' order would become a reality once the political differences between the Chinese and the Dalai Lama are resolved, which might happen sooner or later.

As of now there are no signs of an imminent Sino-Tibetan rapprochement taking a shape. Samdhong Rinpoche's visit to China hasn't yielded any result. Even though, the Dalai Lama has expressed his keenness to return to China but Beijing hasn't yet responded positively. From China's perspective, his return would risk large-scale public frenzy inside Tibet resulting in emotional outburst in favour of the Dalai Lama. This would have adverse impact on China – risk of losing whatever achievements China has made in Tibet during the past six decades.

Instead, China hopes to eventually win over the Tibetans once the Dalai Lama is no more. In fact, the United Work Front that deals with the Tibetan Diasporas outside China is making serious moves to seek reconciliation with the Tibetans living overseas.

Moreover, a gradual process of reconciliation or spiritual merger of the Tibetan and Chinese varieties of Buddhism may already be underway and it may be built on the same premise that Chinese rulers not only readily embraced Tibetan Buddhism but also offered their patronage to the Lamas. In a way, a very subtle and complex process of religious doctrinal merger of the Han and Tibetan Schools seems already at play. This would mean a gradual reinstatement of the imperial era harmonious spiritual coexistence between Tibetan and Han Buddhism, if not accepting the hierarchical order of Tibetan Buddhism by Han Buddhists.

In fact, India may be oblivious to the fact that China is already on the point of harvesting the devotional potential of Tibetan Buddhism—the very religion which the Communists had destroyed several decades ago.

Revival of Buddhism in China and its Impact

It would also be important to illustrate how the revival of Buddhism in China is shaping the Asian landscape – something most readers would be less aware of. Contrary to the conjecture that Buddhism would be dead in China after the founding of the communist controlled People's Republic of China in 1949, the ancient Indian philosophy seemed to have remained firmly rooted in China.

It is a fact that China and Buddhism go a long way back, to the Kushan period (2nd Century B.C. – 3rd Century A.D.) when China became an adopted home for Buddhism. Since then, this Indic philosophy deeply penetrated China's history, culture, ethos, mind, psychology, art, medicine and politics for over 2,000 years. Despite attempts to get rid of religion from Chinese society during the Mao era Cultural Revolution, Buddhism is being greatly reinvigorated and even the state has begun to view it as a potentially valuable asset for China.

China's fervour for Buddhism appears to have grown under President Xi Jinping, who was rather quick to catch on and place China's own Buddhism on the global stage since 2005 through state patronage. He is seeking a renewed campaign for a 'Buddhist globalisation' with the country's growing economic, political and marketing clout, for he surely sees the political leverage associated with Buddhism.

Clearly, at the domestic level, it looks as though Xi is turning to religion not just to bolster his rule, but also to save the party from falling apart. He certainly sees Buddhism as useful for arresting flagging moral values in China's social fabric, and to prevent the angry middle class from crumbling under the weight of a deepening social crisis and an economic downturn.

Externally, Chinese are well aware that Buddhism not only serves as a cementing factor but also a powerful social force that underpins nationalistic sentiments among the Han Chinese as well as the Tibetans and Mongols.

It will be interesting to understand how China's re-embracing of Buddhism, even for serving political exigency will impact Asia, especially the Buddhist Himalayas, where there exists a thinly drawn cultural line between Asia's two major civilisations, in an area comprising countries such as Nepal, Bhutan, Myanmar and India.

In the years ahead, the Buddhist Himalayas cannot escape China's cultural diplomacy. President Xi Jinping, during the course of his journey on the One Belt One Road (OBOR), will mix China's trade/economic and connectivity vision with Buddhism. In recent years, Beijing is seen tapping into Buddhism as a diplomatic resource to win not just goodwill but also economic contracts even in India's backyard. While strengthening its Buddhist linkages with neighbouring Asian countries, China is investing heavily in presenting itself as a patron of Buddhism in the neighbourhood.

Clearly, with China's economic rise and in its bid to protect its interests, Beijing will find it more essential to reflect in its policy thinking on the interplay between Buddhism and the Himalayas and the need to leverage both.

As for the status of Buddhism in India, it has come to be reduced to a political adjunct and a diplomatic tool to serve national purpose rather than a deep philosophical construct that it really is. India's ability to get back to the core philosophy of Buddhism is in question; whereas falling prey to politicizing it for quick gains would be risky and counter-productive. India has already ceded this great Buddhist space to China, which is armed with billions of dollars and the (devotional) ability to change the Buddhist discourse to their advantage. It is also rather disheartening how this great philosophy, which is an Indian invention, is being hijacked and appropriated by the Chinese to be applied to their national discourse.

India's Shortfalls

All in all, the Buddhist Himalayas will continue to remain a contested geo-cultural landscape between the various competing narratives of India and China. However, in the current scenario, India's interests in the Buddhist Himalayas remain even more compromised than during the colonial period, when British strategists were able to play the Himalayan game more perceptively.

For example, in the early twentieth century the viceroy of India, Lord Curzon was able to visualise the Himalayan regions of Ladakh, Sikkim, Bhutan and North East frontier as an 'inner defence line for India protected by a Tibetan buffer region'. The British Raj could also understand, differentiate and manipulate the dynamics of Tibetan vis-à-vis Himalayan Buddhism especially the devotional power of various sectarian groups within Lamaism to achieve the results they desired.

But, contemporary India seemingly lacks sufficient wherewithal to deal with the complexity of the Buddhist Himalayas. Clearly, India, over the years, has relied heavily on playing the so-called "Tibet Card" and perhaps also weighing heavily on the minds of the Dalai Lama and his Government-in-Exile. Of late, the "Tibet Card" is being intensified albeit on the grounds of Buddhist diplomacy.

The recent crisis in Doklam however brought into focus what will be one of the most difficult issues to unfold in the Himalayas in future. It has indicated that the tensions rising from conflicting territorial claims by both India and China in the Himalayan region will almost certainly keep recurring and continue to raise the risk of war.

All these are unfolding at a time when the Western romanticism with Tibetan Buddhism is gradually fading even as India is forced to watch the ensuing developments in askance. More seriously, India's ability to deal with the Buddhist Himalayas vis-à-vis China only through the prism of military power is unlikely to be sufficient.

NOTES

1 James Hilton, *Lost Horizon*, Harper Perennial (first published 1933).

2 https://intothemiddlekingdom.com/category/tibet/, accessed on 30 May 2018.

3 In 1247, Sakya Pandita, the chief of the Tibetan Sakya sect along with his nephew Phagpa paid tribute and pledge allegiance to the Mongol court. In 1260, Kublai Khan granted Phagpa

the title of "Imperial Tutor" resulting in establishing the precedent of a priest-patron relationship between Mongol rulers and Tibetan religious leaders, available at https://tibet-vs-china-nationalisthistories.wikischolars.columbia.edu/Tibet+and+China+Under+Mongol+Domination, accessed on 1 June 2018.

4 Peter Schwieger, "The Dalai Lama and the Emperor of China: A Political History of the Tibetan Institution of Reincarnation," Columbia University Press, March 2015, p. 352.

5 http://shodhganga.inflibnet.ac.in/bitstream/10603/140518/10/10_chapter%206.pdf, accessed on 4 June 2018.

6 P. Stobdan, "Resituating Menser and Darchen-Labrang in the Boundary Negotiations with China", available at https://idsa.in/policybrief/resituating-menser-darchen-labrang-in-boundary-negotiations-china-pstobdan-160218

7 "Letter from the Prime Minister of China to the Prime Minister of India", 8 September 1959, "Notes, Memoranda and letters Exchanged and Agreements signed between the Governments of India and China Correspondence Nehru-Zhou, WHITE PAPER IV, September 1959 - March 1960, Ministry of External Affairs Government of India Letter from the Prime Minister of China to the Prime Minister of India, 8 September 1959, available at http://www.archieve.claudearpi. net/maintenance/uploaded_pics/Correspondence_Zhou_Nehru_Sept-Nov59.pdf, accessed on 7 June 2018.

8 Warren W. Smith, "China's Tibet?: Autonomy or Assimilation", available at https://books.google.co.in/books?id=KM52kp2BeuoC&pg=PA48&lpg=PA48&dq=We+could+ not+launch+an+offensive+ without+a+ pretext.+ And+this+ time+we+ had+a+ good+excuse+and+we+struck& source=bl&ots=Tt6WGRbiaR&sig= HGdlr2NtZBac5Oie PMzR5vha4dY&hl=en&sa=X &ved=0ahUKEwjmq5e8hPbbAhVBv I8KHdW_BuwQ6 AEIKDAA#v=onepage&q= We%20could%20not %20launch%20an %20offensive%20without%20a%20pretext.%20 And%20this%20time%20we %20had%20a%20good%20excuse%20and%20we%20 struck&f=false, accessed on 4 June 2018.

9 P. Stobdan, "Emerging Flashpoints in the Himalayas", available at https://idsa.in/issuebrief/emerging-flashpoints-in-the-himalayas, accessed on 5 June 2018.

10 P. Stobdan, "The Dalai Lama and Tibet's Future", *Strategic Analysis*, Vol. 40, No. 2, 2016, pp. 231-233.

11 "We are not seeking independence since 1974 says Dalai Lama", available at https://timesofindia. indiatimes.com/india/we-are-not-seeking-independence-since-1974-says-dalai-lama/articleshow/63334751.cms, accessed on 7 June 2018.

12 P. Stobdan, "The Dalai Lama Wants to Return Home: Is India bracing for the potential fallout?" *The Wire*, available at https://thewire.in/diplomacy/dalai-lama-india-china-tibet, accessed on 8 June 2018.

6

The Tibet Conundrum

Abanti Bhattacharya

In March 2018, Indian government reportedly asked its officials to keep away from the celebrations organised by the Tibetan government-in-exile on the occasion of the 60th anniversary of the Dalai Lama's flight to India. This directive from the government was quite unexpected and raised questions about India's Tibet policy. In fact, the government was criticised for appeasing the Chinese by giving up its Tibet card. At this point, the pertinent question that arises is, does India have a Tibet card? This chapter delves into this question by taking stock of the long-drawn Tibet conundrum. It addresses the Tibet issue, first by highlighting the divergent perceptions of India and China on the Tibet question; and second by looking from three broad perspectives: India's Tibet policy, China's Tibet policy and the fate of the Tibetan movement. It argues that India has a small window of opportunity vis-à-vis China in using the Tibet card owing to the latter's vulnerability in the arena of domestic and foreign policy.

Tibet in India-China Perceptions

In the post-1947, India did not have a Tibet policy and the reasons were mainly two. One was India's specific view of Tibet, shaped by its strategic culture. And the other was immediate circumstances of the Cold War era, where India had to make a precarious choice between either leaning to the communist Eastern bloc or the Western capitalist bloc. Besides, the role of

Jawaharlal Nehru in making the foreign policy choices and guiding Independent India's foreign policy had been crucial. However, there exists a sharp debate in the academia and policy circles on his role in shaping India's Tibet and China policies. Notably, two statements by Nehru typically portray his misperceptions about China. One, on Aksai Chin, he said, "Not a blade of grass grows there, and the other, on the unlikelihood of war with China, he said, "It is exceedingly unlikely that we may have to face any real military invasion from the Chinese side, whether in peace or in war, in the foreseeable future."[1] These two statements are striking because these not only demonstrate his erroneous perceptions about China, but more so, indicated the influence of strategic culture in shaping his world view.

India, under the leadership of Nehru did not perceive Tibet as a strategic issue, rather viewed it from a cultural and civilisational prism. Historically, Indian traders, pilgrims and saints were the main constituency who interacted with Tibet. The ties that bound the two, were civilisational, not political. For Tibet too, the ties were not political. In fact, India represented the birthplace of Tibetan art, culture, religion and philosophy.[2] Hence, India acquired an exalted position in the Tibetan eyes. However, under the British rule in India, Tibet came to be treated as a buffer between India and China. When Nehru inherited this British legacy, he insisted upon the Chinese to respect Tibet as a buffer. But the idea of buffer was feasible only in the context of a weak China, not any more with the foundation of the People's Republic of China (PRC) in 1949. Nehru did not understand this new China. Also, unlike the Chinese, India did not ever think about bringing Tibet under direct political control. Therefore, India under Nehru unilaterally relinquished the British India mission in Lhasa and trade posts at Gyantse and Yatung. More importantly, on the 1954 Agreement, signed between India and China, the Indian government displayed lack of strategic foresight. Although it was a trade agreement that was to remain effective for eight years, Nehru failed to see that for China, the agreement was essentially to obtain India's concurrence on the Chinese occupation of Tibet. He assumed that the agreement was a gentlemanly understanding that automatically conferred Chinese recognition to India's perspective on the border in return for India's acceptance of Tibet as a region of China. Hence, India unilaterally gave up all its rights in Tibet without gaining from the Chinese government any reciprocal recognition on the British demarcated McMahon line as the border between India and its new neighbour,

China. While India's civilisational links with Tibet essentially coloured Nehru's vision, the Cold War power politics also defined his immediate foreign policy decisions. Deepak Lal and Ramachandra Guha have meticulously spelt out the reasons for Nehru's choice of Hindi-Chini Bhai Bhai approach.[3] They averred that the security problems confronting India in the post-independent and post-partition era essentially led Nehru to give premium on internal security and cohesion, instead of entangling the nascent nation state in the Cold War power politics. And in this larger imperative for internal security and economic development, the need for peaceful border with the largest neighbour was indeed the most pragmatic decision at that juncture. Also, to be noted here is that India turned down the US offer of alliance partnership in 1954.

However, China had a strikingly contrary perspective on both Tibet and the Cold War politics. For China, Tibet was a strategic peripheral region and also the only territory that was left unadministered and unconquered under the last imperial dynasty, the Qing. Under the impact of the 19th century Great Game, Chinese imperial government began to understand the folly of keeping the peripheral territories under 'loose reign' system that allowed the peripheral regions to govern themselves. In fact, many reformist writings of the late Qing era urged the imperial government to implement direct rule over Tibet. One such writings stated that Sichuan would be rendered defenseless if Tibet is lost.[4] By identifying Sichuan as a courtyard and Tibet as a screen or a wall, such writings drew the importance of periphery to the defence of the core. The Qing state, thus, moved to 'nationalise' the frontier. However, they failed to do so due to the ensuing Great Game of the 19th century that precluded the Qing from bringing Tibet under its direct political control. This task was duly completed by the PRC in 1950, when it invaded and occupied Tibet. Arguably, China had a clear-cut Tibet policy from the very inception. This clarity on Tibet particularly dawned upon the Chinese from the post-Opium War era itself, when under the impact of Western imperialism and imposition of unequal treaties, Chinese imperial government realised the strategic need for turning the civilisational frontiers into hard borders. It had already embarked upon this task with the 'provincialisation' of Xinjiang in 1884.[5] Thus, right after the foundation of the PRC, the Chinese government moved with blitzkrieg speed to securitise the Tibetan frontier. While internally, minority policy was crafted to integrate and govern the periphery, externally, the 1954 India-China agreement was signed to settle the status of Tibet as a sovereign part of China.[6]

Thus, Beijing got New Delhi to accept "Tibet region as part of China" and to renounce all special rights in Tibet.

Further, for China, unlike India, external security was a bigger concern. In 1950, the developments in Korea dragged China into a war with the US that ended in a stalemate in 1953. While China confronted the US threat on its northeastern border, it also met with clandestine activities of the Central Intelligence Agency (CIA) in Tibet that tried to destabilise China's northwestern periphery. This CIA interference coincided with the 1959 Tibetan rebellion and the Dalai Lama's flight to India. The Chinese leadership, hence, believed that India too had a role in fomenting the Tibetan rebellion. But more importantly, the 1959 revolt exposed the Chinese vulnerability on the Tibet question, despite its sovereign hold. Thus, the 1959 revolt was the reason for China to escalate the border conflict with India.

What appears from the above narration is that at the root of India-China conflict lay the perceptual differences of the two countries on the issue of Tibet. And this perception mainly arose from their respective historical experiences and Cold War circumstances, and thereby, these impacted on the policy choices that the two countries made on the Tibet issue. These contrary security perceptions and policy preferences adopted by the two nascent states, explain the continuing conundrum on the Tibetan issue.

Additionally, in the post-colonial era, both the countries were engaged in a nation-building process. And since both were sensitive to freedom and sovereignty, upholding the sovereignty rights was central to their nation-building process. It is important, as well, to note that historically India and China did not share a common border. In 1950, when the PLA entered Tibet to claim its sovereignty, the two countries for the first time in history came to share a common boundary. With the Chinese occupation of Tibet, India then began to worry about the fate of the British drawn McMahon line demarcating the international border between India and Tibet. And when China had turned down Nehru's request of keeping Tibet as autonomous, the border issue became a central concern for India. In 1954, thus when Nehru visited China, he raised the issue of inaccurate border alignment in some Chinese maps. To this, the Chinese premier Zhou Enlai replied that those maps were reproductions of the old Kuomintang maps and that the Chinese government had no time to revise them. The next thing that comes to light was the construction of the Aksai Chin road by the Chinese in 1957 which created an uproar in the Indian

Parliament. India regarded it as Chinese transgression of Indian territories. But for China, the need to open up an all-weather road linking Tibet with Xinjiang was prerequisite security need. And hence, Chinese control of the Aksai Chin region was crucial. In other words, more than the border issue that plagued the Indian psyche, the vulnerability over Tibet was most pressing for the Chinese. The first official Chinese response on the border however, came on 23 January 1959, in reply to Nehru's letter of 14 December 1958, in which Nehru had drawn Chinese attention to the incorrect border alignment shown in Chinese maps. Zhou Enlai wrote back saying that the India-China border was never delimited and that the PRC never recognised the McMahon Line. The Chinese side in fact, argued that the McMahon line was an imperialistic relic and hence had to be revisited. It is essential to point out here that the Chinese refused to accept the McMahon line not because it was a product of British imperialism but because under the Simla Agreement, that involved the three countries—British India, Tibet and China, Tibet was represented as a sovereign country with treaty making powers. This was anathema to the Chinese. Evidently, China had no qualms in accepting the same McMahon line as the border between Myanmar and China. Clearly, for China, Tibet was the principal factor in India-China conflict, not the border issue. But for India, the border issue was central. Due to aggressive Chinese nation-building process, Tibet had to lose its sovereignty. And when Tibet lost its sovereignty, India lost its border with Tibet, and this, in turn, dragged India into a conflict with China. In the midst of India-China conflicting perceptions, Tibet was left in a tangle.

India's Flawed Tibet Policy

India has repeatedly messed up its Tibet policy. While under Nehru, India made the mistake of unilaterally surrendering all rights to the Chinese on Tibet, under Rajiv Gandhi, it made yet another mistake by reopening the Tibet issue. It may be pointed out that the validity of the 1954 Agreement was only for eight years and it had expired in 1962. There was no need to reopen the Tibet issue in 1988 and reiterate the 1954 position that 'Tibet region as part of China'. More so, the 1962 War itself was a clear violation of the Panchsheel principles that China so zealously upheld. In fact, India played into Chinese hands when it agreed to keep aside the contentious issues and leave the resolution of the border dispute to future generation. Arguably, China needed a peaceful periphery to focus on economic development in the aftermath of the initiation of reform and modernisation plan of 1978. It was therefore, in China's interest to reach up to the Indian government more than the other way round.

Further, in 2003, under Atal Bihari Vajpayee's China visit, India yet again made a foolhardy decision to recognise Tibet as an autonomous region of China, scarcely realising that for China Tibet autonomous region meant India's state of Arunachal Pradesh. Subsequently thus, China began to claim Arunachal as its own territory calling it, South Tibet. And from then on, the issuance of stapled visa by the Chinese embassy in India and intrusion of the People's Liberation Army (PLA) into Indian territories have become a regular feature. Furthermore, with looming water scarcity in China and the consequent diversion of the Brahmaputra waters, India-China divergences on Tibet have deepened and escalated to assume a clash on river water issue.[7]

What is apparent from the above analysis is that India has time and again exhibited a weak negotiating strategy and gave much leeway to China in having an upper hand on the Tibet issue. However, with the Dalai Lama and 39 Tibetan settlements spread across India, New Delhi indeed possesses a Tibet card. Further, Tibet cannot be regarded as an internal issue, as claimed by China, given Chinese citizens' presence in India as well as the entanglement of Tibet with the border issue. However, so far India has not creatively used the Tibet card. It has not even impressed upon the Chinese that no discussion of the border is possible without bringing the Tibet issue upfront. Rather, it has accepted the Chinese strategy to keep Tibet and border issue separate. Hence, the Special Representative Group (SRG) meetings between India and China to arrive at a border resolution remains inconclusive each time. The second issue that becomes apparent from the above analysis is that India has continued to view the border from a cultural prism. For instance, China claims Tawang on the basis of the birth of sixth Dalai Lama. While India does not lay a claim on Manasarovar, despite being a pilgrimage site for the Hindus from times immemorial. It also does not even table the issue with the Chinese when its entitlement on Manasarovar is historically valid. China's claim on Tawang is not only invalid but also doubly faulty as its claim is based on the claim on Tibet.

China's Vulnerability on Tibet

China's vulnerability on Tibet is rooted in history. Chinese imperial dynasties right from the Qin period, 221 BCE, confronted the problem of barbarian raids and invasion from the north. The construction of the Great Wall was, thus, to ward off the nomadic incursions. The Han dynasty (206 BC-220 AD) in fact, had devised an elaborate mechanism for frontier security and development, the essence of which was two-fold: one, defence through development and two, Hanization of the sparsely populated frontier areas. This twin policy still defines the present China's security and periphery policy. In the post-1949 period, the issue of vulnerability was resolved by occupying Tibet in 1950. Then progressively it moved ahead to integrate Tibet with mainland China. Thus, in 1951, the PRC signed the 17th-Point Agreement with the Tibetan authorities, the central feature of which was granting of autonomy to Central Tibet. This Agreement was essentially a legal mechanism to bind the Tibetan periphery. The Tibetan revolt of 1959, however, exposed the fragility of China's sovereign control over Tibet. And thereafter, in 1965, Central Tibet was constituted into the Tibetan Autonomous Region. In effect, the PRC administratively weaved Central Tibet into the national 'geo-body'.

Moving on, into the post-Mao era, the onset of Tibetan unrest between 1987 and 1989 exposed yet again the failure of China's minority policy that was based on three pillars: ethnic classification, creation of autonomous regions and preferential policies towards the minority. This series of unrest essentially reflected China's vulnerability on the Tibetan issue and the consequent need for adopting ameliorative steps, including the implementation of the Western Development Programme (WDP) in 1999 to meet the threat from Tibetan separatism. It may be noted that the WDP was launched to spread economic prosperity in backward underdeveloped regions of China. It was rationalised that the cause of unrest was lack of development and therefore, it was believed that economic prosperity would help mitigate Tibetan separatism. However, the fault-lines in the programme became apparent with the eruption of massive unrest in 2008 and self-immolation of the Tibetans from 2009 onward, peaking in 2011-12. This again exposed the flawed nature of Chinese policies that addressed the complex identity issues with security-oriented policies alone. Notably, the WDP was primarily a security-driven strategy, based on Hanization, resource extraction, military deployment, infrastructure building and repression, and not a policy for uplifting the minorities and addressing their identity issues.

While internally, the Tibetan unrest kept the Chinese state on tenterhooks, the Dalai Lama's internationalisation of the Tibetan movement with his Five-Point Peace Plan in 1987 and the Strasbourg Proposal in 1988, coupled with the US government's conferring of the Noble Prize on the Dalai Lama in 1989, flustered the Chinese leadership. Since then, the PRC undertook several steps ranging from issuing of White Papers on Tibet to holding of talks with the envoys of the Tibetan Government-in-exile. This was basically to coopt the Tibetans into the national rhetoric of unity and territorial integrity, instead of allowing them to be a force outside the state. After the nine rounds of talks between the representatives of Dharamsala and Beijing that broke down in 2010, China under Hu Jintao began to prepare for a post-Dalai Lama era to tackle the Tibetan issue.[8] These include, the organisation of World Buddhist Forum in 2006, the passage of the Order No. 5 law on incarnation in 2007 and holding of national conferences on the Work Report on Tibet, the fifth such conference was in 2010 that had significant import for the post-Dalai Lama era. Besides, China has also re-cast its Nepal policy, which includes playing a proactive role in determining the future shape of Nepal's politics. Currently, Xi Jinping's extension of the Belt and Road Initiative (BRI) to Nepal effectively means turning the Himalayan Kingdom into China's new periphery and thereby, neutralise the vulnerability emanating from the Tibet issue. If one considers the figures of the Tibetans transiting to India, there has been a substantial decline. If in the pre-2008 Beijing Olympics, the number had been in thousands; in post-2008 era, it had dwindled to just few hundreds.[9] What this essentially demonstrates is that, Tibet has ceased to be a factor in China-Nepal relations. Nonetheless, the above Chinese policies and measures indicate the predominance of vulnerability of Tibet in Chinese foreign and domestic policy. Every policy of the PRC concerning Tibet has emanated from the prerequisite need to end the vulnerability and establish stability on China's periphery. Arguably, therefore, China's policy formulation and strategies on Tibet emanate not from its altercation with India on the border issue per se, but from its deep sense of vulnerability. This psyche of vulnerability has cast a deep shadow on India-China relations.

The Tibetan Response

Arguably, the Tibetans themselves have diluted the goal and purpose of their movement against the Chinese government. The movement, that began with the goal of independence and self-determination in the 1950s, got diluted in the 1980s, when officially the Strasbourg Proposal of 1988 replaced the goal of independence with the Dalai Lama's demands for 'genuine autonomy'. The genuine autonomy proposal, in effect, meant to constitutionally accept Tibet to be a part of the PRC. Further, the dilution of the movement was perpetrated by the US itself when in 1951, the Eisenhower administration turned down the Tibetan request to brand China an aggressor country in the United Nations.[10] Instead, it pressurised the Dalai Lama to project the Tibetan suffering under China as a case of human rights violation, thus effectively, dissuading the Tibetan cause of independence to a mere human rights issue. Nevertheless, this human right dimension has helped the Tibetans to garner considerable international attention. At a time, when terrorism is being denounced worldwide and when China has heightened its repressive measures to curb separatism in the name of terrorism, as is in the case of Uyghur separatists, the Tibetans have managed to escape a similar fate owing to the human rights dimension of their movement.

With regard to the dialogue that started in 2002 between the Tibetan Task force and the Chinese representatives, it too ended without achieving any breakthrough in 2010. A revival of the dialogue process is highly unlikely since the Chinese believed that the Tibetan Government in Exile (TGIE) under an elected prime minister is 'illegitimate' and hence, 'disqualified' to hold talks.[11] Currently, some efforts are now being made to reopen a dialogue with the Dalai Lama primarily because for the Chinese, the Tibet issue is not related to the status of Tibet but is all about the future of the Dalai Lama. In other words, the Chinese government is now trying to bring back the Dalai Lama to China. Once the Dalai Lama enters China, China believes that all controversies about its sovereignty and legitimacy on Tibet would fizzle out. However, the Dalai Lama's devolution of power is an important step towards preparing the Tibetans for a post-Dalai Lama scenario. Seemingly, it is geared to achieve two significant objectives. One is to settle the controversy surrounding the Dalai Lama's reincarnation issue. The Chinese are likely to implant their own Dalai Lama after the present Dalai Lama departs, as they have done in the case of Panchen Lama. But the devolution of power to a democratically elected government has virtually made reincarnation inconsequential for the political future of the Tibetan movement.[12] Two, is to stabilise and legitimise the democratic ethos of the Tibetans. The election of the Tibetan Prime Minister by the Tibetans from almost thirty countries across the globe indeed has strengthened their democratic identity. Over time, this could engender a de-facto character to the Tibetan power outside of China.

Nonetheless, the post-Dalai Lama phase would be critical for the Tibetan movement. It is likely to lose its sheen in the absence of the Dalai Lama. However, the issues of identity are hard to die. And no amount of economic largesse from the Chinese government would help to buy the loyalty of the Tibetans. In fact, the spate of self-immolation among the Tibetans inside China in 2011-12 suggests the resilience and vindication of identity issues despite heightened repression of the PRC.

The Future of Tibet Question and India's Options

For China, Tibet is a sovereignty issue and an internal matter. Therefore, it allows no space for any discussion on the subject. Its sovereignty on Tibet has ramifications for its national integrity and territorial stability. If Tibet falls from Chinese grip, Xinjiang would follow suit. The bottom line of China's Tibet policy has thus been the maintenance of sovereignty at all cost through military and economic means and denial of recognition of Tibetan identity and thereby, eventually submerge the Tibetans into the greater Han identity. Moreover, Beijing's reconfigured Tibet policy under Hu Jintao, based on the promotion of Buddhism and creation of a new monkhood, is aimed at preempting the security threat in the post-Dalai Lama era. At the same time, it is geared towards weakening India's hold on the Tibet card.

In this context, what are the options for India? Is the Tibet card redundant in the face of growing military and economic might of the Chinese? The answer is, the Tibet card is still not lost. Most Indians in the academia, policy establishment and military circles have generally believed that China is all powerful and that India has absolutely no leverage with the Chinese on the Tibet issue. The policy of the Indian government is therefore, largely that of appeasing the Chinese or having no policy at all. But China is not all that strong. There are substantial vulnerabilities in the Chinese system. In dealing with China, India should be aware of the deep insecurities and vulnerabilities that afflict the dragon nation. It should shape its China policy from this 'knowing' and not from a superficial analysis of the immediate global circumstances.

Any mention of China's vulnerability, whose economy is $11 trillion-strong, raises eyebrows. However, this psyche of vulnerability, as mentioned above in the chapter, is deep-rooted in Chinese history. In fact, if one identifies the primary characteristic undergirding China's history and polity, it is the constant tussle between vulnerability and stability. And today, if one asks about the primary goal of the Communist Party of China (CPC), it is preeminently stability. In the current period, China confronts deep insecurity, both internally and externally.

Internally, one-party rule might appear resilient and the People's Liberation Army (PLA) most powerful. But it is quite baffling to see the Chinese Premier Li Keqiang, visiting Tibet between 25 and 27 July 2018 and declaring it an inseparable part of China's "sacred" territory as well as urging religious figures to promote national unity and ethnic harmony.[13] Why has this statement been made now when Beijing has issued more than a dozen white papers on Tibet since the 1990s to bolster its claims, and has rapidly intensified the militarisation of Tibet since the 2000s? Further, the fate of Muslims in Xinjiang is dire as China has detained a million ethnic Uyghurs and sent some two million Uyghurs and other ethnic Muslims to secret camps for indoctrination to Chinese nationalism. Clearly, all is not well inside China. It is spending an enormous amount of money on the People's Armed Police (PAP), deployed to curb internal rebellion and dissent. China's expenditure on internal security is reportedly $196 billion, larger than the PLA's official budget. This suggests internal destabilisation is a greater worry for the Communist Party than external threats. Indeed, internal vulnerabilities have only exacerbated with President Xi Jinping's anti-graft effort, which is apparently the largest organised one in the history of Communist rule in China. More than a million people, including high-ranking military and party officials have been indicted for corruption so far. Many portray this as more of a political purge than an effort to cleanse the rot in the party ranks. Arguably, Xi might confront some kind of a rebellion from within his party ranks and society at large. That presumably explains his holding onto power and the scrapping of the two-term presidential term limit.

Geopolitically, President Trump's outreach to North Korea and advocacy of an Indo-Pacific strategy are eroding China's geopolitical manoeuvrability. In fact, Trump's Indo-Pacific strategy serves as a principal challenge to

Xi Jinping's dream project, the Belt and Road Initiative (BRI) with an estimated cost of $8 trillion. Economically, the ongoing trade war between the US and China is expected to hurt China's growth, and that could very well mean the erosion of the Communist Party's credibility given that it draws its legitimacy from continued good economic performance. Besides the US challenge, more worrying for China is the alleged debt trap issue associated with its BRI strategy that has apparently threatened the economies of eight countries, including Pakistan, Sri Lanka and Maldives in India's neighbourhood. With the veteran leader and Prime Minister of Malaysia, Mahathir Mohammad, cancelling the two Chinese-funded projects in his country, and calling it unviable and unnecessary, the dept-trap issue has considerably gained global attention. His remark at the Great Hall of the People in Beijing on 21 August 2018 that "We do not want a situation where there is a new version of colonialism happening because poor countries are unable to compete with rich countries," has indeed unnerved the Chinese. His remarks literally branded the BRI a neo-colonial project, and China an imperialist. Malaysia's cancellation has created strong reverberations in Pakistan where there are increasing concerns about inability to repay the loans and falling into a debt trap as a result of the $60 billion China-Pakistan Economic Corridor, as part of the BRI project. The case of Sri Lanka is most glaring when it failed to repay the loans and was forced to handover its port of Hambantota to the Chinese on a 99-years lease. In effect, Sri Lanka surrendered its sovereignty rights to the PRC. The dark side of the BRI would seemingly dent China's credibility. In turn, this would exacerbate vulnerability for China, since the BRI is a lynchpin of China's nationalism project and Xi Jinping has steered all resources and energy to the success of BRI.

At this point when there is rising scepticism on the BRI and growing confrontation in US-China relations, China has sought to woo India in a major way. The first such instance was the statement made by Foreign Minister Wang Yi on the sidelines of the parliamentary session in March 2018, when he was quoted saying, "if China and India are united, one plus one will become eleven instead of two." The subsequent Wuhan informal summit in April between Prime Minister Modi and President Xi should also be seen in this context. Again, during the 10th BRICS Summit held in Johannesburg between 25 and 27 July 2018, Xi held the view that the five countries of the BRICS represented the five fingers, and that "when the BRICS come together, we form a fist that can punch." Obviously, it is meant to punch the US. Keeping up the momentum, the Chinese defence minister, Wei Fenghe, visited New Delhi in the third week of August to seemingly re-establish military relations between the two Asian giants. Thus, notwithstanding the 2017 Doklam crisis and New Delhi's refusal to endorse the BRI, China has reached up to India. In other words, vulnerability vis-à-vis the US has caused China to ease its tensions with India. This is indeed an opportune moment for India to be firm with the Chinese.

In fact, India does have a small window to settle the border dispute with China from the position of strength. The window is small owing to two reasons. First, if the larger goal of the BRI is taken into account, it is essentially to fulfil the two centenary goals of China. One, by 2021, the 100th anniversary of the founding of the CCP, China aims to become a 'moderately well-off society' and two, by 2050, the 100th anniversary of the founding of the PRC, it aims to become a fully developed nation. It essentially means that with the fulfilment of the twin goals, China would be the new superpower. Second, to China, the US is the principal hurdle in its path to meet the goals of national rejuvenation. Hence, it has concentrated all its energies in tackling the US challenge. A glimpse at China's foreign policy strategy in the Cold War period, would reveal that China has always based its foreign policy by identifying a principal contradiction (threat) and a lesser contradiction, the purpose of which is to isolate the principal contradiction by tilting towards the lesser one. Notably, the US-China rapprochement of the 1970s came about after the identification of the Soviet Union as the principal hegemon and joining hands with the capitalist United States. Mao Zedong did not regard the rapprochement with the US as an aberration of Marxist ideology. Instead, he vindicated his tilt by advocating the Three Worlds Theory in 1973-74. In other words, ideology mattered the least when China found itself vulnerable. Currently, the US is the principal contradiction, and hence, China is attempting to woo India, the lesser contradiction. By no means, does this current Chinese tilt indicate any real bonhomie between the two Asian giants. In fact, China would never entertain a power equivalent to it because according to the Confucian thought, there cannot be two tigers residing on a single mountain. Therefore, India should not fall into the Chinese trap and give into its machinations. Rather, it should take advantage of the US-China conflict and creatively use the Tibet card. This essentially would mean bringing the Tibet issue upfront in future negotiations with the Chinese. The other option would be to accept participating in the BRI only on condition of Chinese recognition of Arunachal Pradesh as India's territory. This could well mean a grand bargain to settle the Tibetan conundrum.

In sum, the Tibet conundrum is primarily a Chinese creation. China's deep-rooted vulnerability has shaped its Tibet policy from a security perspective, giving no room for any discussion on addressing the identity issues pertaining to the Tibetans. At the same time, its Tibet policy served as a major hindrance to amicably settle the border dispute with India. By regarding it as basically an internal issue, it has closed all doors for any meaningful dialogue with India. But owing to Tibet's entanglement with the border issue, and coupled with the presence of Tibetan exiled population in India, it cannot be regarded as an internal issue of China. Further, the Dalai Lama's internationalisation of the Tibet cause and his March 2011 devolution of power has lent credence to the Tibetan movement and also buttressed its identity. Therefore, a resolution of India-China border dispute is contingent on amicably settling the fate of Tibet and the Tibetans. Finally, India's China policy should factor in the deep insecurities and vulnerabilities that plague China and that which dominates Chinese domestic and foreign policy formulations.

NOTES

1 Claude Arpi, "A New India's Tibet Policy," 24 September 2012, available at http://claudearpi.blogspot.com/2012/09/a-new-indias-tibet-policy.html

2 L.L. Mehrotra, *India's Tibet Policy: An Appraisal and Options*, Tibetan Parliamentary and Policy Research Centre, New Delhi, 1997, available at http://tibet.net/wp-content/uploads/2017/05/Inidas-Tibet-Policy.pdf

3 See, Deepak Lal, "India's Foreign Policy, 1947-64", *Economic and Political Weekly*, Vol. 2, No. 19, 13 May 1967, pp. 879-887. Ramachandra Guha, "Jawaharlal Nehru and China: A study in Failure?," Harvard-Yenching Institute Working Paper Series, 2011, available at https://www.harvard-yenching.org/sites/harvard-yenching.org/files/featurefiles/Ramachandra%20Guha_ Jawaharlal%20Nehru%20and%20China.pdf

4 Giersch, C Patterson, "Grieving for Tibet," *China Perspectives*, No. 3, 2008, p.4.

5 Millward, James A, *Eurasian Crossroads: A History of Xinjiang*, London: Hurst & Company, 2007.

6 Abanti Bhattacharya, "Strategic Significance of Tibet," *IPCS*, Issue Brief, No. 220, May 2013, available at https://www.files.ethz.ch/isn/165109/IB220-Abanti-ChinaPeriphery-Tibet.pdf

7 See, Sujit Dutta, "Managing and Engaging Rising China: India's Evolving Posture," *The Washington Quarterly*, Vol. 34, No. 2, Spring 2011, pp. 127-144.

8 Abanti Bhattacharya, "As China prepares for post-Dalai lama Tibet, what is India to do with

the Tibetan Exiles?," IDSA Comment, 25 March 2010, available at https://idsa.in/idsa comments/AsChinapreparesforpost-DalaiLamaTibetwhatisIndiatodowiththeTibetan Exiles_ abhattacharya_250310

9 The figures are based on the author's field work in Dharamsala in 2012.

10 Melvyn C. Goldstein, "The United States, Tibet and the cold War," *Journal of Cold War Studies*, Vol. 8, No. 3, Summer 2006, pp. 145-164.

11 Abanti Bhattacharya, "Tibet in World Politics," in Prabhat P. Shukla (ed.), *Tibet: Perspectives and Prospects*, New Delhi: Aryan Books International, 2013, p. 19.

12 Ibid.

13 Tibet Part of China's Sacred History, *The Indian Express*, 30 July 2018.

7

Xinjiang under the Shadow of Uyghur Nationalism and Islamic Radicalism

Mahesh Ranjan Debata

Introduction

Xinjiang, known as Xinjiang Uyghur Autonomous Region (XUAR) in the Chinese official parlance, is China's largest province covering an area of 1.6 million sq kms, which is almost one-sixth of the overall landmass of People's Republic of China (PRC). Being located in the northwestern part of PRC, Xinjiang has about 5,600 kms long international border with eight countries such as Mongolia, Russia, three Central Asian Republics (CARs) of Kazakhstan, Kyrgyzstan and Tajikistan, Afghanistan, Pakistan and India. Its neighbours within PRC are the Gansu province, Ningxia Hui Autonomous Region (NHAR), Tibet Autonomous Region (TAR) and Qinghai.[1] Xinjiang's importance as a strategic borderland for China stems from its complex geography, history, ethno-cultural and religious diversity, abundant natural resources like oil, natural gas and minerals, in addition to a sizeable Muslim population living in all the eight bordering countries. Further, the demand of the Uyghurs of Xinjiang for a separate East Turkistan Islamic Republic has compelled Beijing to consider Xinjiang as a highly sensitive region. Uyghurs, who form the majority of the population in Xinjiang with a share of 44 per cent of the total population, are one of the 47 minority groups living in Xinjiang. Against this background, this paper argues that Xinjiang has become

Designed by: Dr. Vivek Dhankar
© Institute for Defence Studies and Analyses
New Delhi, GIS Lab.

Courtesy: Prof. P. Stobdan

a shattered security zone in the post-Cold War period with inimical forces such as terrorism, religious extremism, transnational drug trafficking, smuggling of arms and military technologies, epidemics such as HIV/AIDS and ecological disaster spreading their tentacles and thereby dealing a body blow to regional peace and stability.[2] The paper argues further that rise and spread of ethnic separatism and religious extremism among the Uyghurs and their linkage with international terrorist infrastructure has prompted the Chinese central government to take stern domestic measures in addition to mobilise the world community against anti-state and anti-national activities of the Uyghurs.

Xinjiang Problem: Separatism or Movement?

There has been decades-long debate whether the problem in Xinjiang is a problem of separatism or freedom movement. While the Chinese central government dubs Xinjiang problem mostly as the handiwork of three "evil forces" – national separatism, religious extremism and international terrorism, the Uyghurs call it a nationalistic movement of their freedom from the Chinese yoke. And most of the western countries (American and European) subscribe to the Uyghur view. Thus Uyghur movement across the globe spread by the World Uyghur Congress (WUC)[3] with 28 affiliate Uyghur organisations are overtly and covertly, and financially and intellectually supported by American and European governments, civil society organisations, NGOs, think-tanks etc. However, the Chinese government has assiduously mobilised international opinion against the Uyghurs in the post-9/11 period, and the world community is made to believe that China has been a victim of terrorism. It is worthwhile to note here that the problem in Xinjiang was out and out an issue of ethnic conflict between the Uyghurs and Hans for over two decades (1949-76), which later took an ugly turn in the late 1980s and the post-1991 period.

Uyghur-Han Ethnic Conflict Breeding Uyghur National Sentiment

After taking over power in September 1949, the Chinese Central Government under the leadership of Communist Party of China (CPC) devised a well-thought out policy towards the Uyghurs of Xinjiang. Understanding the dynamics of this restive region, where Uyghurs were able to establish Turkic Islamic Republic East Turkistan (TIRET) in 1930s and 1940s, though short-lived, in addition to the apprehension about the recurrence of Soviet influence that was prominent in Xinjiang for three decades (from 1920 to 1949), CCP supremo Mao Tse Tung used both political and military tactics to keep Xinjiang under Chinese control. At the first instance, Mao was successful in eliminating leading Uyghur leaders, including Ahmetjan Qasimi of the Second East Turkistan Republic, in a mysterious plane crash in Panfilov town of Kazakhstan with the help of Soviet President Joseph Stalin, thus making the Uyghur movement leaderless and dealing a fatal blow to Uyghur aspiration for a separate nation in future on one hand,[4] and keeping the Soviet leadership in good humour on the other. Under the pretext of developing China's underdeveloped western regions such as Xinjiang, the Chinese central government encouraged massive migration of Hans from Mainland China to the sparsely populated northwest. Within a short span, the ratio of the Han population in Xinjiang increased sharply and now it nearly equals the Uyghur population. For example, the Han population in Xinjiang which was a mere 6.7 per cent in 1949, rose up to whopping 40 per cent by now. Ethno-cultural difference between Hans and Uyghurs created an unbridgeable gap between the two nationalities. The government sponsored policies and programmes during the Great Leap Forward period (1958-1966) and Cultural Revolution (1966-1976) under a slogan "Go West Young Han" accelerated the migration process that radically altered Xinjiang's demographic character. Besides, the agrarian economy of Xinjiang was entrusted to a Han para-military structure, Xinjiang Production and Construction Corps (XPCC) or *Xinjiang Shengchang Jianshe Bingtuan*, which not only brought Xinjiang's agrarian sector under its control, but also fulfilled para-military need and responsibility alongside the People's Liberation Army (PLA) in exigency.[5] The predominance of Han in almost every sector in Xinjiang, be it political, social or economic, gave rise to strong ethnic consciousness and a sense of alienation among Uyghurs, which resulted in simmering discontent among them, further prompting Uyghurs to develop an anti-Han and anti-Chinese sentiment.

A sense of nationalism among Uyghurs brewed up because of excesses meted out to them by Chinese authorities during the Mao regime. The hatred for Hans on one hand and building rapport with neighbouring countries and regular contact with the Middle East on the other provided food for a growing national sentiment among Uyghurs. East Turkistan People's Revolutionary Party (ETPRP), a Uyghur organisation, took the centrestage to fan the sentiment of Uyghur identity through intellectual efforts in addition to resorting to some violent means. On the intellectual front, the first and foremost effort was to restore, revive and popularise Uyghur version of the cultural and socio-economic history of Xinjiang, not the way the Chinese government had described. While China claims to have control over Xinjiang since the Western Han dynasty rule (206 BC-221 AD), the Uyghurs believe to have an emotional linkage with Xinjiang for over six thousand years. Two books *The Uyghurs, A Short History of Xionghu* (*Turks*) and *The Literature of the Uyghurs* written and published between 1986 and 1989 by Uyghur intellectual, poet and historian Turghun Almass injected nationalistic fervour amongst the Uyghurs.[6] Earlier, *Sharqi Turkistan Tarikhi* (The History of Eastern Turkistan) written in 1940s by one of the tallest Uyghur leaders Mohammad Amin Bughra provided a systematic historical narrative of Xinjiang from a national perspective.[7] The revival of Uyghur nationalism in 1980s and 1990s was mainly due to the opening up of borders as part of the economic reform programme, liberal Chinese policies allowing religious and cultural freedoms and revival of Islam across the globe following the Great Iranian Revolution of 1979. Slowly and steadily, the Uyghur movement that started with the issue of Uyghurs' ethnic identity coupled with their national sentiment and later on with religion (Islam) thereby created a peculiar situation in Xinjiang. Uyghurs' resistance to Beijing began to be seen in a 'Muslim versus non-Muslim' framework,[8] which is of paramount interest and importance in the light of the dynamic political nature of Islam today and the threat of Islamic radicalism.

Uyghurs and Islamic Radicalism

Even though the Uyghur issue in Xinjiang showed its ethno-national character throughout the Mao Tse Tung rule, religion (Islam) too had played an important role in sensitising the Xinjiang conundrum. The suppression of Uyghurs as a religious minority at the hands of Hans was the veritable cause of adherence to a strict, conservative and radical form of Islam among Uyghurs, especially in the 1990s. External factors such as the Great Islamic Revolution of Iran (1979), revival of Islam in Central Asia and beyond, Haj pilgrimage that led to greater interaction with the Islamic world etc. gave opportunity to Uyghurs to identify themselves more with Islam. The rise of Taliban and Al Qaeda in the neighbourhood (Afghanistan) and their preaching to establish the Islamic Emirate pepped up the religious feeling among the Uyghurs as

Muslims to take up cudgels against the atheist and infidel Han Chinese. Radical Islam, which has diluted the original meaning of Islam, spread into Xinjiang due to freedom of religious practices and regular interaction with the outside Muslim world. Besides, linkages with Saudi Arabia, Pakistan, Turkey and the CARs resulted in greater mobilisation and assertion by the Muslims of Xinjiang (mainly Uyghurs) on ethnic and religious lines.[9] Increasing contacts with the Middle East prompted them to criticise Islamic practices at home and exposed Uyghurs to new radical Islamic ideals. Uyghurs played a significant role in Saudi Arabia's propagation of Sunni Muslim ultra-conservatism in China. The appeal of radical Islamic ideology outside China, which attracted many Uyghurs to participate in violent jihadi activities as part of their religious identity and also as a way to further their struggle against the Chinese was evident when two Uyghur militants in a video (released by the ISIS in 2010) threatened against "evil Chinese communist infidel lackeys" and promised to spill "rivers of blood" in China as "retaliation for the tears that flow from the eyes of the oppressed (Uyghurs)."[10]

However, it is noteworthy to mention here that the strong feeling of Islamic identity among Uyghurs goes back to the reign of Kokandi General Yakub Beg, who established the Great Islamic Republic in Kashgar and ruled over the region for a decade from 1866 to 1876. Yaqub Beg has been revered by Uyghurs as symbol of Uyghur nationalism as well as Islam. In addition, the TIRET established in 1930s and 1940s used the words "Turkic" and "Islamic", symbolising pan-Turkic and pan-Islamic identity of Uyghurs. Even one Uyghur rebel pamphlet "Struggle for Motherland" published during the second TIRET in 1940s stated:

> "We have the right to rise up against oppression for the sake of our liberty, the happiness and prosperity of our sons, and the renaissance of our religion. We also believe that the Allah has said to us, 'I shall punish all oppressors.' We also are fully convinced that the power of the masses is the power of Allah. In this faith we fought and over-throwing the treacherous Chinese sovereignty in three districts established a free Muslim East Turkistan State. At the same time we raised the flag that was handed down from our forefathers."[11]

In the post-independence Xinjiang, Abdimit, a Sheikh from Khotan, who was spearheading Khotan uprising (1956), not only made efforts to establish a pan-Turkic Islamic state in Xinjiang, but also travelled in and around Xinjiang to preach Jihad through religious ceremonies and doled out Islamic literature, posters and pamphlets among the Uyghurs. During Khotan uprising, Uyghurs shouted slogans like "Allah Commands us to Fight for Religion", and "Communists have Stolen the Land, Food, Minerals and Property of the Muslims", which shows assertion of Uyghur identity with Islam. A document titled *The Guidelines for an Islamic Republic* prepared the main agendas of Islamic republic in Xinjiang visualised by Abdimit. Two radical organisations of East Turkistan People's Revolutionary Party (ETPRP) "The Avengers of the Tengritagh (Tianshan)" and "The Avengers of the Urals" vouched for establishment of an independent Islamic state in Xinjiang through violent means. Another Uyghur group Eastern Turkistan Prairie Five Party (ETPFP) was established in Jiashi country of Kashghar in March 1981 to mobilise non-Han people of Xinjiang against the Chinese. Within a couple of months on 26 May 1981, several hundred ETPFP members declared Jihad against the Xinjiang Hans.[12]

Baren Incident: The Turning Point

The most violent separatist act by Uyghurs in Xinjiang since 1949 occurred in April 1990 in Baren, a village 50 km southwest of Kashghar, in the Akto County of Kizilsu Kyrgyz Autonomous Prefecture in southern Xinjiang, close to the Pamir mountain range, which forms China's border with Afghanistan. While offering *namaz* at a mosque in Baren on 5 April 1990, Uyghurs called for Jihad against infidel Hans. The most interesting fact to note here is that the Uyghurs promised paradise for those who sacrifice their lives for this Jihad. With this, the Uyghur separatist activities against the Chinese took a religious overtone in an open manner, and the idea of "Muslims versus infidels" became prominent. Zahideen Yusuf, the main leader of this uprising, was inspired by the Afghan Mujahideen and preached the kind of Jihad professed and practiced by Mujahideen. As the head of the East Turkistan Islamic Party (ETIP), which was set up in December 1989, Zahideen not only recruited Uyghurs as members of ETIP and imparted them training, but also mobilised money, materials, equipment, supplies, horses, motorcycles, explosives, arms and ammunitions. The youth wing of this party was known as "Islamic Dare to Die Corps." The ETIP members aired the virtues of Jihad through audio-visual cassettes and tapes, held ceremonies to swear their support for Jihad and elimination of the betrayers of Islam. The rebels issued Taliban style strictures against the local Han small traders, vendors and even against girls. They gave slogans like "In the Past Marxism-Leninism Suppressed Religion, Now Religion would Suppress Marxism-Leninism," "Revive Islam" and "Independent East Turkistan Islamic Republic."[13] The Xinjiang Academy of Social Sciences (XASS) reported that Muslim separatism had gained a foothold in Xinjiang by veritable means of literature, radio broadcasts, videos, and the use of Quranic schools (madaris) as a cover for indoctrination in Salafi-Jihadism.[14] The lessons learnt from the Baren uprising was that for the first time, a fanatic radical Islamic extremist group dared to challenge Chinese suzerainty. The use of small arms like pistol, sub-machine gun, hand grenades, explosives and dynamites indicated the production and proliferation of small arms across the region. The most important highlight of this incident was the reported involvement of Pakistani Intelligence Agency, the Inter-Services Intelligence (ISI).[15]

ETIM: The Fountainhead of Uyghur Jihadi Activities

The East Turkistan Islamic Movement (ETIM),[16] one of the jihadi extremist groups founded by Uyghur militants in Xinjiang, seeks to establish an independent Islamic state out of China through violent means. As a major beneficiary of covert funding from the Uyghur diaspora population, ETIM has used this funding to acquire a wide range automatic weapons and explosive devices, some of them indigenously made. The actual scale of ETIM's financing and logistical infrastructure was discovered in a crackdown by Chinese authorities in February 1996 as part of its Strike Hard campaign. Nearly 3,000 kg of explosives, 4,000 sticks of dynamite and 600 guns and ammunition were recovered in Xinjiang alone.[17]

The ETIM become a prominent cog in the constellation of globally active jihadist terror groups. Uyghurs' link with international jihadi activities first came to the world's attention during the Global War on Terror in October 2001, when the US and Coalition Forces killed and captured a number of Uyghurs fighting alongside the Taliban and Al-Qaeda in Afghanistan under the banner of the ETIM. The ETIM jihadists have now spread to the Middle East and Southeast Asia, and are part of the Turkistan Islamic Party (TIP) fighting with the Al Qaeda umbrella group Jabhat Fateh al Sham (JFS) in Syria. In the Syrian Civil War, the ETIM operates as TIP, which is also known as "Katibat Turkistani" (Turkistan Brigade).[18] Uyghurs' presence in Syria to fight along with the ISIS terrorists first came to public notice in a report published by the New American Foundation in June 2016.[19]

Uyghur militants, drawing inspiration from sensational Al Qaeda style attacks, like many other militant groups, is evident in an hour long video entitled "Jihad in Eastern Turkistan" posted in an Arabic website in 2006. Being inspired by videos released by Al Qaeda and its affiliates, this video showcased Uyghur militants' operational capability and combat training skill by using rocket propelled grenades, M-16s, AK-47, detonators and small rockets. Interestingly, the Uyghur jihadists even made an unverifiable claim to have brought down an "enemy" (Chinese) plane, besides airing warnings of many more attacks in the coming times. In addition to a video clip of an airplane crashing into the World Trade Centre building on 11 September 2001, this video featured Muslims reading their wills and making last rites, possibly before embarking on suicide missions, and also featured the body of a Uyghur militant, possibly killed in combat and being hailed as a martyr. In a dramatic ending, the video displays the faces of their enemy i.e. the Chinese. Two things can be ascertained from the video: (a) the more radicalised Uyghurs have begun to adopt Jihadi tactics, if not ideology; and (b) the Chinese government is running out of time if it wants to contain the Uyghur struggle.[20]

China's Counter: "Three Evil Forces" Strategy

China was among the first few nations which wholeheartedly supported the US "War against Terror," a massive military crackdown against the terrorists after the deadly attack on World Trade Centre and Pentagon in the US on 21 September 2001. The Information Office of the State Council of China released a government document on 21 January 2002, shortly after the 9/11 attacks, which stated: "under the influence of extremism, separatism and international terrorism, part of the East Turkistan forces, inside and outside the Chinese territory, turned to splittist and sabotage activities with terrorists violence as the main means, even brazenly declaring that terrorist violence is the only way to achieve their aims."[21] In order to stave off any challenge from the anti-Chinese forces in Xinjiang, Chinese central government has opted for multi-pronged strategy at the domestic/national level, regional level and also at the global level.

Domestic Strategy

Chinese Central government considers China a multi-ethnic state of majority Han Chinese and 55 minority nationalities. Any nationalist, separatist or independence movement is considered illegitimate, anti-state and anti-Chinese, because China does not at all recognise the right of national self-determination of the ethnic minority groups.[22] When the critical situation in Xinjiang created by rebel Uyghurs was going beyond control throughout 1990s, the Chinese central government made efforts to strengthen its strategy to contain the anti-Chinese forces by hook or by crook. Xinjiang was made the "Core" national interest along with other two sensitive regions—Taiwan and Tibet. As part of its internal strategy, China devised a sort of "carrot and stick policy." While the "carrot" side is all round prosperity of Xinjiang through socio-economic amelioration, and cultural and religious reformation, the "stick" side is crackdown on the separatists, splittists and anti-Chinese elements.[23]

Beijing realised well that only by improving the economic well-being of the Uyghurs, their attention could be deflected from separatist activities. The Great Western Development Programme undertaken by the Chinese government not only stresses the economic development of the backward western region, but also a part of China's domestic economic strategy to promote trade between Central Asia and Xinjiang. Chinese President Jiang Zemin first used the phrase "Great Western Development" or "Opening up the Great West" in Xian on 17 June 1999 in order to reduce regional disparity and discontent of the people in western regions of China, which lagged far behind the prosperous eastern coastal belt.[24] The Chinese strategy for promoting and accelerating Xinjiang's economic development aims at integrating the region into an emerging Central Asian market. After the disintegration of erstwhile USSR and creation of CARs, Central Asia was tipped to be an important export destination for Chinese products from Xinjiang and other parts of China. Chinese Premier Li Peng's clarion call for revival of the Silk Route during his Central Asia sojourn in 1993 was materialised almost after two decades in September 2013, when Chinese President Xi Jinping announced the ambitious Silk Road Economic Belt and Maritime Silk Road, otherwise known as Belt and Road Initiative (BRI), to revive the old fabled route of trade, commerce and people-to-people contacts. And the first and foremost focus of the BRI was the CARs.

The persistent violence perpetrated by the Uyghur rebels, militants and jihadists in Xinjiang in the post-Cold War period compelled the Chinese authorities to re-initiate military tactic of "Strike Hard, Maximum Pressure Campaign" or *yanda* (also known as "Stern Blows" campaign), which was first taken out in 1983 and continued up to 1986.[25] The Xinjiang Party Committee, which linked separatism with unlawful religious activities, confirmed how Islam was attached to Uyghur separatist activities. Under the Strike Hard campaign, Chinese security forces arrested frontline separatist leaders and activists, destroyed criminal outfits and recovered a huge cache of arms, ammunition and large amounts of hard cash, besides staving off attacks on government officials and security forces. By the end of December 2001, China amended its Criminal Law in order to make the counter-terrorism measures more explicit to punish "terrorists".[26] Shortly after 9/11, China established its National Anti-Terrorism Coordination Group (NATCG). The National Ministry of Public Security also simultaneously launched an Anti-Terrorism Bureau responsible for the research, planning, guidance, coordination and undertaking of the national anti-terror agenda.[27]

China's top legislature the National People's Congress (NPC) Standing Committee adopted the country's first counter-terrorism law on 26 December 2015 in the latest attempt to address terrorism at home and help maintain security and stability. The law, which came into force in January 2016, provides legal support to China's counter-terrorism activities as well as collaboration with the international community. The Chinese central government will provide necessary financial support for key regions listed in the country's counter-terrorist plan, whereas professional anti-terrorist forces will be established by public security, national security authorities as well as armed forces. A National Intelligence Center (NIC) was established to coordinate inter-departmental and trans-regional efforts on counter-terrorism intelligence and information.[28]

Regional Initiatives

Apprehending danger from regional and global actors and factors to create a vicious circle in Xinjiang, Chinese government initiated diplomatic endeavours with friends, foes, big powers, and neighbours and anybody related to the Uyghur issue (CARs, Turkey, Pakistan etc.) or anybody trying to meddle in Xinjiang. With huge economic investment worldwide, Chinese authorities compelled many external actors, especially USA, Russia and Turkey, not to sacrifice their trade and strategic defence relationship with China at the altar of Uyghurs' aspiration. China realised the importance of the newly created independent states three of which (Kazakhstan, Kyrgyzstan and Tajikistan) are direct and closest neighbours along the Xinjiang border. These three CARs are also home to Turkic ethnic groups including the Uyghurs, who had migrated from Xinjiang decades ago. The post-1991 period, especially the year 1996 was important in this context as Xinjiang during this period witnessed violent terrorist attacks by Uyghur militants, which prompted Chinese authorities to initiate the 'Strike Hard' campaign. China also devised a regional security mechanism in 1996 in the form of Shanghai Cooperation Organisation (SCO).

SCO as Bulwark against Three Evil Forces

China spearheaded the establishment of the SCO as part of a security strategy to prevent the Uyghur militants from using Central Asia as a launching pad for separatist and terrorist activities in Xinjiang. In this process of regional strategy, China roped in Russia and the CARs in 1996 to set up Shanghai Five, which later was rechristened as SCO in 2001. Through SCO, China popularised the concept of "three evil forces" in its own territory as well as in the neighbourhood, especially Central Asia. According to the Chinese Central government, the three evil forces have not only been a major security challenge in its troubled northwest province of Xinjiang, but also a constant source of instability in Central and South Asia region. In all the annual SCO Summit documents since 2001, there is at least one clause on joint action against three evil forces. The Tashkent Declaration on 17 June 2004 launched Regional Counter Terrorism Structure (RCTS) to be based in Tashkent. Out of half a dozen main tasks and duties of the Executive Committee of RCTS, four mentioned the "three evil forces".[29] Even the Qingdao Declaration of the Council of Heads of State of SCO held on 9-10 June 2018 stated that they "strongly condemn all forms of terrorism and consider it necessary to make efforts to promote the creation of a unified global counter-terrorism front with the central coordinating role of the UN on the basis of international law, without politicisation or double standards." They confirmed the "key role of the state and its competent agencies in counteracting terrorism, separatism and extremism in its territory, as well as in relevant cooperation within the SCO and in international formats."[30] In addition, China has been taking part in various bilateral and multilateral anti-terror military exercises with the SCO members from time to time.

Mobilisation of International Community

China is perhaps the only country which cashed in on the Global War on Terrorism and justified its military crackdown against Uyghurs and let the world know that Uyghurs are a serious threat to China's unity, stability and territorial integrity. The ETIM was listed as a beneficiary of Osama bin Laden's Al Qaeda network by the Information Office of China's State Council. On 26 August 2002, US Deputy Secretary of State, Richard Armitage announced that the US had placed the ETIM on the US list of terrorist organisations. Because of intense Chinese diplomatic endeavours, the global terrorist list of the UN and the US include other Uyghur terrorist groups including the *Home of East Turkistan Youth*, also known as Xinjiang's "Hamas", which had reportedly been operating along Xinjiang's Tajik and Kazakh borders.[31] In December 2002, China again highlighted the threat posed by "East Turkistan terrorist forces" in a White Paper on "China's National Defence in 2002" published by the State Council. It included a long section identifying "terrorism" as the key security issue. The White Paper reiterated that "China, too, is a victim of terrorism," and that "the 'East Turkistan terrorist forces' are a serious threat to the security of the lives and property of the people of all the ethnic groups and the country's social stability."[32]

In a response to the international criticism about the Chinese policies in Xinjiang that have resulted in human rights violations, China's State Council released a White Paper in May 2003 which stated: "after the 11 September (2001) incident, the voices calling for an international anti-terrorist struggle and cooperation have become louder and louder. In order to get out of their predicament, the 'East Turkistan' forces once again have raised the banner of 'human rights,' 'freedom of religion' and 'interests of ethnic minorities,' and fabricated claims that 'the Chinese government is using every opportunity to oppress ethnic minorities,' to mislead the public and deceive world opinion in order to escape blows dealt by the international struggle against terrorism."[33] In addition to diplomatic efforts, China issued veiled threats to some countries with dire consequences, if any of them tried to fan the Uyghur issue for the disadvantage of China. For example, China threatened to aid and abet the Kurd rebels in Turkey, in case Turkey tried to raise the Uyghur issue in any platform.[34]

Uyghur Movement in Doldrums

The Uyghur aspiration for a separate homeland out of China has become a day-dream or pipedream at the present situation for a variety of reasons. A well-crafted strategy by the Chinese central government, both domestic and external, has been too good and strong for the Uyghurs.

(i) Lack of Inside Support within China

Inside Xinjiang, relations among the major Turkic groups are not so cordial. Local Kazakhs do not have fraternal ties with the Uyghurs and vice versa. Since Uyghurs have failed to garner any support from their Turkic brethren within Xinjiang, there is hardly any hope for pan-Turkic solidarity among the Turkic Muslims within or outside Xinjiang. There is no support from domestic neighbours like Tibet and Inner Mongolia, where the local ethnic minority nationalities (Tibetans and Inner Mongols) have been demanding separate homeland for them since the Chinese independence in 1949. Unlike the Tibetans, Uyghurs have not so far benefitted from a well-defined US policy supporting their political rights, autonomy and cultural identity. Even though some hopes for a separatist triumvirate against the Chinese had arisen after first "International Conference of the Allied Committee of the Peoples of Eastern Turkistan, Tibet, and Inner Mongolia" was held on 16 October 1998 at Columbia University (New York) that did not work out. The present conciliatory stance of the Dalai Lama, who now demands economic and cultural autonomy of Tibet within China instead of the earlier demands of a separate homeland for Tibetans, has dealt a fatal blow to the aspirations of Uyghurs. Lack of cooperation and coordination among the leaders of these three ethnic minority groups has prompted the Chinese central government to fish in troubled waters. In addition to the conventional strategy, Chinese authorities have tried and to create fissures between the Uyghurs and other minority groups living in Xinjiang, especially Central Asians (Kazakhs), and become successful as well. It is noteworthy to mention here that Kazakhs, who are the third largest group in Xinjiang (after Uyghurs and Han) in terms of population, provided all kind of support to Uyghurs to set up the TIRET in 1933.

(ii) Failure of Uyghur Diaspora

There are 5,00,000 Uyghurs living abroad, 5-6 per cent of world's total Uyghur population (approximately 10.5 million). However, the Uyghur diaspora has failed to make any major impact worldwide with regard to their aim and objectives. Further, the World Uyghur Congress (WUC) does not have a leader of the stature of the Dalai Lama, who can influence the global leadership through his image as a spiritual leader and also mobilise money to continue freedom struggle against China. The WUC, established on 16 April 2004 in Munich (Germany), is an international diaspora organisation of Uyghurs that represents the collective interest of the Uyghur people both in Xinjiang and abroad. With the main objective to promote the right of the Uyghur people to use peaceful, non-violent, and democratic means to determine the political future of East Turkistan, the WUC engages in a wide-range of awareness and advocacy campaigns about the human rights situation for Uyghurs in the PRC, concentrating on US Congress in Washington, EU member states, and EU and UN human rights mechanisms. The WUC works closely with the EU Commission (especially the European External Action Service), the EU Parliament (including the EU sub-committee on Human Rights), NGOs, the UN Treaty Bodies, to which WUC regularly submits alternative reports (CERD, CAT, CEDAW) and UN Special Procedures (the Special Rapporteurs, Independent Experts and Working Groups). The WUC participates actively with the United Nations Human Rights Council (UNHRC) throughout the year and submits written statements and reports, delivers oral statements to plenary sessions, and organises side events that focus on Chinese human rights abuses. It has so far organised six general assemblies the last being held on 10-12 November 2017. The World Uyghur Congress has 28 Uyghur affiliate organisations across the world—mostly in Central Asia, Turkey, USA, Europe (Germany, Switzerland, UK, Belgium, Norway etc.), Japan and Australia.[35]

(iii) Changing Global Perception about Uyghurs

The international community understands the strength and stature of China in the global corridor and hence does not want to meddle in its internal affairs, especially the complex issue of Xinjiang. No country in the world now openly buys the Uyghur argument about Chinese repression and human rights violations against Uyghurs. Further, separatism, religious extremism and terrorism not only in Xinjiang, but also in any part of the world, are considered as greatest dangers humanity faces today, and the world community is in no mood to tolerate these menaces. Thus the linkage between Uyghur militants with international terror infrastructure is not accepted by the international community. With a land mass spanning from Russia in the north to Vietnam and Thailand in the south, from India and Pakistan in the west to Korea and Japan in the east, China has the world's third biggest territory, with a total land area of 9.6 million sq. kms, next only to Russia and Canada. One out of five people in the world lives in China (1.2 billion people). China is also the second largest economy in the world after the US and is a major investor with investments across the globe amounting to a whopping $1,778 billion in between 2005 and 2017.[36] China's indispensability in the global economic scenario is ironically felt through its grand strategy of BRI that aims at boosting trade, transit and traffic connectivity, besides facilitating and augmenting people-to-people contacts, covering over 60 countries in Asia and Europe with a total land area of 50 million sq kms and a population of three billion people. Any country desiring to compete in the global market cannot ignore the gigantic and increasingly prosperous Chinese market. Besides, China is a big military power with the largest army in the world.

Uyghurs and *Hindistan* (India)

It is worthwhile to mention here that Uyghurs, in their quest for an independent state, believe that in due course of time, *Hindistan* (as they fondly address India) will support their cause, even help them establish an independent East Turkistan republic. A couple of reasons they ascribe to justify this argument are: (i) historically, there were cultural and economic linkages between Uyghurs and the people of India; and (ii) use of Uyghur card by India. The disagreements between India and China are many, both are involved in competition and even confrontation, and most importantly, India is worried, even concerned about Chinese encirclement following conspicuous Chinese presence in India's neighbourhood, which will force India to use the 'Uyghur card' against China, once it outmanoeuvres China as an important economic and military power in the coming 30-40 years. However, no one in India buys or will buy this argument, at least as far as its relationship with China is concerned.

Till 1949, Uyghur factor was nowhere in the relationship between India and China. Following the Communist takeover of China in 1949, China eyed India with suspicion after two top Uyghur leaders, Mohammad Amin Bughra and Isa Yusuf Alptekin, left Xinjiang for the Indian State of Kashmir, along with over 100 Uyghur families. Since both Bughra and Alptekin were spearheading the Uyghur movement in Xinjiang, the Communist leadership in China suspected Indian patronage to these two Uyghur leaders. However, this was proved wrong after Bughra and Alptekin left for Turkey in 1950 without getting any patronage or help from India. Even today, the Uyghur rebels and separatists do not at all curry India's favour or sympathy for their cause – a separate Islamic republic exclusively for Uyghurs. India, having its own problems of separatism and terrorism in Jammu and Kashmir, deplores any kind of separatist and terrorist violence not only in Kashmir or Xinjiang, but also anywhere across the globe. India did even cancel the e-Visa earlier issued to Dolkun Isa, a prominent leader of the Munich-based World Uyghur Congress, to attend a Conference in Dharmshala (India) in April 2016. Further, India's involvement with Shanghai Cooperation Organisation (SCO) as an Observer earlier and now a full-fledged member, India subscribes to SCO members' campaign against three 'evil forces' (separatism, religious extremism and terrorism).

Conclusion

After analysing the Uyghur issue in Xinjiang threadbare, it is found that the situation in this northwestern region of China is grave because of Uyghur opposition to Chinese policies, post-Cold War realities, internal subversion and external influences, rise of religious extremism and terrorist activities. There has been a conflict of interests between Uyghur aspiration for a separate homeland and Chinese bid to uphold its national unity, territorial integrity, security and stability of its sensitive northwestern frontier. In comparison to the Uyghur argument, Chinese logic is simple, straight-forward, factual and clear-cut. For China, Xinjiang is China's strategic frontier with eight countries, three of which are nuclear powers (India, Pakistan and Russia), and the main duty and responsibility of the Chinese Central government is to secure peace and stability in this region. As discussed earlier, the current state of affairs in South and Central Asia region being marred by non-traditional security threats (religious fundamentalism, terrorism, narcotics, nuclear arms etc.) has put the adjacent regions like Xinjiang in jeopardy. Further, it is an established fact that Xinjiang has been an integral and inseparable part of China for the last seven decades of its independence in September 1949 and cannot be offered to Uyghurs to establish a separate homeland, because this will lead to a Soviet like situation and dismemberment of the Middle Kingdom as there are 55 minority nationalities living in China. In addition, Xinjiang that nurtures the economic interests of the world's second largest economy (China) has been dubbed as the gateway to resource-rich Central Asia and beyond. This northwestern borderland is also the fulcrum of China's gigantic transnational strategy of Belt and Road Initiative. So, the question does not at all arise for China to make any compromise on the issue of Xinjiang. Hence there is an amalgamation of well-crafted domestic policy (sometimes soft and sometimes stringent), astute foreign policy and sound economic policy by the Chinese central government to ensure China's national unity and integrity as well as to keep this strategically important region under control. Further, the linkage between Uyghur militants with international terror infrastructure such as Taliban, Al Qaeda and the ISIS is well known and proved as well, and thus prompts the international community to tilt towards China dubbing terrorism as a crime against humanity. Against such undercurrents, it is not wise for the Uyhgurs to think of a separate nation out of China, which is a global power with economic prowess and impeccable military might. The only option left for the Uyghurs is to relish China's astounding economic development by shunning anti-Chinese activities. Last but not the least, the Chinese Central government has thus an impregnable task of bringing this dissenting minority group (Uyghurs) to national mainstream so that peace and stability is established for the greater benefit of the people of South and Central Asia.

NOTES

1 *The Facts and Figures on Xinjiang, China,* Beijing: China Continental Press, 2013, p. 9.

2 Mahesh Ranjan Debata, "Xinjiang in Central Asia's Regional Security Structure", *International Studies,* Vol. 52, Nos. 1-4, 2017, p. 1.

3 "World Uyghur Congress homepage", available at www.uyghurcongress.org, accessed on 2 July 2018.

4 Nabijan Tursun, "Yearning for a Republic Erased from the Map", available at http:// www.uyghur congress.org/en/wp-content/uploads/uyghur_history.pdf, accessed on 12 July 2018.

5 "The History and Development of the Xinjiang Production and Construction Corps", Beijing: The State Council of People's Republic of China, 5 October 2014, available at http:// english.gov.cn/archive/white_paper/2014/10/05/content_281474992384669.htm, accessed on 31 October 2015; Also see "Bingtuan: China's Paramilitary Colonizing Force in East Turkistan", Uyghur Human Rights Project, 26 April 2018, pp. 1-45.

6 Mahesh Ranjan Debata. *China's Minorities: Ethnic-Religious Separatism in Xinjiang,* New Delhi: Pentagon Press, 2007.

7 Michael Dillon, *Xinjiang-China's Muslim Far Northwest,* London & NY: Routledge, 2004, p. 52.

8 Mahesh Ranjan Debata, op. cit

9 K. Warikoo, *Xinjiang: China's Northwest Frontier,* London & NY: Routledge, 2016, p. 162.

10 Rohan Gunaratna, Arabinda Acharya and Wang Pengxin, "Uighur-Separatism: East Turkistan

Groups", in Rohan Gunaratna, Arabinda Acharya and Wang Pengxin (eds.) *Ethnic Identity and National Conflict in China*, US: Palgrave Macmillan, 2010, pp. 47-88.

11 US Department of State, Division of Chinese Affairs, "Signs of Unrest in Tihwa," American Consul J. Hall Paxton to the Secretary of State, Urumqi, 13 January 1947, enclosure no. 2, quoted available at http://www.eastturkistangovernmentinexile.us/etr_archive.html, accessed on 15 August 2017.

12 Michel Dillon, op. cit., p. 59.

13 Ibid, p. 63.

14 Kendrick T. Kuo. "Revisiting the Salafist-Jihadist Threat in Xinjiang", *Journal of Muslim Minority Affairs*, Vol. 32, No. 4, 2012, p. 530.

15 K. Warikoo. op. cit, p. 172.

16 Beina Xu, Holly Fletcher and JayashriBajoria, "The East Turkistan Islamic Movement (ETIM)", Council on Foreign Relations homepage, 4 September 2014, available at https://www.cfr.org/backgrounder/east-turkestan-islamic-movement-etim, accessed on 15 September 2016.

17 Rohan Gunaratna and Kenneth George Pereire, "An Al-Qaeda Associate Group Operating in China?", *China and Eurasia Forum Quarterly*, Vol. 4, No. 2, May 2006, pp. 58-59.

18 Colin P. Clarke and Paul Rexton Kan, "Uighur Foreign Fighters", ICCT Policy Brief, November 2017, available at https://icct.nl/wp-content/uploads/2017/11/ClarkeKan-Uighur-Foreign-Fighters-An-Underexamined-Jihadist-Challenge-Nov-2017-1.pdf, accessed on 2 January 2018.

19 Patric Meyer, "China's De-Extremization of Uyghurs in Xinjiag", *New America*, June 2016 availble at https://www.newamerica.org/international-security/policy-papers/china-de-extremization-uyghurs-xinjiang/, accessed on 15 June 2017.

20 Rohan Gunaratna and Kenneth George Pereire, "An Al-Qaeda Associate Group Operating in China?", *China and Eurasia Forum Quarterly*, Vol. 4, No. 2, 2006, p. 58.

21 "'East Turkistan' Terrorist Forces Cannot Get Away with Impunity", Beijing: Information Office of the State Council, People's Republic of China, 21 January 2002. Reproduced in *News from China*, 29 January-11 February 2002, p. 8.

22 Eric Hyer, "China's Policy towards Uighur Nationalism", *Journal of Muslim Minority Affairs*, Vol. 26, No. 1, April 2006, pp. 75-86.

23 "Strike Hard Campaign Targets Violent Crimes", *China Daily*, 15 June 2010, available at http://www.china.org.cn/china/2010-06/15/content_20267402.htm, accessed on 15 June 2015.

24 "Introduction to the Implementation of Great Western Development Strategy in China", Ministry of Ecology and Environment, People's Republic of China, 2 November 2000, available at http://english.mep.gov.cn, accessed on 15 September 2007.

25 Susan Trevaskes, "Courts on the Campaign Path in China: Criminal Court Work in the 'Yanda 2001' Anti-Crime Campaign", *Asian Survey*, Vol. 42, No. 5, September/October 2002, p. 675.

26 Amnesty International, *People's Republic of China: Gross Violations of Human Rights in the Xinjiang Uighur Autonomous Region*, ASA 17/021/2004, April 2004, p. 10.

27 Pan Guang, "East Turkestan Terrorism and the Terrorist Arc: China's Post-9/11 Anti-Terror Strategy", *The China and Eurasia Forum Quarterly*, Vol. 4, No. 2, May 2006, p. 21.

28 "China Adopts First Counter-Terrorism Law", *Xinhua*, 27 December 2015, available at http://www.xinhuanet.com/english/2015-12/27/c_134955905.htm, accessed on 20 January 2017.

29 "The Executive Committee of the Regional Counter-Terrorism Structure", available at http://www.sectsco.org/EN123/AntiTerrorism.asp, accessed on 15 July 2018.

30 Shanghai Cooperation Organisation (SCO) homepage, available at http://eng.sectsco.org/documents/, accessed on 15 July 2018.

31 "'East Turkistan' Terrorist Forces Cannot Get Away with Impunity", Beijing: Information Office of the State Council, People's Republic of China, 21 January 2002.

32 White Paper, "China's National Defence in 2002", Beijing: Information Office of the State Council, People's Republic of China, 9 December 2002.

33 White Paper, "History, Development of Xinjiang", Beijing: Information Office of the State Council, People's Republic of China, May 2003.

34 Yitzhak Schichor, "Ethno-Diplomacy: The Uyghur Hitch in Sino-Turkish Relations", Policy Studies, No. 53, Honolulu: East West Centre, 2009, p. xi.

35 "Introducing the World Uyghur Congress", World Uyghur Congress Homepage, available at www.uyghurcongress.org, accessed on 15 June 2018.

36 "Worldwide Chinese Investments", available at http://www.aei.org/china-global-investment-tracker/, accessed 5 July 2018.

8

Uyghurs: China's Missing Minorities

Prabha Rao

China has unleashed a prohibitory pogrom, in the form of internment centres against its Uyghur Muslim minorities, resembling in scope and magnitude Nazi concentration camps during the Second World War. These centres, ostensibly for 'vocational training', are more in the nature of high security prisons. Xinjiang today resembles the proverbial dystopian state, with invasive surveillance, and arbitrary detentions. China dismisses these allegations stating that they are examples of Western interference and double speak, and that re-education of the Muslim minorities is a concrete and important step towards their de-radicalisation, which will not only benefit China and Central Asia, but the larger global security scenario. Below is an effort to evaluate both contentions.

Introduction

On 6 November 2018, the United Nations' Human Rights Council (UNHRC), in its Universal Periodic Review (UPR), castigated China's human rights record, and asked Beijing to address the issue of its treatment of ethnic minorities, specifically the Uyghurs in Xinjiang. According to information garnered by the Human Rights Council through satellite imagery, reports from Uyghurs who have managed to leave Xinjiang, and activists/journalists who have managed to enter the Province, over a million Muslims of Turkic descent-Uyghurs and Khazaks had been interned in high security camps/re-education centers in the region. Unsurprisingly, China has responded by terming the camps as workshops for vocational training, and to quote Le Yucheng, Chinese vice minister of foreign affairs, who was heading the Chinese delegation at the forum, the UN assessment was 'politically driven' and 'fraught with biases'. Reacting to the accusation, the UN's high commissioner for human rights, Michelle Bachelet, has requested direct access for UN observers into Xinjiang, as did 15 western ambassadors spearheaded by Tamara Mawhinney, Canada's deputy permanent representative at the UN.[1] The Chinese foreign ministry spokeswoman Hua Chunying reacted angrily to the accusation in the Human Rights Council and claimed that the ambassadors had gone beyond their their diplomatic brief. Significantly, during the debate in Geneva, the award winning photographer Lu Guang went missing while visiting Kashgar in Xinjiang, and his wife Xu Xiaoli got official confirmation of his arrest—without details of the charges against him, and location of detention only in mid-December.[2] Now, activists who have been able to escape the camps are giving inputs about forced labour channeled from the camps into factories. Beijing has rebutted the contentions, claiming that the "vocational centres" set up by the state offered free training in law, language, and workplace skills, and that the initiative was well within the purview of Chinese domestic law.[3] This contention has been met with widespread disbelief and derision, but to little effect; the incarcerations remain, and the numbers continue to swell in the camps.

The Backdrop

Xinjiang—the Xinjiang Uyghur Autonomous Region (XUAR), is China's largest province, whose terrain is mainly either desert or mountain ranges. Turkic speaking Uyghur Sunni Muslims, mainly of Sufi persuasion, who were earlier a majority in the province, but now constitute only 44 per cent of the population, due to the systematic re-settlement of Han Chinese in the area, and migration of Uyghurs. Demographically, there are four distinct waves of human displacement from Xinjiang. The first was in late 1949, following the Communists' seizure of Xinjiang and consolidation of the province into PRC, when Uyghur political leaders and intellectuals, fled to Turkey, mainly through India. Many of them settled in the West, and set up the World Uyghur Congress, etc, which acted as focal points for the Diaspora. The second wave started in late 1959 and culminated in large scale migration mainly as a reaction to the extreme hardships faced by the Uyghurs due to the 'Hundred Flowers Movement' and the 'Great Leap Forward', which drove more than 60,000 of them out of China to the then USSR, and over 50,000 to the Central Asian republics—Kazakhstan, Kyrgyzstan and Uzbekistan. This exodus, which embarrassed the Chinese Government, caused Beijing to bring out the "compulsory order of residence"—a no exit policy, via the hukou system; which made crossing borders and procuring travel documents and visas extremely difficult. During this period there was simultaneous sustained settlement of Han Chinese into the XUAR administration and the region, causing quantifiable demographic changes. After the death of Mao in 1976 and the end of the Cultural Revolution, Beijing adopted a policy of greater tolerance to avoid ethnic unrest. This was changed post the Tiananmen Square incident in 1989, which brought in an authoritative clampdown in the whole country and particularly in Xinjiang and Tibet. It was only in mid 1990s that the end of the Cold War brought in reforms due to economic imperatives, which made the Chinese government reopen the borders, causing another wave of immigration.[4] The fourth wave, which is continuing till date, is the movement out of Xinjiang to radical Islamic movements—the ISIS, al Qaeda, Islamic Movement of Uzbekistan (IMU) etc.

The genesis of Uyghur discontent and causes of migration can be contextualized by studying Xinjiang's situation pre 1949, and the subsequent impact of the Chinese takeover. There were two main influences in the area[5]—Turks from Turkey, and the Tatars of Russia, both adhering to variants of pan-Turkism. The pan Turkist movement gained momentum as early as 1880s in Tatarstan, Russia, with the objective of restoring political influence to the Muslim Turkish peoples, and served as a nascent anti colonial movement. This movement closely aligned with Uyghur nationalism, the embers of which are active to this day.[6] Consequently, two independent republics were formed in Xinjiang—the Turk Islamic Republic of East Turkistan (TIRET) led by the emirs of Khotan centred on the region of Khotan and Kashgar which espoused an anti-communist ideology, and the East Turkistan Republic (ETR) propped by the Soviets in the three northern districts of Xinjiang along the border with the USSR; a reflection of the 'Great Game' politics being played between Britain and Russia at that time.[7]

After 1949, China asserted full control over the area, and the communist regime, introduced a Nationalities Policy –'Shaoshu Minzu', which promised to guarantee recognition of linguistic and cultural identities. Moving in this direction the PRC converted Xinjiang into an autonomous province XUAR

(Xinxiang Uyghur Autonomous Region) in 1955, but the pan Turkist adherents maintained that the autonomy was only emblematic, and initiated an underground fight against what they termed Han domination and overt colonialism. Pent up frustration resulted in underground cells propagating ethnic nationalism and covert radicalisation—problems which the Chinese state has been unable to expunge despite myriad draconian measures.

The above led to the formation of the East Turkistan Islamic Party (ETIP)—'Sherqiy Türkistan Islam Partiyisi,' in 1989 by Ziyauddin Yusuf, with nationalism and ethnic revivalism as its main platforms. Ziyauddin had revolted against the PLA forces in Baren Township Riot, in several towns of Kizilsu in 1990, which was termed as the 'Baren rebellion' by Beijing. He was killed in the riot and after his death, his party was taken over by Hasan Mahsum,[8] a native of Shule County, who came to notice for preaching Jihad against Chinese authorities He was arrested in October 1993 by Chinese Authorities and sent, interestingly enough, to a 're-educational/vocational training camp' in Yecheng County, which completely radicalised him. After his release, he fled from China in 1997 to Mecca, and from there to Afghanistan, where he trained with the Taliban, who gave him Afghan nationality and issued him an Afghan passport. The ETIM's headquarters was shifted by him to Kabul in 1998, and became an integral part of the al Qaeda under Osama bin Laden, who reportedly offered/gave $300,000 of financial assistance to the ETIM in 1999. Mahsum remotely controlled a network of criminals and extortionists in Urumqi, the capital of Xinjiang province in early 1999, and directed a series of deadly knife attacks in Khotan province, China in December 1999. Significantly, Uyghur detainees at Guantanamo Bay have confessed that they were trained by Hassan Mahsum and his associate Abdul Haq in Afghanistan.

Abdul Haq incidentally, was the leader who threatened terror attacks on the 2008 Beijing Olympics, and joined the Shura Council of al-Qaeda in 2005. The duo moved with impunity across the Durand line, integrated into the Taliban caravan, which enjoyed a degree of patronage from the Pakistani state. Under pressure from Beijing, Mahsum was later killed by Pakistani troops in 2003 during a raid on a suspected al-Qaeda hideout in South Waziristan, near the Afghanistan border. Abdul Haq, who took over from him was wounded in an air attack by Pak forces at Zor Babar Aidak town, Mir Ali, North Waziristan, Pakistan in 2010. The ISI claimed that his neutralisation was a success of the

Zarb e Azb programme, but the TIP did not confirm his death, and he resurfaced in 2014. Members of Afghanistan's NDS have been sceptical about Pakistani intentions about targeting the Uyghurs, which they claimed was only being done in a superficial manner, to maintain Islamabad's all important relationship with China. They further claimed that Abdul Haq who was popularly called Maimaitiming Maimaiti in Central Asia, was looked after by the Pak army, and returned to the Jihadi fold in 2014, as an agent of the ISI.

In the intervening period, between 2010 and 2014, the TIP was headed by Abdul Shakoor Turkistani, a jihadi from Turkmenistan, whose ascension underscored the reach the TIP/ETIM had in Central Asia, and the close links between the then Turkmen regime and the Talban/al Qaeda leadership. International pressure forced Pakistan to put muscle into the Zarb-e Azb programme, and the ISI popularised the distinction between the "good and bad Taliban", and took stringent measures to clear the North West Frontier Province (NWFP) of foreign Jihadis, which included cadres from the TIP. Subsequently, Abdul Shakoor Turkistani, who was carrying a political death warrant on his head, was killed along with several cadres of the Islamic Movement of Uzbekistan (IMU), in South Waziristan, again reinforcing the fact that these groups, who had fled their countries were working in tandem.[10]

Abdul Shakoor was succeeded by Abdullah Mansour in 2012, who rose to prominence due to his fiery writing in the TIP's mouthpiece Islamic Turkistan.[11] Earlier (2018) Mansour, speaking from a secret location in Waziristan to a Reuters correspondent, in a video, along with Abdul Haq, had threatened mass attacks during the Summer Olympics to be held in Beijing, and claimed that his group was a part of the larger Islamic war.[12].In another dramatic gesture, Mansour claimed responsibility for the 28 October 2013, Tiananmen Square attack, which killed five and injured 38 others.[13] In his accompanying message he warned of waves of future attacks including targeting of the Great Hall of the People. He stated that for Uyghurs, fighting the Chinese state was a religious obligation, and that they should eschew democracy and follow the 'prophetic methodology' of Jihad. These remarks were followed up with the horrific attack on Kunming Railway station when eight Uyghurs armed with knives hacked passengers on the platform killing 31, and wounding several others. The Kunming and the Tiananmen Square attacks seriously impacted public morale, and the people's trust in the CCP to control random terrorist occurrences.

In an immediate response, Xi Jinping's government, in May 2014, launched a renewed 'campaign against the 'triple evils' of religious extremism, separatism and terrorism in Xinjiang by scaling up its military presence in the region and introducing stringent restrictions on freedom of movement and assembly, which included draconian measures like prohibiting beards in Xinjiang, headscarves for women, permission only for state sponsored muftis to deliver Qutbahs in mosques where President Xi's policies would be praised, prohibiting fasting during Ramazan etc.

The direct fallout was bloody clashes on 28 July 2014 between Uyghur protestors and Chinese military personnel, in Yäkän, Xinjiang, which left at least 100 people dead (World Uyghur Council put the death toll at around 2000). Three days later, on 31 July, Jume Tahir, Deputy President of the Xinjiang Islamic Association and the Chief Imam of the Kashgar's Id Kah mosque, who had supported the communist regime was publicly lynched.[14]

In an attempt to contain the situation, Beijing issued an official public admission of China's 'all weather friend' Pakistan's ties to Uyghur militants in August 2014, which was carried in China's State sponsored newspaper The Global Times. The paper released a report stating that Memetuhut Memetrozi, a co-founder of ETIM, who is currently serving a life sentence in Urumqi jail for his involvement in terrorist attacks, had repented his actions and had exhorted Uyghur youth not to join the TIP or any other militant outfit, which he reportedly asserted was a crime against Islam and humanity.[15] The Global Times further added that he had been radicalised in Deobandi Madrassas in Pakistan, and that he had been in touch with Hasan Mahsum in Waziristan. since 1997.

While it was evident that the Global Times article was an ill-disguised attempt at propaganda, the incident highlighted Beijing's mounting disquiet about radicalisation within the Uyghur ranks. The disquiet was amply justified, as the Russian intelligence gave out information that scores of ethnic Uyghurs in Kazakhstan had joined the Islamic Renaissance Party, and in Uzbekistan and Kirgyzstan some of them joined the Islamic Movement of Uzbekistan (IMU) or the Hizb-ut Tahrir. Chinese press, quoting Russian intelligence sources has published figures of around 200 Uyghurs in the "bin Laden camps", and that and several thousand had been to Pakistan to receive religious education. Specific mention had been made of the Binori Mosque Karachi, and Syed Mawduddi Institute, Lahore. Many of them, according to Chinese researchers were in contact with Jamaat-e Islami, Jamaat al-Tabligh, Hizb ul-Mujahidin and the Lashkar-e Taiba, apart from the Taliban and IMU, which enabled their participation in military skirmishes.[16]

This transformed the Uyghurs into battle hardened Jihadis, rated at a premium by international Jihadi groups like the ISIS/ Daesh and the al Qaeda. Videos of Uyghur Jihadis appeared in both the ISIS sponsored Furat media, and the al Qaeda sponsored As-Sahab media. Chinese contentions that Uyghur nationalism had morphed into extremism, and that the ETIM/TIP was linked with international groups was adequately justified. The actual numbers of Uyghur fighters in the Levant is not known, but UAE think tanks who are monitoring the situation put the number at close to 20,000. ISIS administrative documents and records recovered in Syria by the US forces, giving statistics about 1,139 women who had joined the Islamic State, showed that 76 were from Xinjiang. Data retrieved in the same ledger on 290 child soldiers showed that 12 were from Xinjiang, mainly from the city of Aksu, which had witnessed major riots in 2014.[17]

Also, according to Syrian army officials, an Uyghur colony has been established in the city of al Zanbanki, on the border with Turkey, which is said to be housing around 18,000 people. These people claim to be affiliated to al Qaeda and not the ISIS, speak mainly Turkic, and have told Syrian army interlocutors that they refuse to return to China. The city is likely to be overtaken soon, and with Turkey refusing to take them, and their facing a very uncertain future in China, a humanitarian crisis is in the offing, which has little chance of clean resolution.[18] There are also thousands of Uyghurs in Idlib, which is the last remaining Jihadi stronghold in Syria. The Syrian Army is likely to over-run the area, and without US support for the Free Syrian Army, which was cooperating with al Qaeda aligned forces will be unable to withstand the onslaught. China had been warning the international community that Uyghurs were leaving Xinjiang to join the al Qaeda since 2012, and it is now clear that there are thousands of Uyghur Jihadis in Idlib, Aleppo, Homs and Latakia. Jihadis are attempting to flee that theatre and this could pose an evolving security concern for China. To illustrate, in May 2016, the Emir of al Qaeda, Ayman al Zawahiri had sent out a message asking Uyghurs to take action against China. This was followed up in September 2016, when the Chinese embassy was bombed in Bishkek, Kyrgyzstan, and the accused Uyghurs were found to have links with Al Nusra, the al Qaeda affiliate in Syria. Shortly thereafter Abu Bakr al-Baghdadi, leader of the ISIS, also threatened China in its main propaganda magazine the Dabiq.

The TIP/ ETIM's international links were demonstrated in November 2018, when the Katibat Ghuraba al Turkistan (KGT), an Uyghur jihadist group operating near Idlib and Lakatia in Syria, showed in a video that it was cooperating with the Malhama Tactical, an elite jihadist unit comprised of battle hardened fighters from Chechnya, Ingushetia, Dagestan, Uzbekistan, Kyrgyzstan, Georgia, Belorussia etc. This unit, which was started by Abu Rofiq, an ethnic Uzbek, who was a Russian military commando, is reputed to have trained the best warriors in the Al Nusra and Hayat Tahrir al Sham, the premier al Qaeda affiliates in the Levant. Abu Rofiq, who was killed in 2017, was succeeded by Abu Salman Belarussi, a Belarussian from the Belarus Army, who has claimed that he has trained TIP leader Ajnad Kavkaz, and has issued a video that he is preparing the Uyghurs for a sustained assault on China. Affiliation and training with the Malhama Tactical has raised KGT's Jihadi profile and honed its skills to a dangerous level.[19]

The Chinese Response

Beijing is now underscoring and emphasising the premise that it faces a very real threat from Jihadis, and claims that it has intercepted over 100 Jihadis entering from Tajikistan and Uzbekistan. This has offered it an iron clad reason to proactively enter Afghanistan and help Kabul set up a 'mountain brigade' in the Wakhan corridor area in Badakshan province, which links the country to Xinjiang province. The ostensible aim is to aid counter terrorism efforts, and intercept in the country's north to boost counterterrorism efforts. The PLA is working closely with the Afghan National army and the Afghan National Directorate of Security (NDS) for this project. While with the mountain brigade, the Chinese Government is strengthening its ties with the National Unity Government (NUG) of Afghanistan, lines of communication to the Taliban have been well established to ensure that extremism in Xinjiang is contained and that obstacles to the Belt and Road Initiative (BRI) are minimised.[20]

On the political front, in May 2017, Chinese President Xi Jinping, speaking at the National People's Congress, said that Beijing would build a "great wall of iron "to safeguard Xinjiang and that Islamist separatists posed the "most prominent challenge" to the country's integrity and stability.[21] The contours of the wall are now clear. The building blocks of the policy were laid during

President Xi's speech during the 18th party congress, in which he laid maximum stress on the concept of "Zhonghua Minzu Weida Fuxing." The operational part is "Zhonghua Minzu"—which loosely translates as "the Chinese nation". Xi appears to have used the word Minzu like the word Minzoku in Japanese, which has its roots in race supremacy. The word "Zhonghua." It can be translated simply as "China," but the suffix "hua"—literally meaning "flourish" While the statement is benign in itself, the connotation and iconography that it carries is significant. It was a term frequently used by Mao Zedong during the 'Great Leap Forward', which implied the merging of the 56 nationalities into the Han Chinese mould. Xi articulated his vision of the Chinese dream in which was filled "with glory, hardship, and sacrifice," and as a rival to the American and European dreams which he termed superficial and plastic. He has further emphasised that the Chinese Dream promotes "world peace and development", a loaded statement which incorporates elements of control and expansionism. He has made it clear that the aspirations of the minorities have to be subsumed in this larger objective, and according to analysts has used the word 'Minzu' more like the Nazis used the word 'Volk'—individuality has to merge with the larger national ethos.[22]

In furtherance of his objectives, President Xi made a significant new appointment in August 2016—that of Chen Quanguo, a soldier turned party functionary, as the XUAR party Secretary, replacing the previous party secretary Party Secretary Zhang Chunxian. Chen had served in the difficult Tibet Autonomous Region (TAR), when it had erupted into violence in 2008, and in five years had brought in more than a semblance of good governance, by establishing an efficient network of surveillance and control. Chen was handpicked by Xi, to replicate his success in TAR in Xinjiang, and has forged out a securitization programme surpassing the one in TAR in scope and magnitude. He has used local divisions and has established a corps of Uyghurs who will be monitoring their neighbours and relatives, again much in the mould of the Gestapo surveillance systems in Nazi Germany.

His primary step has been to ramp up police recruitment. In response to the July 2009 riots in Urumqi. Xinjiang had advertised about 5,800 police positions, which had come in for criticism from Human Rights groups. Now Chen enhanced the intakes to over 40,000 by 2016. These positions were by and large contract based and out of the regular civil services stream. They were grabbed by the local Uyghur population, who were being forced out of the labour market by the Han Chinese and had little choice but to accept them. This strategy has aided the cost-efficient expansion of the police force, and the better-equipped regular police units have a organization of lesser paid, poorly trained subordinates, who are fluent in the local language and customs, and are a part of a system where their subordination can be guaranteed. For international consumption, Beijing has put out that it is increasing job opportunities for local Uyghurs and cite the statistic that 90,866 positions—were advertised in 2017 and a similar number in 2018. 95 per cent of the jobs were assistant police positions, and consequently over 7,500 new police stations have been established across Xinjiang in 2017 and 2018. Now in the province, private sector jobs, and civil administration jobs are predominantly cornered by Han Chinese, and for the locals, the primary employer, is the police, and the related prison services.[23]

Enhanced recruitment into the Security Services is not the only indicator of burgeoning internments in camps. PRC government's own budget figures appear to contradict Beijing's assertions that attempts are being made to increase employment opportunities through 'vocational training, re-educational' centres. Instead, the outlines of expenditure show an emphasis on construction of highly secure prisons. For instance spending security-related facility construction rose by an astounding 213 per cent, nearly RMB 20 billion in 2017. In contrast, spending on vocational education in Xinjiang actually decreased from 2016 to 2017 and the trend continued in 2018. In fact, Xinjiang spent below the national average on vocational education, and three times the national average on its justice system. It needs to be noted that the justice system in China is separate from the prosecutorial and court systems which administer Justice including the formal prosecution and conviction of criminal suspects, which is funded separately. One of the main objectives of the justice system is re-education. Hence, the emerging picture from analysis of the budget figures of Xinjiang is that there is disproportionate budgetary allocation for building of security facilities, and a larger allocation of budget for re-education as compared to vocational training and skilling.[24]

Azadliq, Azabliq

'Azadliq'—liberation, and 'Azabliq'—pain are two words in Uyghur Tili, which are often used, albeit covertly, by the Uyghurs in Xinjiang. Conversations with members of Uyghur Diaspora in the west or in Kazakhstan reveal that a majority of Uyghurs in China feel economically and socially discriminated and racially profiled. The CCP has gradually phased out the use of the Uyghur Tili, the Turkic based language of the Uyghurs from the curriculum in Xinjiang's schools. Though "experimental bilingual classes" are being held in the province, Mandarin is used for all math and science courses. While Uyghurs are expected to learn Mandarin very few Han Chinese, even those in the government learn Uyghur Tili. Language discrimination has ensured that though the Xinjiang region's GDP is flourishing and the region is an integral part of the Belt and road initiative, few Uyghurs are reaping its benefits.[25] Consequently, the fear of Uyghur nationalism, in tandem with Islamic recidivism is a frightening prospect for Beijing. This has led to massive suppression, even of moderate voices, with even mild criticism of the state termed 'splittist propaganda', attracting extreme punitive measures.

For instance, a moderate scholar/activist like Ilham Tohti who never advocated separatism or violence was arrested in September 2014, after President Xi announced the " Peoples War on Terror" following a number of attacks linked to the region. He has been condemned to life imprisonment and the Chinese government has castigated the West, for calling him China's Mandela, and honouring him with Martin Ennals award for human rights defenders in 2016.[26]

A more extreme case is the disappearance of the erstwhile Interpol Chief Meng Hongwei, in April last year. The announcement of his arrest, ostensibly on charges of corruption came months after. The Ministry of Public Security, for which Mr Meng worked as a vice minister, issued a significant statement on October 8th to the effect that the Communist Party committee had not only condemned Mr Meng's alleged graft, but also his lack of "absolute loyalty" to the party, and President Xi's vision. The Committee decreed that all party members needed to maintain a high level of conformity![27] An interesting recap is that in February 2018, Interpol rescinded a red corner notice for Dolkun Isa, the President of World Uyghur Congress based in Munich, Germany, to enable him to attend a conference in Dharamshala, India. China, which has termed Dolkun Isa a terrorist was infuriated at the red corner notice being rescinded and in April, Meng was removed from his post as a member of the public-security bureau's party committee and subsequently arrested, during a home visit. Deviation from the Party line is seriously culpable, even in an international milieu.[28]

China's insecurity about the Uyghurs is gauged by the fact that today, one in every ten Uyghurs are in internment camps. The indoctrination that occurs in the camps, which are mainly around the city of Hotan, Xinjiang, include inmates being forced to renounce their religion, eat pork, sing propaganda songs etc, apart from torture which occasionally results in death. Islam is treated as a "mental illness" and the local Government refers to Muslims as "societal tumours". Uyghur police officers have told activists that they are under orders to meet targets for arresting people—the targets have reached up to 40 per cent of the population in restive areas.[29]

Conclusion

With Beijing facing the twin djinns of Uyghur nationalism, and Islamic extremism, no resolution of the Xinjiang province is in sight. Muslim minorities continue to disappear into the mammoth internment camps, and dissenting voices, even subdued ones, are silenced with impunity. Muslim countries, who come out with clarion calls for the safety of the Ummah in Palestine and Kashmir, are significantly silent when it concerns the Uyghurs. Pakistan made a feeble protest when some people from Gilgit-Baltistan complained that their Uyghur wives had been put into detention camps,[30] and that the Khunjerab pass between GB and Baltistan was under strong surveillance. There was no follow-up on the protests. China has maintained a below the radar stance regarding Mohammad bin Salman and his involvement in the Khasoggi murder case, and consequently there is signal silence from Saudi Arabia, which is normally the vanguard of Muslim activism on the Uyghur issue. And Iran, with its myriad problems with the US has raised no demur.

Will these draconian measures translate into tangible security for China? It is hard to read the Chinese tea leaves on this subject. But, it needs to be noted that excessively repressive measures almost always result in further radicalisation. China needs to learn from its own experience with Hasan Mahsum, the founder of the ETIM, who emerged from prison completely radicalised. China needs to revert to its policies in the aftermath of the Cultural Revolution, of calibrated accommodation of minorities. A leaf out of the Indian playbook would be apposite.

NOTES

1 https://www.theguardian.com/world/2018/nov/06/china-un-criticism-human-rights-record
2 https://frieze.com/article/award-winning-photographer-lu-guang-went-missing-xinjiang

3 Made in China journal vol 3 Oct-Dec 2018
4 https://www.rsc.ox.ac.uk/files/files-1/wp61-making-states-displacing-peoples-2010.pdf
5 https://journals.openedition.org/chinaperspectives/648
6 Andrew D. Forbes, *Warlords and Muslims in Chinese Central Asia, A Political History of Republican Xinjiang 1911-1949*, Cambridge: Cambridge University Press, 1986,
7 https://journals.openedition.org/chinaperspectives/648
8 "China: The Evolution of ETIM", *Stratfor.com*. 13 May 2008.
9 Mackerras, Colin (Winter 2004), "Ethnicity in China: The Case of Xinjiang". *Harvard Asia Quarterly.*
10 https://jamestown.org/program/al-qaedas-uyghur-jihadi-a-profile-of-the-turkistan-islamic-partys-abdul-shakoor-turkistani/
11 Zenn, Jacob, "Beijing, Kunming, Urumqi and Guangzhou: The Changing Landscape of Anti-Chinese Jihadists", *China Brief.* The Jamestown Foundation, 23 May 2014.
12 Wong, Edward, "Group Says Video Warns of Olympic Attack". *The New York Times*, 7 August 2008.
13 Kaiman, Jonathan, "Islamist group claims responsibility for attack on China's Tiananmen Square", 25 November 2014.
13 https://www.theguardian.com/world/2014/jul/31/china-jume-tahir-imam-kashgar-xinjiang-mosque-stabbed-death-violence
14 Source: *Global Times* Published: 2014-8-28 1:08:03
15 https://journals.openedition.org/chinaperspectives/648
16 https://jamestown.org/program/returning-uighur-fighters-and-chinas-national-security-dilemma/
17 Conversation with Syrian journalists.
18 https://www.longwarjournal.org/archives/2018/11/uighur-jihadist-group-trains-with-elite-unit.php
19 https://www.reuters.com/article/us-china-security-xinjiang-idUSKBN16H04J
20 http://www.xinhuanet.com/english/2017-03/10/c_136119256.htm
21 https://mail.google.com/mail/u/0/#search/geoplotical+futures/FMfcgxvzLDzsPBGTkJr CdFh HsdJsPSfr
22 https://jamestown.org/program/chen-quanguo-the-strongman-behind-beijings-securitization-strategy-in-tibet-and-xinjiang/?mc_cid=3c93d1fdb6&mc_eid=cade98a992
23 https://jamestown.org/program/chen-quanguo-the-strongman-behind-beijings-securitization-strategy-in-tibet-and-xinjiang/?mc_cid=3c93d1fdb6&mc_eid=cade98a992
24 https://thediplomat.com/2014/08/empire-and-the-rising-violence-in-xinjiang/
25 https://www.theguardian.com/world/2016/oct/11/ilham-tohti-uighur-china-wins-nobel-martin-ennals-human-rights-award
26 https://www.economist.com/china/2018/10/09/some-clues-on-why-china-arrested-the-president-of-interpol
27 https://www.theatlantic.com/international/archive/2018/10/meng-hongwei-china-interpol/572728/
28 https://www.theatlantic.com/international/archive/2018/08/china-pathologizing-uighur-muslims-mental-illness/568525/
29 https://www.dawn.com/news/1393081

9

Nepal and Bhutan: Changing Dynamics

Ranjit Rae

Despite numerous similarities in terms of geographical location, the basket of natural resources and their close, even intimate ties with India, both Nepal and Bhutan have followed dissimilar trajectories for political advancement and economic development. Today, Nepal is a Republic, a multiparty democracy ruled by communists. It remains amongst the poorest nations of South Asia with a per capita income of $1000. Bhutan is a constitutional monarchy and one of the richest countries of the region, with a per capita income of $3000. Both countries are landlocked; physical access to the outside world is largely through India. India is also the largest trade and investment partner for both countries. Sovereign and independent, both Nepal and Bhutan have Treaty relations with India. With the Himalayas traditionally representing India's security frontier and both Nepal and Bhutan sharing open borders with India, developments in each country clearly have a bearing on the security of India. This was demonstrated most recently in the Doklam imbroglio between Bhutan and China which drew in India.[1] Furthermore, the flow from North to South of Himalayan Rivers from the two countries into the Ganges and Brahmaputra link the economic destinies of both countries with India.

This article provides a broad based assessment of some of the major developments in these societies, India's role as well as the implications of the ever growing presence of China. It concludes with some recommendations on the manner in which future challenges should be addressed by India to safeguard and promote her interests.

Internal Developments

Both Nepal and Bhutan are undergoing major political transitions and economic transformation of their societies. The transition has been relatively smooth in the case of Bhutan, but has run into serious roadblocks in Nepal. The new Constitution of Nepal has transformed it from a Monarchy to a Republic, from a Hindu Rashtra to a Secular Nation and from a Unitary to a Federal State. Nepal also aspires to graduate from its status of a Least Developed Country to a Developing Country. Considering, the nature and scope of these changes, there is occasionally a pushback from forces that feel that they have lost political or economic power. A widespread perception amongst sections of the ruling elite is that federalism will weaken national cohesion and unity and may give rise to fissiparous tendencies. On the other hand, there is discontent among groups such as the Madhesis[2] and Janajatis[3] that the progressive agenda for political representation, inclusion and federalism has not been fully accomplished. Nevertheless, a series of elections at municipal, provincial and national level, critical for the implementation of the new Constitution, have been held successfully in 2017 and have brought a degree of political stability hitherto unseen in Nepal.

Political change in Nepal has not been easy. It has generally been a response to mass agitations as well as violent insurgencies. Multiparty democracy which replaced the non-party Panchayat system and made the King a Constitutional Monarch was a consequence of Jan Andolan 1 (people's movement) in 1989. The rise of identity politics with demands for federalism and inclusion of groups hitherto un- or under-represented in State organs, viz. Madhesis and Janjatis, is directly related to the Maoist insurgency during 1996-2006[4] and the Madhesi Agitation of 2007.[5] The end of Monarchy is a consequence of Jan Andolan II and the intransigence on the part of the then King Gyanendra.

In Bhutan, change has been driven from the top, unlike Nepal, where ruling elites resisted change. It is King Jigme Singye Wangchuck, widely revered by his people and deeply conscious of the mood of the times, who was instrumental in supporting a new Constitution that has transformed the Monarchy from an Executive to a Constitutional one, introduced multi-party democracy and has even set a retirement age for the King. And all this was pushed through in the face of strong opposition by common Bhutanese who wanted the King to remain an Executive Monarch. Bhutan has held several rounds of Parliamentary elections and is forging ahead in the implementation of its new Constitution.

Inclusion

Political change without meaningful efforts to evolve a more inclusive system, particularly in countries with diverse populations is unlikely to bring durable stability. Indeed, one of the more complex challenges faced by both Nepal and Bhutan relates to the management of their diversity and accommodating the aspirations of all their citizens. Both countries have followed policies of majoritarian nationalism that have left significant sections of their populations excluded from the mainstream. In Nepal during the 1960s, King Mahendra gave voice and strength to an exclusivist hill nationalism based on the slogan "*Euta Bhasha euta Bhesh, euta Raja euta Desh*", automatically excluding a third of the population that did not have Nepali as their mother tongue or the *daura saruwal* as their dress.[6] The Madhesis of the Terai in particular, who spoke Maithili, Bhojpuri, Awadhi and Hindi, wore the *dhoti kurta* and were culturally aligned to the people of Bihar and UP felt "othered" by this nationalist narrative. Indeed, an erroneous view gained strength that the Madhesi were not indigenous inhabitants of the Terai but had migrated from India! While in the past, there may have been some migration for better economic prospects, especially from Bihar, the reality is that the Madhesis have always lived there; some found themselves on the Nepalese side after the delineation of the India-Nepal border under the Sugauli Treaty of 1816.[7]

The dominance of the hill *Bahun-Chhetri* community in political and state organs, including the bureaucracy and security forces has resulted in deep rooted grievances among the Madhesis of the plains. Following the Madhesi Andolan of 2007 an agreement for greater inclusion and political representation as well as a Federal Province in the plains was arrived at with Indian support in 2008 but was not fully incorporated into the new Constitution. Indeed the polarisation between the hill and plains communities is evident in the manner in which they voted in the last General Elections in 2017. Madhesh centric parties won a sweeping victory in Province No 2 in the Terai plains whereas the communist alliance led by Communist Party of Nepal (Unified Marxist-Leninist) (CPN-UML), a party that was adamantly opposed to concessions to the Madhesis, swept the other provinces. Following the elections however, given the large mandate received by the Communist Alliance and subsequent merger of the CPN-UML and Maoist Centre, even Madhesi parties sought accommodation with the new Government. One group led by Upendra Yadav joined the Government; the other, the Rashtriya Janata Party extended outside support, which has since been withdrawn.[8]

In Bhutan, the Driglam Namzha policy, of a national dress and Dzongkha as the national language alienated the Nepali speaking population of southern Bhutan. This ultimately resulted in large groups of Southern Bhutanese either voluntarily or forcibly leaving Bhutan for refugee camps in eastern Nepal. It is only after some two decades that most of the Lhotsampas[9] have been resettled abroad, principally in the USA. The issue for the present stands resolved, though how a new generation of Bhutanese refugees that have grown up in the West will impact on their mother country, only time will tell.

Economic Development

Together with the march of democracy and a more inclusive society, the third biggest challenge facing both countries is to meet the aspirations of the people for economic advancement and a better life. Both societies have young populations. Economic progress in both Nepal and Bhutan has been asymmetrical. Nepal has been consumed by its struggles for political emancipation and has been plagued by short lived Governments. In Nepal, the youth are voting with their feet. The hills are emptying, even the youth of the plains are migrating abroad in the absence of opportunities for gainful employment at home. The dependence on remittances from expatriate Nepalis creates a semblance of prosperity in the major towns of Nepal but is not a firm basis for sustainable development in the long run and is also extracting a heavy social cost. Bhutan, on the other hand, has been stable and able to focus on economic development. Bhutan has followed a conscious policy of promoting hydropower development with Indian support and participation and has implemented projects effectively. In the case of Nepal however, even though the hydropower potential is significantly larger than in Bhutan, the trust deficit between India and Nepal has made cooperation in this win-win sector difficult. Installed generation capacity in Nepal today is less than 1000 MW. Ironically, it is India that supplies some 500 + MW of power to Nepal every year. With major hydropower projects such as Pancheshwar, Arun III and Upper Karnali on the anvil, hopefully things will change.[10]

India's Relations with Nepal and Bhutan

Contemporary relations of both Bhutan and Nepal with India to some extent emanate from their relations with British India. Both countries were linked to British India by Treaty relations, the core of which was that internal affairs would be the domain of their respective governments whereas on foreign policy issues they would be guided in various degrees, by British India. The relationship with Nepal was greased by the steady supply of Gorkha troops for the British Indian Army by the Ranas of Nepal. As for Bhutan, the establishment of the Wangchuck dynasty was directly linked to the support extended by the Trongsa Penlop and first King of Bhutan Ugyen Wangchuck to the Younghusband expedition to Tibet in 1904.[11]

India's independence and the departure of the British created a new context for relations with Bhutan and Nepal. Apprehensive about the Communist victory in China in 1949 and Chinese machinations in Tibet, both Nepal and Bhutan sought Treaty relations with India, which were in effect an insurance policy. India's new compacts with Bhutan and Nepal, signed respectively in 1949 and 1950 required both countries to be mindful of mutual concerns on foreign policy and security issues. Specific clauses governed the importation of arms and lethal equipment into both these countries.[12] Over time, both sets of clauses were viewed by the two countries as derogating from their sovereignty. Indeed, a major objective of both the countries in their relationship with India became a modification of what they saw as unequal treaties and a less than equal relationship with India. The review and amendment of the Treaty became an extremely contentious issue in the bilateral relationship of Nepal with India and was used to whip up anti-India sentiment. The issue continues to remain contentious though high level discussions have taken place in the Eminent Persons Group set up by the two countries, the Report of which is awaited. Bhutan handled the matter of the revision of the 1949 Treaty in a low key manner, with quiet negotiations at high political levels. Bhutan successfully revised the Treaty in 2007 well before the advent of multi-party democracy and before it could become a contentious issue in the relationship.[13]

Contemporary India' broad policy objectives in both Nepal and Bhutan are stability, security and development. Given the open borders India shares with both countries, India is naturally keen to ensure that the territory of the two countries is not used for activities inimical to her interests. The hijack of

IC 814 from Kathmandu to Kandahar in 1999 and the presence of Indian Insurgent Groups in southern Bhutan remain fresh in memory, to name only two instances. Clearly, security cooperation remains a key priority in both countries.

Second, India's long term strategic objective is to bind the sub-region into a web of mutually beneficial economic linkages. Neighbours should develop a vested interest in India's growing economic prosperity. This is the surest way to better relations. The one sector that represents a win-win situation is hydropower. Several initiatives both at bilateral and sub-regional like BBIN levels are already underway.[14] Similarly, connectivity projects—roads, railways, Integrated Check Posts, pipelines that are being developed would create the required infrastructure for greater economic engagement. Clearly progress on these and other initiatives require a high degree of mutual trust, understanding and confidence; considerable historical baggage in the relationship, particularly with Nepal, needs to be shed. So is this possible? Yes, but significant efforts will be required on both sides.

Nepal

The India-Nepal relationship is extremely complex and multi-layered. It is close, even intimate and filial. The destinies of the two countries are intertwined. However, given the asymmetry in size and the overwhelming dependence of Nepal on India, there is some resentment against India. Nepali leaders sometimes find India's embrace too claustrophobic and seek greater political space.

In part, this is also due to the fact that India has been closely involved with virtually every major political transformation in the country. This includes the Delhi Pact of 1950 that arrived at a compromise between the Rana regime and the democratic forces. The Jan Andolan I of 1989 was strongly supported by former Prime Minister Shri Chandrashekhar. The agreement between political parties and the Maoists that ended the insurgency and brought the Maoists into the democratic mainstream was signed in Delhi in November 2005. India also played an important role in the agreement between Madhesi political forces and the Government of Nepal that ended the Madhesi agitation of 2007 elements of which were later incorporated into the Interim Constitution of Nepal. From the Indian perspective, at all major turning points in Nepal's political history, India has been on the side of the people and has supported their aspirations even at the cost of temporarily riling ruling elites. However, the cost that India had to pay is that a certain resentment against it has built up amongst the political elite, particularly the communists and the royalists, who viewed this as interference in Nepal's internal affairs.

Some of the elites have responded by inflaming anti-India passions. Thus for instance, King Mahendra responded to India's criticism of his abolition of multiparty democracy in 1960 as anti-Nepal. He sought to rally the royalists, Hindu groups and leftists against the "external threat" on the basis of anti-India nationalism. His policy of hill nationalism sought to consolidate his power among ruling elites by "othering" the Madhesis of the plains who were occasionally conflated with Indians. He sought to exploit the Hindu sentiment both in Nepal and India by declaring Nepal to be a Hindu Rashtra. In order to dilute the popularity and support of the Nepali Congress whose Government he had dismissed and leaders of which went into exile in India, the Monarchy started supporting leftist groups. And Nepal played the so-called China card with the agreement for the Kathmandu-Kodari road in the face of Indian opposition. Even during the Maoist insurgency, when Nepal was still a monarchy, the narrative in Kathmandu was that somehow India was supporting the Maoists since some of them were underground in India.

Historically, in Nepal the leftists and monarchists have coalesced together under the umbrella of anti-Indian nationalism. This was witnessed most recently in the leftist royalist coalition under PM KP Oli in 2015. In the face of the Madhesi agitation prior to and after promulgation of the new Constitution and the so called "blockade" by protestors of transit points along the India-Nepal border that led to severe shortages, particularly of petroleum products in Nepal, UML leader KP Oli successfully projected this as an Indian blockade, polarised Nepali society between *Pahadis* and *Madhesis* and emerged as the tallest Nepali leader who could stand up to India. Anti-Indian nationalism was again successfully used by UML during the recent national elections that catapulted the Communist Alliance led by KP Oli to power.

Nepalese nationalism is also complicated by the fact that there are huge similarities in language, culture, religion with India. If most aspects of Nepalese culture are derived from Indian civilisation, what is it that makes Nepal a unique nation state? There is thus an effort to define Nepalese nationalism by identifying elements that are different from India, by emphasising its non-Indianness. Thus, it is a matter of great national pride that the Buddha was born in Nepal or that Mount Everest is located in Nepal. The use of rhetorical flourishes of a "special relationship" and a *bhai-bhai ka rishta* by Indian political leaders make Nepalese communists cringe. Indeed, a former PM once remarked to the author that Nepal does not want brotherly relations with India, since this implies that India is the elder brother and Nepal the younger! Nepal only wishes to have friendly, and hence equal, relations with India.

Whenever there have been serious differences between Nepal and India, Nepal has sought to play the so-called China card. In the past, King Mahendra used it following India's criticism of his abolition of multi-party democracy. The merger of Sikkim with India in 1974 was viewed with great concern in Nepal. The proposal for Nepal to become a Zone of Peace, equidistant between India and China emerged soon thereafter. Most recently, during the Constitution drafting process, India's broad approach was to counsel accommodation of aspirations of all communities. India's anxiety was that if the contentious issues of political representation and inclusion were not resolved, there would be tensions, frictions and even violence in Nepal. Given a nascent movement for secession in the plains, India felt that the grievances of the Madhesis should be addressed in order to achieve durable stability. This is important for Nepal, given that its principal access to the outside world is through the Terai; equally for India with borders contiguous to the Terai and strong cross border relationships, a disturbed Terai, and specially one where the youth is alienated or where the secessionist idea gains greater traction will give rise to innumerable difficulties. The Indian view was projected as interference in the internal affairs of Nepal. The blockade of border crossing points by Madhesi political parties was projected within Nepal as being instigated by India. In addition to whipping up anti-India sentiment Prime Minister KP Oli signed far reaching trade, transit and connectivity arrangements with China in order to obtain alternative routes for supplies, including petroleum products. Though these proposals would take several years to fructify, they made huge headlines in the Indian media that India was "losing" Nepal to China. Of course, following the General Elections, the Communist led alliance was catapulted to power on the plank of anti-India nationalism as well as a seat share arrangement between the second (CPN-UML) and third (Maoist Centre) largest parties that subsequently merged. Under the changed situation in Nepal, India has rightly built bridges with the new Government under PM Oli.

Bhutan

Bhutanese culture and civilization, on the other hand is more akin to Tibet. The historical experience of Bhutan with Tibet and the Dalai Lama is fraught with tension. Bhutan has defined its culture, dress and language as distinct from those in Tibet. Further, Bhutan has seen the manner in which Tibetan culture and religion were suppressed following the Chinese takeover. Bhutan also has a long standing border dispute with China that recently flared up on the Doklam plateau. They, therefore, have their own reasons for not wanting to come too close to China. Even though they share borders, Bhutan has not established diplomatic relations with China. Of course, with a young generation that has few memories of the past and sees a wealthy China next door, there are and will be efforts for greater contacts. While in the past, it was relatively easy for India to deal with the King, the final authority on all critical issues in the bilateral relationship, today, with Bhutan as a multiparty constitutional monarchy, India's outreach to key elements in a more decentralized system of decision making, needs to be strengthened. It should be India's endeavour to prevent Nepal style competitive politics based on anti-India sentiments from emerging in Bhutan.

The China Factor

In India's approach towards dealing with neighbours, the China factor inevitably becomes a complicating one. The role of China in India's neighbourhood is an issue that policy makers in India will have to grapple with for the foreseeable future. Today, China is determined to play a more assertive role globally, and particularly in Asia. It not only has the desire but also the capability to do so. The Belt and Road Initiative and the developments in the South China Sea point to increasing Chinese dominance in Asia. China is the single largest trading partner for a large number of countries. In fact most countries and leaders are eager to benefit from projects being offered by China, without paying due attention to the long term implications of such cooperation. The report in the New York Times with regard to the Hambantota Port deal in Sri Lanka during the Presidency of Mahinda Rajapaksa is very telling.[15] The alacrity with which countries of South Asia, with the exception of Bhutan, have joined the Belt and Road Initiative (BRI) bandwagon without heed to India's reservations, the speed with which China has signed agreements of far reaching strategic significance with countries such as Sri Lanka, the Maldives, Nepal leave alone Pakistan, will pose a challenge to Indian foreign and strategic policy. Even in the context of Bhutan, we have seen China's aggressive actions on the Doklam plateau. Inevitably, India's ties with her neighbours will be influenced by the relations of each with China and of India's own relationship with China.

In the past, China's principal concerns in Nepal related to Tibet. They were apprehensive of the role of western countries and their anti-China activities emanating from Nepal. China was comfortable with India's role in Nepal and counselled visiting Nepalese dignitaries to China to maintain cordial relations with India. Today, the situation has changed and China is not averse to taking advantage of opportunities arising from difficulties in the India-Nepal relationship as was demonstrated during the border disruptions of 2015. The two visits of PM Oli to China have resulted in a comprehensive upgradation of the Nepal-China relationship. Connectivity initiatives involving North South Roads, Railways, transmission lines, optic fibre cables and additional checkpoints, once implemented will change the political dynamics of the region. New investments in the form of hydro-power projects, land ports and airports, and in other areas will further enlarge Chinese presence. Politically too, China is more active than in the past. The merger of the two communist parties, UML and Maoist Centre, had the blessings of the Chinese. China has also stepped up its defence cooperation with the Nepalese Army and held for the first time a joint military exercise on counterterrorism. Chinese Defence Minister General Chang Wanquan made an official visit to Nepal in March 2018, making it the first ever visit to Nepal by a Chinese Defence Minister.[16]

How should India address the challenge posed by China in its own vicinity? Is it a zero-sum game? If so, what are the options available to India? Alternatively, could there be some opportunities for mutual cooperation and benefit as well? Clearly, in instances such as on the Doklam plateau, China's actions are crossing a threshold that India can never accept and must be resisted. However, in other areas relating to joint projects and connectivity initiatives, can India identify some win-win situations?

At one level, since Chinese presence is growing worldwide, it is natural that it will also grow in our immediate neighbourhood, specially Nepal. In Bhutan, given the absence of formal diplomatic relations, the prospects for major Chinese investments at the current juncture are not significant. But this situation could change in the future. Further, Chinese investments in India too are growing. How then can India tell its neighbours that such investments in their countries pose a threat? Further, even if India wishes to, it will not be easy to prevent Chinese projects. India would expend a lot of political capital, and would also need to come up with alternatives. India does not have the kind of resources required to take up developmental projects that China is funding in India's neighbourhood. In fact some projects were offered to China only after India found them unviable. The question naturally arises as to why China is taking on these unviable projects. For instance, what incentive would China have to invest billions of dollars in a trans-Himalayan railway network from Xigatse to Kathmandu? What would the financing modalities for such a project be? Would a poor country like Nepal be able to meet the financial liabilities that such a project would entail? Is China prepared to fund such projects on a grant basis? Clearly, such a project may become potentially viable only if it facilitates overland trade between China and India through Nepal. Both China and Nepal are therefore advocating the concept of Trilateral Cooperation or Nepal as a bridge between India and China. When seen together with some preliminary discussions that Nepal and China are undertaking on a possible bilateral FTA (this is mentioned in the Joint Statement following PM Oli's last visit to China), clearly this is an issue that could have serious implications for India and would need to be examined in detail. India would not wish to see Bihar and UP flooded with cheap Chinese products coming through Nepal. Further, the economic viability of such projects would need to be viewed against the present mode of sea transport between China and India/Nepal. The situation today is such that the bulk of China's trade with Nepal does not go through the trans-Himalayan land route but through the ports of Shanghai and Kolkata.

While cautioning the neighbours on the pitfalls of some of the grandiose schemes under the BRI, it may not be prudent to opt out of the entire scheme given that there is now a certain inevitability to these projects coming on stream. Even as India maintains its reservations on CPEC and conveys its concerns about some projects in her immediate neighbourhood, it should be open to exploring ways in which India and Indian companies could also benefit from some of the connectivity projects.

India should be prepared to enter into a dialogue with China on the BRI. The dialogue could be covered under the rubric of "strategic communication" at all levels between India and China as agreed at the Wuhan informal summit. It would assist in preventing misunderstandings about each other's role in what the other country considers to be its traditional region of importance. In addition, a sharing of views and assessments with regard to the situation in third countries would undoubtedly contribute to greater understanding and assist in allaying concerns. It would also prevent third countries from playing one neighbour against the other.

In addition to sharing assessments, both countries could also consider undertaking joint projects similar to the one being undertaken by India and China in Afghanistan. Could India not think in terms of a joint India-China project in Nepal, say in the hydro-power sector. Given that India's long term strategic interest is to have a South Asia that is economically integrated, a Joint India-China or India-third country hydro-project in Nepal, will contribute towards this goal.

Apart from considering the possibility of joint projects, what is extremely important is to improve India's own project implementation capabilities. A constant refrain heard in Nepal is that India does not deliver on time unlike the Chinese. India tends to treat projects in Nepal similar to those in India. Projects have been held up for years on account of some obstacle or the other. A new bilateral project monitoring mechanism has been established, but much more remains to be done for efficient and timely project delivery.

Finally, India also needs to step up its engagement with other players such as the US and EU that are active in its neighbourhood by intensifying its dialogue with them on South Asia.

China is going to be a formidable presence in India's neighbourhood, especially in the Himalayan region in the foreseeable future. India's effort should be to increase cooperation for mutual benefit while reducing the possibility of countries in the region playing one country against the other. While India should do everything possible to prevent conflict, but as in the case of the Doklam incident, India should also be fully prepared for the worst case scenario.

NOTES

1 Doklam problem started in June 2017, when Chinese army engineers attempted to build a road through the Doklam plateau in Bhutanese territory, but claimed by China. After "coordination" with Bhutanese authorities, Indian soldiers intervened. A standoff between Indian and Chinese troops lasted several weeks. After intense negotiations, both the countries agreed to withdraw to their original positions. Joel Wuthnow, Satu Limaye and Nilanthi

Samaranayake, "Doklam, One Year Later: China's Long Game in the Himalayas", available at https://warontherocks.com/2018/06/doklam-one-year-later-chinas-long-game-in-the-himalayas/, accessed on 24 March 2019.

2 Madhesis are people living in *Terai* plains, who are sometimes considered by the people living in hills as the migrants from India. The word Madhesi has originated from Sanskrit word "madhya desh" meaning "middle country", which refers to region between the Himalayas and the Vindhya mountains. Also see Ravi Bhandari, Nanda R. Shrestha and Dev Raj Dahal, "Rising Ethno-Cultural Nationalism in Nepal: Postmodern Illusion or Democratic Delusion?" *Sociological Bulletin*, Vol. 58, No. 1, Special Issue on Development of Democratic Routes in the Himalayan 'Borderlands' (January-April 2009), p. 22.

3 Janajatis refer to a general term in Nepal meaning indigenous ethnic groups akin to the Scheduled Tribes in India.

4 The 'Maoist people's war' that started on 13 February 1996 and officially ended on 21 November 2006, also see Hari Tamalsina, "Maoist Insurgency And The Aftermath", The rising Nepal, available at http://therisingnepal.org.np/news/9624, accessed on 3 April 2019.

5 It should not be confused by the Madhesi agitation and blockade of 2015-16. To read more about the Madhesi agitation please see Krishna Hachhethu, "Madheshi Nationalism and Restructuring the Nepali State" A paper presented at an international seminar on "Constitutionalism and Diversity in Nepal" Organized by Centre for Nepal and Asian Studies, TU in collaboration with MIDEA Project and ESP-Nepal 22-24 August 2007 Kathmandu, Nepal.

6 Nepali hill nationalism was particularly nurtured during the rule of King Mahendra in the mid 20th century. He proclaimed the policy of 'one language, one dress and one culture' in a land of ethnic and cultural diversity. Please see Binit Gurung, "Nepali Nationalism and Media: A Critical Review", *International Research Journal of Social Sciences*, Vol. 4, No. 2, February 2015, p. 68.

7 Treaty of Sugauli was signed on 2 December 1815 and ratified by 4 March 1816. It was signed between the East India Company and the then king of Nepal, King Girvan Yuddha Bikram Shah after the Anglo-Nepalese War in the years 1814-1816. Raj Guru Gajaraj Mishra aided by Chandra Shekhar Upadhayaya was the signatory for Nepal while Lt. Col. Paris Bradshaw was the signatory for the Company.

8 The Rashtriya Janata Party Nepal – an amalgamation of several Madhesh-centric parties, finally withdrew support to the government on 7 March 2019. Also see, "Nepal: Rashtriya Janata Party Nepal quits prime Minister KP Oli's government", available at https://www.wionews.com/south-asia/nepal-rashtriya-janata-party-nepal-quits-prime-minister-kp-olis-government-201733, accessed on 4 April 2019)

9 Lhotsampasa meaning 'southerners' is a term used to describe Bhutanese of Nepali origin who live or lived in Southern Bhutan. Many of them left Bhutan (either voluntarily or forcibly) to live in refugee camps in Eastern Nepal. Most of them have now been resettled in western countries.

10 For more details, please see, Prakash Kaini and George Annandale, "Hydro Review: The Way Forward for Nepal's Hydropower Development", available at https://www.hydroworld.com/articles/2019/01/hydro-review-the-way-forward-for-nepal-s-hydropower-development.html, accessed on 4 April 2019.

11 Younghusband expedition to Tibet was effectively a temporary invasion by British Indian forces under the auspices of the Tibet Frontier Commission, whose purported mission was to

establish diplomatic relations and resolve the dispute over the border between Tibet and Sikkim. The expedition began in December 1903 and lasted until September 1904. It was assisted by the Penlop of Trongsa in Bhutan, who subsequently became the first king of Bhutan Ugyen Wangchuck. He was recognised as the ruler of Bhutan in the Treaty of Punakha of 1910.

12 Indo-Bhutan Treaty of 1949, provided for, among others, "perpetual peace and friendship, free trade and commerce and equal justice to each other's citizens." It specifically called for Bhutan to seek India's advice in external matters, while India pledges non-interference in Bhutan's internal affairs. For more details read Lopamudra Bandyopadhyay, "Indo–Bhutanese Relations: A Historical Perspective", available at http://www.globalindiafoundation.org/Bhutan%20History.pdf, accessed on 4 April 2019. India and Nepal signed the Treaty of Peace and Friendship at Kathmandu on 31 July 1950. For complete text see https://mea.gov.in/bilateral-documents.htm?dtl/6295/Treaty+of+Peace+and+Friendship, accessed on 4 April 2019.

13 The Indian-Bhutan Friendship Treaty, which was signed in New Delhi on February 8, 2007, came into force following the exchange of Instruments of Ratification between the two governments in Thimphu on March 2, 2007. See "INDIA-BHUTAN FRIENDSHIP TREATY" from Ministry of External Affairs Website https://mea.gov.in/Images/pdf/india-bhutan-treaty-07.pdf, accessed on 4 April 2019.

14 The Bangladesh, Bhutan, India, Nepal (BBIN) Initiative is a sub-regional initiative for greater cooperation. It meets through official representation of member states to formulate, implement and review quadrilateral agreements across areas such as water resources management, connectivity of power, transport, and infrastructure.

15 Maria Abi-Habib, "In Hock to China, Sri Lanka Gave Up Territory", *The New York Times*, New York edition June 26, 2018, p. A1.

16 "Nepal, China hold first-ever joint military exercises", *The Economic Times*, July 12, 2018.

10

The Making of 'Space': Changing Geo-politics in Himalayas

Medha Bisht

'Bhutan is a small landlocked country in South Asia sandwiched between two larger neighbours-China and India.' This is the general introduction to Bhutan, as it is introduced in textbooks of foreign policy and international relations. This chapter attempts at understanding the geographical location of Bhutan by engaging with the spatial context within which Bhutan as a sovereign country is located and the manner in which the Doklam plateau, which was a witness to a subsequent stand-off in 2017 could be perceived in geo-political calculations of the South Asian neighbours. The key analytical framework chosen to take this analyses further are the contributions that geographical approaches have made to the field of war and conflict. These contributions need to be revisited and reckoned with because of the meaning they endow to the foreign policy and strategic undertones of the concerned countries (particularly China, India and Bhutan), who are major stakeholders in the changing geo-politics of Himalayas.

Bhutan's case in the context of power contestation between India and China, serves as illustration of how strategic foresight could transform physical space into cognitive place. It highlights what role can material and ideational factors play in the process of strategic, political choices. In this regard, this chapter is divided into three distinct parts. The first section contextualises the need for understanding borders in the larger South Asian context and Bhutan in particular. It also examines the relevance and applicability of some of the key discourses that would highlight the role that geography plays in giving meaning to foreign policy choices. The second section focuses on the material and ideational developments that have been fundamental in the making of the Himalayan space. The third section foregrounds the consequences of some of these developments as changing the meaning of geographical space for strategic choices. An illustration of the Doklam face-off which happened in 2017 is useful for this analysis. A key question that animates this discussion, in this context is the probability or the degree of war/conflict between India and China in near future. Will the probability be high, medium or low becomes significantly predictable from such conceptual analysis.

Borders in the South Asian 'Space'

Borders in South Asia have animated the geopolitical contours of the region in myriad ways. Where the spatiality of borders between Afghanistan, Iran and Pakistan have often given way to cognitive understanding leading to Pashto, Baloch, Pakistani, Kashmiri, or Indian nationalism, borders between India-Bangladesh and India-Nepal have often been an irritant to national security / sovereignty concerns having a debilitating impact on the bilateral relations between these countries. One can even argue that the borders of South Asia in many ways have fossilised the imagination of the 'post-colonial' South Asia to a mere strategic chess board, where often the historical traditions and cultural—civilisational pasts have faded in front of political narratives, which seek to perpetuate the divisive understanding of the South Asia region. The cultural, spiritual, ecological legacy of Himalayas is an appropriate reminder to this.

Amidst these political discourses, the Himalayan country of Bhutan, which is roughly around 38000 sq km, offers a unique and distinct understanding of how it has managed its borders. While it had cautiously moved towards India in the last few decades, it has also sought to balance Chinese interests. Given its policy of not establishing diplomatic relations with P-5 countries, Bhutan has no diplomatic relations with China. By the dint of its small-state diplomacy, it has managed to avoid China and India in exercising collaborative or antagonistic interest in its own domestic policies.

One of the areas of contention between Bhutan, India and China are the border disputes along their territories. Both China and Bhutan have had sustained interaction on resolving the demarcation of boundaries between them since 1980s. While, India had officially stated that the Sino-Bhutan boundary dispute is of bilateral concern to both countries, both Bhutan and India had been in touch with each other on Sino-Bhutan negotiations. Significantly, both countries were also concerned over the infrastructure construction which was being undertaken by China since 2004. However, no official objection was communicated to China by India. Bhutan, on its part had been discussing these concerns in its National Assembly sessions since 2007. While borders in Himalayas have been continuously expanding and shrinking and there is often an existential threat to the places which dot this region, Bhutan has been able to maintain its territorial integrity and sovereignty. Thus, while externally border disputes have been managed cautiously by Bhutan, domestically Bhutan has also consciously addressed some of these challenges. Unlike some of its other Himalayan neighbours, it has been consciously articulating the cultural and political markers which determine and define its territorial space. An explanation to this uniqueness can perhaps be put into perspective by understanding how these markers have given meaning to political order and citizenship in Bhutan. Domestically, these have not only tamed and redefined notions of power and authority in significant ways but have also given rise to select cultural and ideational values —which historically have been cognitively influential in giving meaning to the very definition of who a Bhutanese is. While Bhutan has been quite successful in shaping its domestic policies in terms of cultural values, externally, it is yet to surmount challenges related to contested spaces, which has strategic value for its 'big' neighbours China and India. This chapter concerns the recent Doklam face-off and highlights some of the strategic challenge which the Himalayan country will have to witness in the coming years. The choices which it makes will therefore have a consequence on its foreign policy orientations. A key question which becomes important in this context is that will the understanding of geographical space play a deterministic role in catalysing Sino-India conflict?

Theorizing Geography and Conflict

One of the critical lessons that the intersecting strands of international relations and geography has offered to the students of statecraft is the discourse around spatiality. Spatiality has not only contributed to physical and cognitive understanding of 'space' and 'place' respectively but it has also illuminated the difference between corporeal and critical boundaries. The difference between the two can be broadly understood through two broad discourses—classical and critical geo-politics.

The classical view emphasises the deterministic relationship between geography and state-behaviour. It can appropriately be summed up through the following quote of Napoleon who noted that the politics of the state is in its geography. Thus classical geo-politics, a term which emphasised the interface between geography and politics was coined by a Swedish political scientist Rudolf Kjellen."[1] Often identified with the Haushofer school, which was influenced by Nazi ideology, classical geo-politics came to be defined as a set of ideas which contributed to a 'deterministic and reductionist' understanding of geo-political theory. So much was Haushofer's influence in Nazi ideology that it was often claimed by some social scientists, that Hitler's military campaigns could not have started if Haushofer was not ready."[2] This as many have argued primarily shaped the cartographic consciousness of Germany's role in the World Wars.[3] Also influenced by the work of Mackinder, it is often said that the Haushofer school made a whole generation think spatially.[4] This spatial reification of world politics, was also deterministically treated in historical terms. Richard von Kuhlman, another German diplomat noted, "geographical position and historical development are so largely determining factors of foreign policy that, regardless of the kaleidoscopic change of contemporary events, and no matter what form of government has been instituted or what political party may be in power, the foreign policy of a country has a natural tendency to return again and again to the same general and fundamental alignment."[5] Friedrich Ratzel's term *Lebensraum* is another example of classical geo-politics, which emphasised on the Darwinist idea that only the fittest would survive. Ratzel's seven laws which informed his theory of spatial politics, can be most appropriately quoted in his own words, "The space of states increases with the growth of its culture. The growth of states follow other symptoms of development: ideas, commercial production, missionary activity. The growth of states process by the amalgamation and absorption of smaller states. The frontier is the external organ of the state and as such, it is the measure of growth, strength and health of that organism. In its growth the state tends to include its politically valuable sections—coastlines, river-beds, plains, regions rich in resources etc. The general trend towards amalgamation transits the tendency for territorial growth from state to state and increases the tendency in the process of transmission."[6] While essentially inspired from a positivist outlook of the world wars, such views became popular with strategic studies, which emerged as a distinct discipline in its own standing, and were taken further by scholars such as Liddell Hart, Andre Beufre, Collin Grey, amongst others.

However, with a distinct genre of strategic theorising becoming popular since the late twentieth and early twenty-first century, strategic studies have taken a leap, thus going beyond the very deterministic understanding of geography and history. The critical theorists for instance have challenged the mainstream understanding of geography playing a deterministic role in war and state behaviour. Interrogating the causality between geography and wars/ conflict, the role of perceptions and socialisation is highlighted in giving meaning to spatial reasoning. How these perceptions need to be understood and communicated vis-a-vis the changing geopolitical realties on claimed/ contested spaces is therefore the main argument of critical geopolitics. Thus to challenge this spatial perspective which was deterministic and reductionist to a certain extent, some scholars offered the notion of opportunity and willingness. Harvey Starr, who advocated these concepts derived it from the framework of Boulding and Sprout, who have argued for 'environmental possibilism'.[7] Starr defined opportunity as the "possibility of interaction between entities or behavioral units of some kind,"[8] where the nature of interactions that states undergo determines the possibility of cooperation and conflict. The second element that Starr talked about was the notion of willingness, which was indicative of understanding the desirability of the decision-maker to go for war. In the words of Starr, willingness refers to "the processes by which (decision-makers) recognise opportunities and then, given these opportunities, become willing to choose war as a behavioral alternative."[9]

While environmental possibilism/opportunity and willingness question determinism and reductionism which has been established between geography and conflict, a genre of scholars also attempted to liberate the deterministic relationship which has been associated with geography and conflict and looked at the making of space and place. For instance, Gearoid O Tuathail and Simon Dalby have challenged this understanding of geo-politics and geo-political reasoning by revisiting and engaging with the phenomenon of geographical representations that gives meaning to the notion of space in world politics. With an attempt to bring back the notion of geo-politics into the field, they illuminate the understanding of the world and its demarcation into the respective terminologies such as place, space, landscape through the lens of critical geopolitics.[10] Critical geopolitics defines geo-politics as a "social, cultural and political practice", which often offers a counter narrative of a nation or that of classical geopolitics.[11] Critical geopolitics thus moves away from the Cartesian logic of the absolute space, where the sense of space was measured in absolute geometrical term along latitudinal and longitudinal lines. David Harvey writes, "absolute space is fixed and we record and plan events within its frame. This is the space of Newton and Descartes and it is usually represented as a pre-existing and immoveable grid amenable to standardised measurement and open to calculation. Geometrically it is the space of Euclid and therefore the space of all manner of cadastral mapping and engineering practices. It is a primary space of individuation—*res extensa* as Descartes put it—and this applies to all discrete and bounded phenomena including you and me as individual persons. Socially this is the space of private property and other bounded territorial designations (such as states, administrative units, city plans and urban grids). When Descartes' engineer looked upon the world with a sense of mastery, it was a world of absolute space (and time) from which all uncertainties and ambiguities could in principle be banished and in which human calculation could uninhibitedly flourish."[12] On the other hand, relative space is a concept associated with Einstein that frames of references depend on the observer. Liebniz is another philosopher who has deliberated on the notion of relational space. According to him, "the relational view of space holds there is no such thing as space outside of the processes that define it. Processes do not occur in space but define their own spatial frame. The concept of space is embedded in or internal to process."[13] The making of the space is therefore important and the factors that contribute to the making of space thus merit attention. The making of the himalayan space in the past few years, where China has emerged as a key player and the discourses that are associated with it, become relevant in this context.

Lefebvre has defined this understanding as the 'science of space'. According to him, the science of space consists of three essential pillars. First, its use implies that knowledge constructed has political underpinnings. The construction of knowledge is political because it responds to forces of production and reflects the social relations of production. Second, space can be considered as a type of ideology, which governs the constitution of knowledge and belongingness. Third, the notion of space carries itself a technological utopia—which is a framework for the future modes of production. This notion of space is reflected in other modes of production such as architecture, urbanism or social planning. These three factors when combined constitute the truth of space. This truth of space according to Lefebvre operates at three levels—physical—which is the cosmos; the mental—the logical and formal abstraction of space and social—the space of social practice and the one occupied by sensory phenomenon—which includes "products of imagination such as projects projections and symbols and utopia."[14]

This understanding of space by critical geographers is significant in illuminating the changing geo-politics of Himalayas. It is in this regard that the development in the NorthWestern border of Bhutan merit attention. These developments therefore should not only be restricted to border negotiations and border skirmishes but also to some projects which are being planned out in the Himalayas and could substantively change the physical and cognitive understanding of the Himalayan space in the years to come. These developments are important for two primary reasons. First, they exhibit 'perceptions in making' vis-a-vis the Northwest border of Bhutan. Second, they also highlight the prospects for conflict and cooperation which the Himalayas could be witnessing in the coming years.

The Making of the Himalayan Space: Bhutan's Northwest Borders

Maintaining the status-quo—this seemed to be the primary concern of India as it challenged and objected to the building of infrastructure by China along the North-Western sector of Bhutan. While the building of roads and access points by China to the site of disputed area, is not a recent development (see Figure 1),[15] June 2017, was the first time that an 'offensive' position was taken by India, asking China for a "return to the status-quo pre-2017." Post 2017, Minister for External Affairs, Sushma Swaraj stated that the bilateral issue between Bhutan and China is of strategic concern to India, thereby implying that India is a legitimate stakeholder to the boundary demarcation between China and Bhutan.[16] This posturing by India can be interpreted in two ways. First, it could represent a breach of trust between India and Bhutan, where New Delhi expressed its desirability of being more proactively engaged and concerned about the developments along the Bhutan's North-Western

Figure 1: The Cartographic 'space' in Doklam: Physical and Cognitive Changes

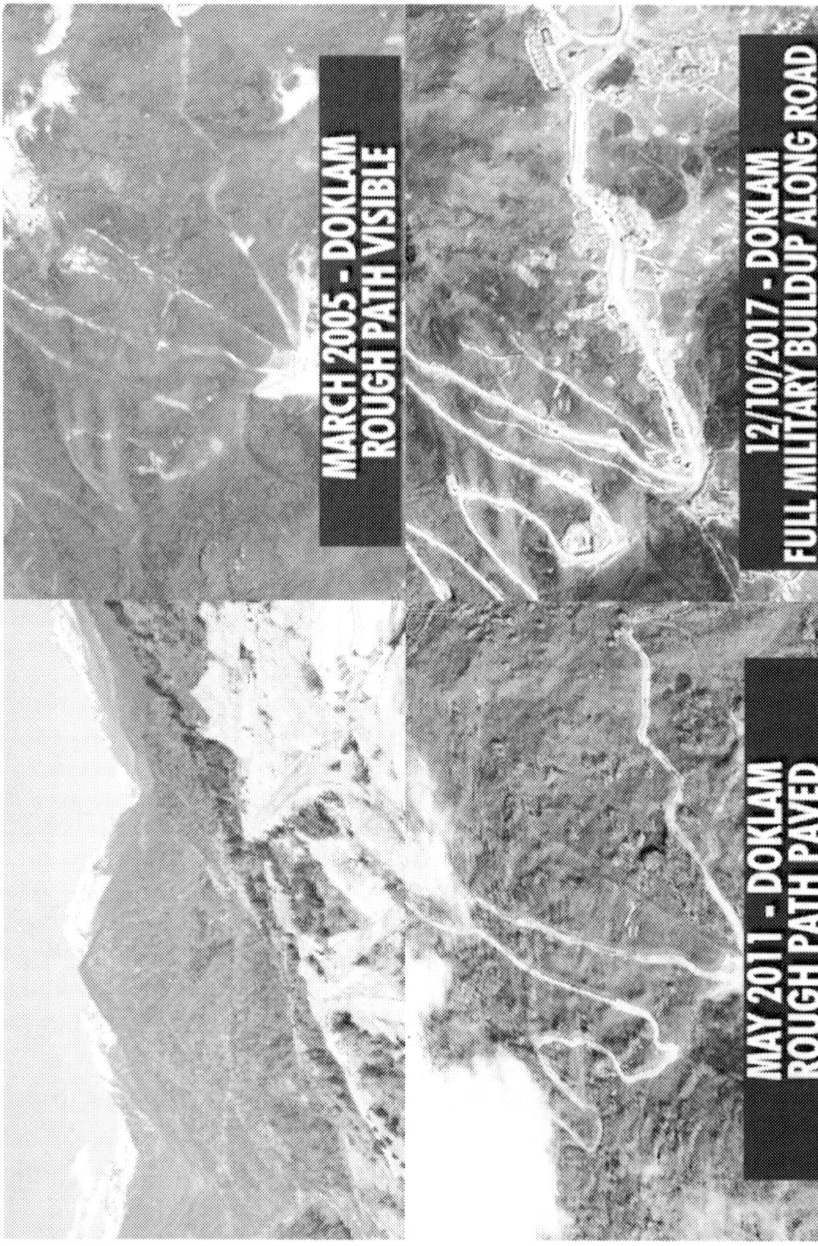

area. Second, it represents a shift from defensive posturing to offensive posturing, as pre 2017, there was no explicit official reservation expressed by the Indian Government. In order to understand the reasons for this shift, it is important to explain the material and the ideational elements which have contributed to the making of this Himalayan space to help us address questions related to 'what' has changed and 'why' these changes appears to be a pertinent factor in changing geo-political environment.

The history of border dispute between Bhutan and China go back to the 1950s when China published maps claiming Bhutanese territory as Chinese, thus bringing the issue into the public domain. The disputed areas that China claimed, covered a total of 764 square kilometres covering the North West (269 sq km) and Central parts of Bhutan (495 sq km). While the North West part constitutes the Doklam, Sinchulung, Dramana and Shakhatoe in Samste, Haa and Paro districts respectively, the Central parts constituted the Pasamlung and the Jakarlung valley in the Wangdue Phodrang district. The intrusion by Chinese soldiers and Tibetan herders has often been an issue of concern in Bhutan's National Assembly discussions, where many *chimis* (district representatives) have claimed that traditionally the land always belonged to Bhutan and historically there has been no precedence of Bhutan paying taxes to the Tibetan government for any of the disputed claims.[17] However, in 1984 formal negotiations started between Bhutan and China with a focus on North, North West and Central regions. In 1996, China proposed a package deal, under which it offered a swapping arrangement, where 495 sq km of Central Bhutan with that of 269 sq km of North Western Bhutan. The 269 sq km stretch is a space for contested aspirations as the strategic Chumbi Valley is located there; which is a vital tri-junction and is 5 km from the Siliguri corridor. The siliguri corridor, also known as the 'chicken neck' connects the rest of India to its North East and Nepal to Bhutan and is considered important for India's national security interests.

China and Bhutan have held twenty-four rounds of border talks so far (2018). The nineteenth round, which took place in 2010 was particularly significant as both sides decided on a joint field survey, in order to harmonise the reference points and names of the disputed areas. The focus of the stated joint-field survey was on the disputed areas in the western sector which constitute the pastoral lands of Doklam, Charithang, Sinchulumpa and Dramana. This exclusive focus on the North-Western sector is important due to its close proximity with the Chumbi Valley. However, while negotiations were underway on the disputed regions, China had been continuing its infrastructural activities. If one looks at the satellite images from 2004, there is remarkable progress on the visibility of pathways that China has built.

Figure 2

Source: June 2017 Faceoff (Adapted from Burgess 2012[18])

If one casts a look at the June 2017 stand-off between India and China, the debates revolved around the change of status-quo. While Bhutan claimed that China had built a road inside its territory and the road construction efforts had entered the Doklam area, which was not the case before. India on its part, approached the Chinese construction area and urged them to desist from changing the status quo[19] (See Figure 2).

It is interesting to note the positions that have been unfolded in public domain in the past one year. As far as the Chinese claims are concerned, the 1870, Anglo-China Convention, is the primary frame reference. Article 1 of the Convention is significant in this context which notes "the crest of the mountain range separating the boundary of the Chinese territory starts from the "waters flowing into the Sikkim Teesta and the beginning point of the boundary line would be "Mount Gipmochi on the Bhutan frontier". In an interesting analysis, Manoj Joshi has noted that the 1861 British Map shows that Mount Gipmochi is near the tri-junction but within Bhutan.[20] India and Bhutan have rejected these claims and India along with Bhutan has stated that the boundary line follows from Batangla to Merugla and Sinchula then down to Amochu. Bhutan, meanwhile also passed an official statement, which stated that China should adhere to 1998 Convention where both countries had agreed to maintain peace and tranquility in their border areas and till a final settlement on the boundary question is achieved, both countries would maintain status-quo on the boundary pre March 1959. Bhutan in its official statement had also mentioned that China had agreed to refrain from taking unilateral action, or use of force, to change the status quo of the boundary.

Meanwhile, the Ministry of External Affairs, on China's unilateral attempt on altering of the 'tri-junction' retorted that "where the boundary in the Sikkim sector is concerned, India and China had reached an understanding in 2012 reconfirming their mutual agreement on the "basis of the alignment". "Further discussions regarding finalisation of the boundary have been taking place under the Special Representatives framework." The press release (MEA) 2017 further noted that, "In this context, the Indian side has underlined that the two Governments had in 2012 reached an agreement that the tri-junction boundary points between India, China and third countries will be finalised in consultation with the concerned countries. Any attempt, therefore, to unilaterally determine tri-junction points is in violation of this understanding."[21] It needs to be noted that the Indian position on the legitimacy of its claims recalls the India-China Agreement on "Working Mechanism on Consultation and Coordination" which was held with China during the 15th Round of Sino-Indian Special Representative (SR) dialogue."[22] However, interestingly, no information in the public domain is available in the Indian media (official and non-official), mentioning the term 'tri-junction' and 'consultation with third countries'. As far as the Chinese sources go, it briefly mentions with some ambiguity that, "the SRs discussed bilateral, regional and global issues. The discussions were wide ranging, productive, forward-looking and marked by a commonality of views on many issue." However, the mention of the 'tri-junction' and 'consultation with third countries is also clearly absent in the Chinese press releases. In terms of clarifying the official Indian position on the same, an official statement from the Chinese Embassy is worth recalling. It states that, "what was agreed in the 2012 understanding was that in the future, the parties will conduct demarcation on the side of the tri-junction area. The bone of contention is not what is stated in the 2012 understanding, but what is stated in 1890 convention."[23] This explicit acknowledgement by

China for the first time to the frames of reference reveals the differing perceptions that China, India and Bhutan have over the boundary question. What is also evident is how the discourse on the understanding of the Doklam space has been reconstructed and represented for framing purposes.

A question which needs to be asked at this juncture is therefore what are the reasons for this understanding or alternatively how this understanding by China and the differing perceptions over the North-West space were achieved over a period of time.

As mentioned before, the story for understanding these differing perceptions can be traced to the nineteenth round of border talks between Bhutan and China which started way back in 2010. In fact, by 2006, National Assembly debates in Bhutan claimed six roads were built by China near Bhutan's North and North-West areas. By 2010, China had made some progress on infrastructure build-up and the same year, Secretary of International Boundaries, Royal Government of Bhutan Government had protested road building activities and PLA incursions which had been happening since 2008-09. Interestingly, by 2013, Indian intelligence reports claimed that China had been operating military camps in the disputed areas in North–West sector, hosting Chinese flags.

Given these developments, it could be concluded that the negotiations on the disputed border have witnessed some progress since 2010. One could even go on to state that, Bhutan could have almost decided to surrender the patches of disputed land in its north-west region to China.[24] Events post 2010, have revealed that People's Liberation Army camps have been established inside Bhutanese territory. The author of the report had also claimed that China has been operating three military camps inside Bhutan since 24 May 2013 with the Chinese flag being hoisted there. This action (not officially refuted by the Chinese then) could lead one to conclude that while the Chinese presence "seems" to be an encroachment—a deal may well have been concluded.[25] These facts as they appear in the media, thus force the analysts to ask a simple question: Have Bhutan-China border negotiations already reached some political compromise, or is it that Bhutan had been surrendering slowly to Chinese tactics on its north-western border?

Chinese actions on the ground and the recent claims made by China, have revealed the perceptions on the border more clearly. While in 1980s, when the border talks started, there was little clarity on the spatial representation in the North-Western region, in 2018, the space has been represented and reproduced in a different way. The representation is not in physical, as evident through the satellite images, depicted in Figure One, but it also has an ideational structure. The ideational structure has well been represented by the historical claims which have been put forth through the 1890 Convention.

Production and Representation of Space

If one was to reflect on the rationale behind the production and reproduction of space, Chinese overtures in the last few decades merit some attention. An important frame to understand this is China's go-west policy and trade diplomacy towards South Asia. While the debate on China's go west policy started in 1990s, it has over a period of time taken a concrete shape through gradual initiatives which China has undertaken. These initiatives can be considered a part of the 'China's dream of the great rejuvenation of the nation, which has been promised by Xi Ping to be fulfilled as "Chinese dream of great rejuvenation by 2049.[26] Scholars believe improving connectivity between Tibet and India, by extending the railway to Eating in the Chumbi valley and onwards to Siliguri can be the beginning of an important strategic North-south corridor for China. The other two are the Irrawady corridor connecting Myanmar to Yunnan and the Karakoram Corridor which connects Gwadar to Xinjiang, both of which are on either side of India. These, given the Chinese strategic designs can be considered as the building blocks of Border Roads Initiative.

This strategic rejuvenation of China, where it has offered the neighbouring countries to jump "aboard the Chinese development train" throws useful insights on the transformation of space. Putting some perspective in the North-Western borders of Bhutan it can be said, particularly after the Doklam stand-off, which has given rise to varying perceptions, on either sides of the border, Doklam is a small dot in completing the circle. China will not stake a war with India on Doklam, as the motivations for the same are guided by economic rationale as much as it is military motivations. Significantly, the debates surrounding the dispute has been intertwined with perceptions, on which there is no convergence of views. While this might take a route of protracted negotiations and stalemate, the physical modification of space is there to stay for the years to come. Borrowing from Lefebvre understanding of 'science of space', the making of North-West borders of Bhutan along with the grand strategic design of China governed by the Border Roads Initiative will have ramification in the years to come. While it will be too myopic to look at the Doklam issue in isolation, it appears that China's approach to its construction activities along the border areas was not to change the immediate status-quo, but to create conditions for a more gradualistic change in near future. These changes will be there to stay and have the potential for a economic vision as well gaining military/offensive leverage over a period of time. It would be appropriate to conclude by saying that for the time being the objectives of China have been achieved and there is low probability of a order skirmish in near future. Unless challenged overly, it is unlikely that China will take any military action to change the status-quo in Bhutan's North-Western frontiers.

NOTES

1 Osterudd, , 1988, p. 98 cited in Harvey Starr, *On Geopolitics: Space, Place and International Relations*, New York: Routledge, 2013, p. 3.

2 Cited in Karl Polelle, Raising Cartographic Consciousness: The Social and Foreign Policy Vision of Geopolitics in the Twentieth Century, Lanham, Md.: Lexington Books, p. 93.

3 Karl Polelle, *Raising Cartographic Consciousness: The Social and Foreign Policy Vision of Geopolitics in the Twentieth Century*, Lanham, Md.: Lexington Books.

4 Neumann cited in Karl Polelle, *Raising Cartographic Consciousness: The Social and Foreign Policy Vision of Geopolitics in the Twentieth Century*, Lanham, Md.: Lexington Books, p. 94.

5 Richard von Kulhman, cited in Harvey Starr, *On Geopolitics: Space, Place and International Relations*, New York: Routledge, 2013, p. 14.

6 Ratzel cited in Karl Polelle, *Raising Cartographic Consciousness: The Social and Foreign Policy Vision of Geopolitics in the Twentieth Century*, Lanham, Md.: Lexington Books, p. 97.

7 Gary Goertz and Paul Diehl, *Territorial Changes and International Conflict*, New York: Routledge, 2010.

8 Gary Goertz and Paul Diehl, *Territorial Changes and International Conflict*, New York: Routledge, 2010, p. 2.

9 Harvey Starr, *On Geopolitics: Space, Place and International Relations,* New York: Routledge, 2013.

10 Tuathail, Dalby, Routledge, *The Geo-political Reader,* London, Routledge, 1998, p. 2.

11 Ibid.

12 David Harvey, "Space as a Key Word", paper for Marx and Philosophy Conference, *Institute of Education*, London, 29 May 2002, available at http://frontdeskapparatus.com/files/harvey2004.pdf.

13 Harvey Starr, *On Geopolitics: Space, Place and International Relations*, New York: Routledge, 2013.

14 Henry Lefebvre, The Production of Space, Oxford, Blackwell, 1981, p. 12.

15 Vishnu Som, "Full-Fledged Chinese Military Complex In Doklam, Show Satellite Pics", *NDTV*, 23 January 2018, available at https://www.ndtv.com/india-news/full-fledged-chinese-military-complex-in-doklam-show-satellite-pics-1801323

16 Indrani Bagchi, "Sushma Swaraj rebuts China's Doklam statement", *Times of India*, 3 August

2017, available at https://timesofindia.indiatimes.com/india/sushma-swaraj-rebuts-chinas-doklam-statement/articleshow/59904638.cms

17 Medha Bisht, "Sino-Bhutan Boundary Negotiations: Complexities of the 'Package Deal'", *IDSA Web Comment*, 9 January 2010, available at https://idsa.in/idsacomments/Sino-BhutanBoundaryNegotiations_mbisht_190110

18 Steven Lee Myers, Ellen Barry and Max Fisher, "How India and China Have Come to the Brink Over a Remote Mountain Pass", *New York Times*, 26 June 2017, available at https://www.nytimes.com/2017/07/26/world/asia/dolam-plateau-china-india-bhutan.html

19 Ministry of External Affairs, "Recent Developments in Doklam Area", *Ministry of External Affairs, Government of India*, 30 June 2017, available at http://www.mea.gov.in/press-releases.htm?dtl/28572/Recent_Developments_in_Doklam_Area

20 Manoj Joshi, "To start at the very beginning", *ORF Special Repor*t, August 2017, p. 1, available at https://www.orfonline.org/wp-content/uploads/2017/08/ORF_SpecialReport_ 40_ Doklam.pdf

21 Devirupa Mitra, "Construction at Bhutanese Tri-Junction Will Harm Our Security Interests, India tells China", *Wire*, 30 June 2017, at: https://thewire.in/diplomacy/construction-doklam-will-harm-security-interests-india-tells-china

22 Jabin T. Jacob, "China-India Special Representatives Talks: Moving Beyond the Boundary Dispute?" *RSIS Commentaries*, No. 029/2012, 20 February 2012, available at https://indiandchina.com/2012/02/21/15th-sino-indian-sr-talks-moving-beyond-the-boundary-dispute15th-special-representatives-talks-between-china-and-india-moving-beyond-the-boundary-dispute/

23 Liu Jinsong, Deputy Chief of Mission, Chinese Embassy, New Delhi, 2018.

24 Medha Bisht and Dil Rahut, "Assessing Bhutan Elections", *Economic and Political Weekly*, Vol. 48, No. 39, 28 September 2013.

25 Ibid.

26 United States House of Representatives, "Testimony before the House Committee on Foreign Affairs", *Subcommittee on Asia and the Pacific*, United States House of Representatives, 15 November 2017.

11

New Nepal under Chinese Shadow and Indian Influence

Nihar R Nayak

Nepal has remained an important sub-theater of major power rivalries in the Himalayan region ever since its unification under Prithvi Narayan Shah in 1769. Its relevance was further enhanced during the Cold War period. After a short break, Nepal once again attracted global attention due to the Maoist insurgency and emergence of China as an important partner in Nepal's development process besides India. During this period, Nepal remained an important actor because of its strategic location and its effort to survive as a sovereign nation.

Nepal's political transition from 2006 to 2015 and adoption of democratic, secular and federal system under the new Constitution brought major changes in its foreign policy (FP) as well as that of its two important neighbouring countries. While India has been supporting democratic movements in Nepal since 1950s, Nepal's transition from monarchy to multiparty democracy forced China to readjust its southern Himalayan policy. Ever since the establishment of diplomatic relations with Nepal, China worked closely with monarchy for political stability and security reasons. India's 'democracy project' also brought the Monarchy and China together. In absence of monarchy, China was worried that lingering political instability could facilitate anti-Chinese elements, especially agitations by Tibetan refugees, in Nepal. In fact, its suspicion turned true when anti-China protests began in Nepal during Olympic Games in August 2008.

Nepal in China's Foreign Policy

Nepal has a special place in Chinese foreign policy now, though it is described as a country of "peripheral" concern by many scholars in China. China has been following a moderate policy towards Nepal ever since the two countries established diplomatic relations in 1955. There are several concerns that underpin the Chinese policy towards Nepal. First, Nepal shares the longest border with China—after India—and a larger part of this border remains unguarded due to the mountainous terrain. Second, geographically Nepal has remained the southern gateway to Tibet and has had closer economic and cultural linkages with Tibet than China since times immemorial. Third, India's leverage in Nepal as well as presence of western countries has led China to better its relationship with Nepal.[1]

A new dimension to China's approach towards Nepal was added after the introduction of OBOR by Chinese President Xi Jinping in 2013. The objective of this policy is to expand Chinese soft power by sharing its economic and technological achievements across the world. Like many other neighbours of China, Nepal too reciprocated the OBOR initiative by signing an MoU in May 2017. As a multidimensional project, the OBOR gave the perfect opportunity to China to expand its engagements with Nepal beyond the existing state-to-state relationship.

Neo China-Nepal Relations

Since security issues have been embedded in the bilateral relations, China readjusted its approach towards Nepal in the post-monarchy period. Some important developments propelled China to take that decision. First, China was worried about emergence of new democratic forces like the Maoists and Madhesis and also the restoration of dissolved Parliament under the leadership of G P Koirala after the 19-day *Jan Andolan-II* in April 2006. Since India played a major role in bringing about the new changes in Nepal, China felt that the new government, suspected as pro-India, could be lackluster in taking action against Tibetan refugees living in Kathmandu. Second, China was also equally worried about growing influence and pro-active roles shown by the EU, UK and US in the political transition of Nepal. Third, in the absence of monarchy, which was a stable political institution in Nepal from Chinese point of view, China looked for a new trusted political partner in that country. In the absence of a strong government and lingering negotiations between the Maoists and the mainstream political parties, China adopted a four pronged approach through: (1) cooperation at the institutional level (bureaucracy, armed police, intelligence and army) to take care of its immediate security concerns, (2) negotiations with the political parties by sending frequent political delegations from Beijing as a medium term plan, (3) strengthening people-to-people relations, and (4) diversifying economic engagements for long term benefits.

Political Visits

The frequency of high level visits since 2006 from China to Nepal reflect elevation of Nepal's position in China's external periphery policy. While only two high–level visits took place in 2006, the number jumped to 11 by the end of 2011. At the same time, the number of bilateral personnel exchanges with Nepal touched 74,000. The same reached to 168,000 in 2013.[2] The relationship strengthened further with the visit of the Chinese Premier in January 2012. During these visits, both sides discussed issues of mutual interest, regional issues and many agreements were also signed. Following are the major high level exchanges since 2008:

- In June 2013, the then Vice President Parmanand Jha attended the opening ceremony of the First China-South Asia Expo and State Councilor Yang Jiechi visited Nepal.
- In July 2013, Chief of Army Staff of Nepal Army General Gaurav Rana visited China.
- Foreign Minister Wang Yi visited Nepal in 2015 to attend the 'International Conference on Nepal's Reconstruction.'
- Chinese Vice Premier Wang Yang visited Kathmandu from 14-17 August, 2017.
- Vice President Nanda Bahadur Pun visited China in June 2017.
- Prime Minister Pushpa Kamal Dahal visited China from 23-29 March 2017.
- Prime Minister K.P. Sharma Oli visited China in March 2016 and again in June 2018.

- General Chang Wanquan, State Counselor and Defense Minister of China, visited Nepal in March 2017.[3]

Economic Engagements

There has been a phenomenal increase and expansion of Chinese economic engagements with Nepal in the last one decade. China has emerged as the second largest trading partner of Nepal after India. In 2015-16, total exports to china reached $181 million with marginal increase from $179 million in the previous fiscal year. In contrast, import from China has been growing at the rate of 39 per cent per year. It rose from $421 million in fiscal year 2009-10 to $1,247 million in fiscal year 2015-16. As a result, the trade deficit with China has risen from $401 million in 2009-10 to $1228 million in 2015-16. Nepal exported goods worth $17 million to China during the first seven months of the current fiscal 2017-18, a rise by 72.3 per cent over the same period last fiscal year.[4]

There has been a significant increase in grant-in–aid since 2006-07. China has increased its annual aid assistance to Nepal from $0.14 million in 2005/06 to $35.48 million in 2010-11, while Indian aid went up from $5.75 million in 2005-06 to $92 million in the same period. After regime change, Chinese aid assistance to the country increased more than 200 times and India's more than 19 times. Interestingly, during former Chinese Premier Wen Jaibao's visit to Nepal in January 2012, China committed $1.18 billion in aid to be spent over a period of three years in Nepal. Even in Overseas Development Assistance (ODA), China overtook India in 2015. China's ODA has been growing steadily from $19 million in 2010-11 to $38 million in 2014-15. In 2014-15, India's ODA in Nepal was $22 million.[5]

There has also been significant increase in Chinese investments in Nepali market in the post conflict period. Since 2008, Chinese investments in Nepal have been increasing and in 2014, it overtook India for the first time in terms of total investments in Nepal. In 2015-16, 42 per cent of total FDI to Nepal came from China. China accounted for $51.77 million out of $76.39 million pledged as FDI in the first half of the 2017-18. In 2015-16, while China made the highest FDI pledge to Nepal at $57 million, whilst India's was third at $18 million.[6] China committed foreign direct investment of $8.2 billion to Nepal out of the total pledge of $13.52 billion proposed at the Nepal Investment Summit in 2017.[7] China has invested mostly in hydro, services, infrastructure and agriculture sectors.

China is deeply engaged in infrastructure development projects in Nepal. It is currently directly and indirectly involved in seven hydro projects, six highways construction, three airports, three telecom projects and one each in railway and transmission lines.

In the tourism sector, China overtook India as the top source country for inbound tourists to Nepal with a 38.04 per cent jump in arrivals in the first three months of 2018. According to the figure released by Nepal Tourism Board, Nepal received 40,976 Chinese tourists from January to March. During the same period, the number of Indians visiting Nepal dropped by 0.98 per cent to 34,133 individuals.[8]

Security Cooperation

The Chinese engagement in Nepal goes beyond the political domain. At a meeting between Defence Minister Ram Bahadur Thapa and the Deputy Commander of the PLA, Lieutenant General Ma Xiaotian, held in Kathmandu in December 2008, China pledged to provide $2.6 million in military assistance for the modernisation of the Nepal Army. Earlier in September 2008, China announced military aid worth $1.3 million, the first such assistance to the Maoist government. Beijing had keenly supported the Maoist government's proposal to integrate some 19,000 Maoist guerrillas into the army. During Prime Minister Wen Jiabao's visit to Nepal in January 2012, China announced a one-time grant of $20 million for the rehabilitation of former Maoist combatants. During Madhav Kumar Nepal's regime, Defence Minister Bidya Devi Bhandari visited China in March 2010 and the Chinese reiterated their keenness to provide military modernisation assistance to Nepal. In 2011, during the then Chinese Army Chief General Chen Bingde's visit to Nepal, China signed an agreement for providing military aid to the tune of $7.7 million to the Nepal army in an effort towards deepening the military relations. During Wen Jiabao's visit, again, the Chinese side pledged $2 million for strengthening the Nepal Police, including setting up an Armed Police Force College.[9]

In 2018, both the countries agreed on border security and cooperation, including the establishment of a 'joint action center' in a town on Nepal's border to further tighten movement of Tibetans at the borders. The Chinese People's Liberation Army and the Nepal Army have established a military assistance program in recent years, including the supply of equipment, training, infrastructure development and the exchange of high-level delegations. The military cooperation was strengthen further during China visit of Nepalese Deputy Prime Minister and Defence Minister Ishwor Pokhrel in October 2018. During that visit both the countries signed a memorandum of Understanding (MoU) on military cooperation. As per the MoU, China would provide an assistance of RMB 150 million to Nepal for the purpose of humanitarian and disaster relief equipment over a period of five years.[10]

Marking an extension of this engagement, the first joint Nepal-China military exercise-Sagarmatha Friendship 2017—was held in April 2017 "with a special focus on combating terror and disaster".[11] The second military exercise was held in September 2018 in Sichuan province.

In order to ensure quick and effective response system to control anti-China activities in Nepali soil, China has targeted the bureaucracy and the Armed Police Force (APF) which guards the Nepal-China border. In this regard, during State Councilor Yang Jiechi's visit to Kathmandu in June 2013, China pledged NPR 3.6 billion in assistance for the construction of APF training academy at Matatirtha near Kathmandu. China also increased the number of seats and scholarships in its various training colleges for Nepali bureaucrats as well as at its National Defence University for Nepali police officers. It has also supported joint exercises with the Nepal Armed Police in Tibet. Besides, China has increased the number of war college seats for Nepal Army officers. The current ratio of Chinese to Nepalese Army personnel in China's War College short term training programs may be around 4:1. During the training period, China arranges trips for Nepali officials to various parts of the country to provide them first-hand knowledge about modern China. As a result, China has over a period of time created a constituency within the Army. Some senior officers of the Nepal Army argue in favour of deeper military cooperation with China to reap more benefits.[12]

People-to-People Relations

Keeping tight watch over the Tibetans living in Nepal has been the primary objective of Chinese penetration in multiple sectors of Nepal. Party officials equate political 'stability' in Tibet with the security of the entire PRC, and this approach has been extended to Nepal, which shares close historic and cultural ties with Tibet, and since Nepal is the gateway to exile for Tibetans.[13] In recent years, China has been perceiving developments in its periphery as constituting a national threat. Its 2008 Defence White Paper identified Tibet as a national security threat for the first time – the earlier versions had only mentioned Taiwan. The White Paper observed: "China is encountering many new circumstances and new issues in maintaining social stability.... 'East Turkistan independence' and 'Tibet independence' pose threats to China's unity and security."[14] A series of anti-China protests by Tibetan refugees in Kathmandu in March 2008 gave credence to this threat perception.[15] Deepening people-to-people relationship is one such project to keep a tab on the Tibetans and spread Chinese soft power. Following activities are undertaken in this program.

- Arranging youth, journalist, academician, parliamentarian, party officials and business delegations to different parts of China. It is believed that every month one delegation from Nepal departs for China.
- Nepal-China media cooperation by holding cultural and film festivals.
- Providing technical assistance during the elections.
- Organise training programs for Nepali bureaucrats, police and army at Chinese institutions.
- Promoting Chinese language, scholarships and culture through numerous Chinese study centers that have sprung up in Nepal, including in the Terai region of Nepal that borders India. China has around 35 study centers across Nepal. China also offers more than 100 scholarships to Nepali students. As of 2018, China is offering 160 scholarships to Nepalese students for higher studies in China.
- China has also been funding several social development projects, including construction of schools, hospitals and other basic necessities to create a favorable constituency in Nepal. In 2011, China agreed to develop infrastructure in Lumbini with a master plan proposed at a cost of $3 billion.[16] China has also come up with special packages for the economic development of northern Nepal.

India-Nepal Relations in Post-Conflict Period

Nepal has an important place specifically in India's neighbourhood policy and in its foreign policy in general because of Nepal's geo-strategic location and as the two countries share an open border. Himalayas has long been considered vital security guarantor to India's northern frontier in the context of traditional and non-traditional security threats. Articulating India's approach towards defending its north-eastern frontiers, Prime Minister Nehru made a statement in the Indian Parliament on 6 December 1950 stating that "from time immemorial the Himalayas have provided us with magnificent frontiers...we cannot allow that barrier to be penetrated because it is also the principal barrier to India."[17] Radio Peking's announcement in November 1949 to liberate Tibet[18] forced India and Nepal to sign the Peace and Friendship Treaty in July 1950. By having this agreement, India created a northern frontier defence mechanism to protect Nepal and its own territory against Chinese aggression.

Although there are asymmetries, both the countries acknowledge that they are equally dependent on each other. While Nepal is dependent on India for its rapid economic growth and development, India needs a politically stable and peaceful Nepal to take care of its security concerns. At the same time, a deeper relationship reassures each other's support during crisis periods and indirectly they stand as each other's security provider. That is the reason why Nepal finds a special position in India's 'neighbourhood first' policy.[19]

Moreover, India-Nepal relation is embedded with common geography, history, culture, people-to-people relations and diplomatic relations. The relationship goes beyond formal ties, which started in June 1947. The open border has made the relationship special in the region. The treaty of peace and friendship signed between both the countries in July 1950 formalised the relationship further. It recognised each other's sovereignty, dependency on one another but as equal partners, guaranteed multidimensional and people-to-people relations.

Political Relations

Frequent high level political exchanges have consolidated the Indo-Nepal relations. In the post conflict period, except Jhalanath Khanal, all the PMs of Nepal paid official visits to India at different points of time. Ram Baran Yadav, as the first President of Nepal, paid a State visit to India in February 2010. Indian President Pranab Mukherjee paid a State visit to Nepal in November 2016. Immediately after assuming office, PM Modi planned his second foreign visit to Nepal in 2014. A number of factors propelled Modi's visit to Nepal: (1) no Indian PM had visited Nepal for 17 years, (2) Introduction of neighbourhood first policy by Modi government, (3) Nepal seen as one of the friendliest neighbours, and (4) being a Hindu majority country Nepal has important pilgrimages like Pashupati, Lumbini, Janakpur and Muktinath, among others. Politically and culturally, the August 2014 visit was a huge success. PM Modi offered a special prayer at the Pashupatinath temple. Modi visited Nepal on three different occasions from 2014 to 2018. Similarly, Prime Minister Oli and former Prime Minister Dahal visited India twice on different occasions from 2016 to 2018. During these visits a number of bilateral agreements were signed.

Economic Engagements

India is the largest trading partner of Nepal and major transit route for doing business with third countries. Around 65 per cent of Nepal's annual trade is with India. The bilateral and transit trade through India has increased in recent years due to implementation of GST in India, operationalisation of ICPs and railways connectivity to Birgunj and Biratnagar, agreement on using Vishakhapatnam port for transit trade and Motor Vehicle Agreement (MVA) under the BBIN.

While India maintains its status as the largest trading partner, it has slipped into second position as an investor in Nepal. China replaced India as the top investor in Nepal for the third consecutive year since 2013. Nepal's Department of Industry (DoI) in August 2018 found that China contributed highest FDI to Nepal in fiscal years of 2015-16 and 2016-17 with $76 million and $57 million respectively. India stood second with FDI pledge of $46 million. Surprisingly, since the Maoist conflict Nepal has not received major investments from India in the manufacturing sector. It was only in 1990s that Indian MNCs like Dabur, Asian Paints and Unilever entered Nepal to set up joint ventures (JVs) or wholly owned subsidiaries. While manufacturing sector still accounts 20 per cent of the total Indian FDI in Nepal, the energy sector is still neglected.[20] Even in the 2017 Kathmandu Investment Summit, India committed a mere $317 million in comparison to $8.3billion by China.[21]

Even in the last decade, India's official development assistance has not increased as per its commitment to Nepal as a key development partner. China overtook India in 2015. China's ODA has been growing steadily from $19 million in 2010-11 to $38 million in 2014-15. In 2014-15, India's ODA in Nepal was $22 million.[22] However, India committed a fund of $250 million in grant and $750 million soft loan for earthquake reconstruction projects. In 2014, India committed two lines of credit ($100 million and $250 million) and $1 billion to be utilised in financing development projects of Nepal's choice.[23] Other than this, India has committed to be a key development partner in hydro, railways, waterways, highway, police training centers, hospitals, transmission lines, ICPs and services sectors in Nepal.

No doubt Chinese economic engagement with Nepal has increased. It appears larger than India because just one decade earlier China had a limited role in Nepal's socio-economic development projects. On the other hand, India has constantly engaged in these sectors since 1952. If we compare Chinese investments, trade and ODA with that of India in the last five years in Nepal, China seems to be at the top. But a cumulative assessment of external contribution to Nepal's overall development reflects India as the largest development partner.

Security Cooperation

Modern India-Nepal relations stand on five pillars—geography, common history and culture, deepening people-to-people contacts, formal diplomatic relations and security cooperation, including military-to-military relations. Amongst these five pillars, military cooperation has been the most stable and less averse to diplomatic skirmishes in the last 70 years of diplomatic relations despite not having a formal bilateral military agreement. In fact, it has to some extent helped in re-booting the formal diplomatic relations during crisis situation. For example, armies of both countries reportedly played an important role in removing border blockade by the anti-Constitution agitators in January 2016.

As per the 1950 Treaty, India has been supplying military equipment to the Nepal Army. The army has been trained and equipped by India since 1952 and was even briefly manning joint check posts on the Northern border.[24] Till today, the Indian Embassy in Kathmandu has the biggest military mission, including Pension and Welfare Wings at four major Gurkha recruitment centers. In a unique arrangement, both the countries confer honorary general position to each other's Army chiefs. Other than that, every year thousands of Nepali Gurkhas join Indian Army under the tripartite agreement.

India and Nepal also have a robust security bilateral institutional mechanisms starting from Joint Commission at Foreign/External Affairs Ministers level to regular meetings between border security forces. During these meetings, both the countries reiterate their commitment to address each other's security concerns. Every year, since 2009, armies of both the counties meet for annual bilateral military exercise called Surya Kiran. The objective of this joint exercise is to ensure better coordination between armies of both the countries in disaster management, anti-terrorism operations and strengthening of the bilateral relations.[25]

People-to-people Relation

India-Nepal P2P is unique because it is not supported by the state. The volume and quality of P2P relations indicate that it is mostly driven by culture, geography and people themselves. Linkages between pilgrimages, exchange of priests and marital relations, Nepali participation in India's freedom struggle, Gurkha regiment in the Indian Army and use of open border, etc., make the relationship unique. India provides about 3,000 scholarships under 12 schemes to Nepali students to study in India.[26] This is highest amongst the foreign countries offering scholarships to Nepali students per year. Besides India has been a job destination for the Nepalese since the colonial time. As per one estimate, more than five lakh Nepalese work and live in India.

China and India in Nepal: A comparison

Ever since Nepal emerged as the buffer state between China and India, both the countries have factored in their respective relations with Nepal. Previously, Nepal took advantage of competition between the two large powers. But there were occasions when Nepal lost its relevance as China and India engagements improved. For example, in the post-election period, the new government in Nepal could not play the so called 'China card' against India due to frequent meetings between PM Modi and President Xi Jinping since 2014.

Despite its recent multi-layer engagement in Nepal, China still believes that India has better leverage in Nepal. There are occasions when China has suggested to the Nepali leaders to resolve differences with India. First, when Nepali leaders approached China to supply essential goods during economic blockade by India in late 1980s, China made such suggestion. Second, China did not intervene when India tried to bring the Maoists into the mainstream in 2005. Third, during Prachanda's visit to China in October 2009 and 2010 when he tried to get the help of Chinese leaders in forging a consensus between the major political parties of Nepal and support a Maoist-led national unity government in Kathmandu, the Chinese reportedly refused to intervene.

Fourth, the Nepali proposal on tri-lateral cooperation has not been formally discussed between India and China at the bilateral meetings. Rather, both have reportedly agreed to have 2+1 dialogue on Nepal.[27] Fifth, once again China suggested Nepal to resolve differences with India when Madhesi rebels blocked major trading points with India from September 2015 to February 2016. Therefore, at any given point of time, China would prefer an Indian-influenced Nepal rather than any other extra-regional presence in Nepal.

New Nepal and Foreign Policy (FP)

As Nepal formalised the new Constitution, it attempted to pursue a 'resilient foreign policy'[28] keeping in mind the strong domestic appetite for rapid infrastructure and economic growth, international obligations and strategic competition between its immediate neighbours over the Himalayas.

The new government's FP was mostly driven by domestic requirements like development and independent FP. Keeping in view domestic and contemporary regional and global developments, the new constitution emphasised upon "pursuing an independent foreign policy considering national interest to be of utmost importance"[29] and negotiating with countries over new treaties or revision of existing ones as an equal partner. In this regard, Nepal recalibrated its foreign policy with an objective of addressing pressing domestic issues like energy security, food security, climate change and modernisation of security forces.

People's Expectations

Unlike 2008 and 2013 parliamentary elections, issues like political stability, economic and infrastructure development and curbing of migration, etc., dominated the 2017 electoral debates. Both the left and democratic alliances promised 'rapid economic growth' if voted to power. In fact, during the election campaigning, voters demanded better roads, jobs, hospitals, schools, and electricity in their regions.

It has been a major challenge for the new government to address people's expectations with limited resources. Two separate World Bank studies suggest that Nepal needs $10 billion Foreign Direct Investments (FDI) per year in order to become a middle income country. Nepal also needs to spend $13 billion to $18 billion till 2020 to improve its infrastructure.[30] As of 2018, Nepal received less than $1 billion FDI per year. It received more ODA than

FDI. Moreover, although ADB has agreed to support infrastructure projects in Nepal, these proposals have not materialised due to strings attached to them. FDI flow from India, which was the largest investor in Nepal, have shrunk over a period of time due to tensions in the bilateral relations. The US, Japan and European countries do not show much interest in investing in Nepal. Therefore, future governments in Kathmandu would look towards investments from China, which has both resources and technology. China has already agreed to develop mega projects in Nepal under the ambitious BRI project. In March 2017, Chinese companies had announced to invest around $8.3 billion in different sectors of Nepal.[31]

Final Observations

The growing Chinese footprint and its popularity in every sector of Nepal indicate the success of its policy towards Nepal despite the geographic and cultural constraints. An average Nepali perceives China as a non-interfering and benign neighbour. Since 1955, China has successfully managed the security threats emanating from Tibetan refugees living in Nepal and India. Nepal's reiteration to the 'One-China' policy during every bilateral meeting and acknowledgement of TAR as an integral part of China could be a major diplomatic success for China. It has also successfully prevented Western forces from supporting the Tibetan refugees in Nepal. Although it has not reached the level of India while engaging in Nepal, it has certainly reached a stage to challenge India's influence in the south of Himalayas. For example, China reportedly played a decisive role in the merger of the left parties in the post-Constitution period. It has emerged as an alternative to India in terms of trade, transit, energy and economic developments in Nepal.

Given that China has been able to acquire a visible presence and influence in other continents like Africa and South America, it would not be very difficult for it to play a decisive role in Nepal in the future. It seems, however, that China does not want to disturb its relationship with India because of Nepal. It perhaps understand that the Tibet issue can be managed by improving overall relationships and dialogue on border issues with India. China wants to play a major role in South Asia without impacting the normal course of China-India relations.

More importantly, neither China nor India on their own can fulfill the development aspirations of Nepal. Because, while the southern neighbour offers transit facilities and easy market for Nepal's trading activity, the northern neighbour has the ability to extend technological and financial support.

Given the geographical situation, the new government in Kathmandu could have some edge in its bargaining power with its neighbours due to unfolding favorable domestic and regional competition between China and India. Despite that it could be a litmus test for the new government to strike a balance between domestic aspirations and neighbours' sensitivities.

NOTES

1 For details see Nihar R Nayak, *Strategic Himalayas: Republican Nepal and External Powers*, Pentagon Press, New Delhi, 2014, p. 80.

2 China and Nepal, Ministry of Foreign Affairs of the People's Republic of China, available at https://www.fmprc.gov.cn/mfa_eng/wjb_663304/zzjg_663340/yzs_663350/gjlb_663354/2752_663508/ , accessed on 26 August 2018.

3 "Nepal-China Relations", Ministry of Foreign Affairs, Nepal, available at https://mofa.gov.np/nepal-china-relations/ .

4 "Nepal's export to China surge by 72 percent", *Xinhua*, 19 March 2008, available at http://www.xinhuanet.com/english/2018-03/19/c_137049557.htm

5 Lt Gen S L Narasimhan, "How Candid is China's Good Neighbourhood Policy?", *Defence Aviation Post*, 9 January 2017.

6 "India watches warily as China further ramps up FDI into Nepal", *The Times of India*, 7 February 2017.

7 "Chinese investors commit highest amount of FDI at Investment summit in Nepal", *China Daily*, 4 March 2017.

8 "China overtakes India as top source country for tourists", *The Kathmandu Post*, Kathmandu 13 April 2018.

9 For details see Nihar R Nayak, *Strategic Himalayas: Republican Nepal and External Powers*, Pentagon Press, New Delhi, 2014. p. 91.

10 Source: http://kathmandupost.ekantipur.com/news/2018-10-27/nepal-china-sign-mou-on-military-cooperation.html

11 "High-level Chinese visit to Nepal highlights difficulties for Tibetan community" *International Campaign For Tibet*, 28 August 2017, available at https://www.savetibet.org/high-level-chinese-visit-to-nepal-highlights-difficulties-for-tibetan-community/

12 Nihar R Nayak, "China's growing military ties with Nepal", IDSA Strategic Comments, 31 March 2017.

13 "High-level Chinese visit to Nepal highlights difficulties for Tibetan community" *International Campaign For Tibet*, 28 August 2017, available at https://www.savetibet.org/high-level-chinese-visit-to-nepal-highlights-difficulties-for-tibetan-community/

14 White Paper on China's National Defense, 2008, The Central People's Government of The People's Republic of China, available at http://www.china.org.cn/government/whitepaper/node_7060059.htm (accessed on 17 July 2013). Also see China's National Defense in 2006, at http://www.china.org.cn/english/features/book/194421.htm, accessed on 12 February 2014.

15 Kunda Dixit, "A New Himalayan Game", *The Fletcher Forum of World Affairs*, 34(1), Winter 2010, pp. 125–34.

16 "Chinese foundation plans $3 billion project in Nepal" *The Hindu*, 17 July 2011.

17 "Nehru speeches, 1949-1953", Publication Division, GoI, 1963, p. 252.

18 Leo E Rose, "Nepal Strategy for Survival" UCP, Berkeley, 1971, p. 184.

19 For details see Nihar R Nayak, "Nepal and Bhutan in India's Security Architecture", in Satish Kumar (ed), *India's National Security: Annual Review 2018*, Pentagon Press, New Delhi, pp. 231-243.

20 "Nepal to push for more Indian investments", *The Kathmandu Post*, 9 August 2018.

21 "Investment summit draws $13.51bn FDI commitment", *The Himalayan Times*, Kathmandu, 4 March 2017.

22 Lt Gen S L Narasimhan "How Candid is China's Good Neighbourhood Policy?", *Defence Aviation Post*, 9 January 2017.

23 Nepal-India Relations, Ministry of Foreign Affairs, Nepal, available at https://mofa.gov.np/nepal-india-relations/

24 Ashok K Mehta, "Nepal quake and the Gorkha bond", *The Hindu*, 15 May 2015.

25 http://pib.nic.in/newsite/PrintRelease.aspx?relid=179508

26 Embassy of India, Kathmandu. For details see http://www.indianembassy.org.np/index1.php?option=Xgc4cACnML2T1_DC21jA58Ttm2KiX8IXemmj5VvU8ug&id=7cKojsLDqP5MqnsrwVgI8y6IKjP3Nnful4NzPKSVPus

27 "China proposed 2+1 format for India talks", *The Hindu*, 26 June 2018.

28 Resilient foreign policy means effective bargaining power with India and China on issues related to mutual interests, pro-active role in multilateral organisations like BBIN, BIMSTEC, BRI, SAARC, LDC, LLDC, etc., and look for development related funds and investments beyond China and India without undermining security concerns of China and India and making any compromises with its national interest.

29 Article 51 (M-1&2), Constitution of Nepal 2015.

30 Kuvera Chalise, "Infrastructure development key to propel growth", *Republica roundtable*, *Myrepublica*, Kathmandu, 6 February 2017, available at http://www.myrepublica.com/news/14405/

31 Nihar R Nayak, "What Nepal's Elections Say About Its Foreign Policy", South Asian Voices, hosted by the Stimson Center in Washington, D.C., 12 December 2017.

12

Gilgit-Baltistan and Aksai Chin: Indian Territories under Foreign Occupation

Alok Bansal

Himalayas have traditionally been perceived as a protective wall for India against any aggression from the North. Climatically they protected India from the extreme cold winds that emanate from Siberia. They also provide bulk of fresh water resources to most of North India and Pakistan. They have a huge hydropower potential and are also rich in minerals and other natural resources. There is, therefore, no doubt that Himalayas have a great geostrategic significance as far as Indians are concerned. Despite its salience, there is a general ignorance about the region amongst common public, especially about the regions that have not been under the political control of the Indian government.

Historically, the Himalayas were perceived as an impregnable wall that could not be breached. Unfortunately, this myth was rudely shattered, when large swathes of Indian territory were occupied by Pakistan and China in quick succession after Indian independence. Indian territorial claims are based on the perceived extent of the territorial limits of the former princely state of Jammu and Kashmir that was ruled by Maharaja Hari Singh in 1947. This chapter deals with these occupied territories especially the largest chunks under Pakistani and Chinese occupation, namely, Gilgit-Baltistan and Aksai Chin, and is more informatory than analytical.

Although both the territories are constitutionally integral part of India and under foreign occupation, the two cases differ significantly. The region under Chinese occupation, which includes the trans-Karakoram Shaksgam Valley, unilaterally ceded by Pakistan to it in 1963 as part of a boundary settlement, and Aksai Chin and Western Ladakh, militarily occupied by China in 1962, is almost totally devoid of any habitation, and as such needs to be dealt with separately.[1] It would be infructuous to analyse its administration and the treatment of its people as there are virtually none. Moreover, China does not claim Jammu and Kashmir but only a part of it and its dispute with India is a border dispute not a territorial one. On the other hand, both India and Pakistan, claim the entire state as their integral part, although Pakistan has bequeathed a part under its occupation to China in 1963. More significantly, since the Simla Accord of 1972, the Line of Control (LoC) between India and Pakistan from International Border to Point NJ 9842 has been clearly delineated on map and demarcated on ground. On the other hand, Line of Actual Control (LAC) between Indian and Chinese positions in Jammu and Kashmir has neither been delineated on map, nor demarcated on ground.

In subsequent paragraphs, the territories under Pakistani and Chinese Control in general and Gilgit-Baltistan and Aksai Chin in particular, have been covered.

Territory under Pakistan's Occupation

In 1947, when Maharaja Hari Singh, the ruler of princely state of Jammu and Kashmir was deciding which of the two dominions he should accede to, Pakistan virtually forced his hand by unleashing tribal militia led by Pakistani army officers to invade the State. On 20 October 1947, armed Pathan tribesmen backed by Pakistani troops, crossed the border from North Western Pakistan.[1] Initially, they enjoyed considerable success as many Muslims from the Maharaja's army who had been subverted by a carefully planted propaganda blitz by Pakistan, deserted their posts and joined the tribesmen. By end October, they were within striking distance of Srinagar.[2]

Maharaja, threatened by the advancing raiders, quickly acceded to India, and the Indian Army landed just in time to save Srinagar, the capital of the state. Subsequently, Pakistan's army openly entered the arena in support of 'tribal raiders' many of who were in any case former soldiers or soldiers on leave. Pakistan also succeeded in instigating a small section of State Forces, to revolt and join the raiders. Consequently, the pace of liberating the territory that had been captured was slow in areas where the enemy had dug in. Meanwhile, India, conscious of its 'superior' moral and legal position, approached United Nations (UN), against Pakistan's aggression. The UN brokered a ceasefire, which came into effect on 1 January 1949, and wanted Pakistan to ensure complete withdrawal of its troops and 'tribal raiders' from Jammu and Kashmir. However, Pakistan to this date has refused to do so; consequently, the territory of Jammu and Kashmir under the illegal occupation of Pakistan constitutes Pakistan occupied Jammu and Kashmir (POJK).

Pakistan for its own vested interests has divided POJK in two parts, Mirpur Muzaffarabad, which it calls 'Azad' (independent) Jammu and Kashmir ('AJK') and Gilgit-Baltistan, which till 2009, was called The Northern Areas. 'AJK', which has less than 15 per cent of the territory of POJK, has been given a facade of an independent state. Consequently, it has its own 'President,' 'Prime Minister,' 'Supreme Court' and all other vestiges of state. However, the government in AJK changes, every time there is a change of government in Pakistan.

Gilgit-Baltistan

Gilgit-Baltistan constitutes over 85 per cent of the territory of POJK and till 2009 was virtually treated as a colony of Pakistan, where citizens hardly enjoyed any democratic rights. The sparsely populated region has a rich pre-Islamic culture and vast cultural and linguistic diversity. The region historically evolved as two separate entities and the two were administered separately till 1947. Gilgit region was historically known as Dardistan, the land of Dards, or people speaking Dardic Languages, which are part of Indo Aryan group of languages.[3] The region in 1947 was divided into Gilgit Agency, which comprised of territory on the Right Bank of Indus, and Gilgit Wazarat, which comprised of the territory on the Left Bank of Indus. While Gilgit Wazarat was directly ruled by the Maharaja, his control over Gilgit Agency was notional, whose day-to-day administration was being taken care of by the British. However, the modicum of Maharaja's rule was maintained by flying his flag at the Agency Headquarters and other government buildings, as well as by granting holiday on his birthday. The only real power exercised by the Maharaja over the Agency, was granting of mining leases in this resource rich region.

Baltistan, or the land of Baltis, was an independent state, till it fell under the suzerainty of Mughals. Unlike Gilgit, in 1947, it was part of Ladakh Wazarat, under the direct administrative control of a Wazir-e-Wazarat (Governor) appointed by the Maharaja. The governor shifted his office between Skardu, Leh and Kargil. The region had become part of the Dogra Empire in 1840, much before Kashmir Valley or Gilgit came under its sway. Baltis unlike Dards, are Mongoloids and speak Balti, a language of the Tibetan group.[4] Pakistan's illegal occupation of Gilgit and Baltistan has brought these two disparate regions under one administrative entity. There were also numerous princely states in the region, who had accepted Maharaja's suzerainty and paid tribute to him as well as received subsidy from Maharaja to run their administration. While, these rulers periodically travelled to Srinagar to pay tribute to the Maharaja, their routine interaction was with Wazir-e-Wazarat in Ladakh and the British Governor at Gilgit.

Since 1947, the region has been treated by Pakistan's rulers as a virtual colony. Local residents were denied any role in their own governance and were governed under barbaric Frontier Crimes Regulation (FCR), enacted by the colonial masters to subdue recalcitrant tribes in Federally Administered Tribal Areas (FATA). Even the historical identity of the region was diluted by naming the region as 'The Northern Areas'. Till 1967, an official sitting in Karachi, thousands of miles away from Gilgit-Baltistan, lorded over the destiny of its residents. To compound matters, Pakistan gave away 5180 km^2 of its territory to China as part of Sino-Pak Agreement on 2 March 1963. In 1967 Pakistan created a post of 'Resident' based in Gilgit and in 1969 for the first time a local elected body 'Northern Areas Advisory Council' was established, with purely advisory functions. In 1971, India managed to retake approximately 804 km^2 of territory in Gilgit-Baltistan. This was followed up with firm military actions to prevent Pakistan from occupying the glacier region in 1984. Pakistan perceives that India captured 3000 km^2 of territory in the region.[5]

Northern Areas Advisory Council initially transformed into Northern Areas Council and finally into Northern Areas Legislative Council (NALC) by 1999. However, all these bodies remained mostly advisory with extremely limited legislative power.[6] Growing pressure from the local population, eventually forced Pakistan to grant them a modicum of self-governance and Gilgit-Baltistan (Empowerment and Self-Governance) Order-2009 was promulgated by the then Pakistani President Asif Ali Zardari. The order renamed the region as Gilgit-Baltistan, a long-standing demand of the residents. It also gave the region its own Chief Minister, Governor and Judiciary. However, all these organs were in reality powerless and the real power remained with Islamabad. More significantly, by giving the region structures similar to a Pakistani province, Islamabad has attempted to amalgamate this region into Pakistan.[7] Finally, in 2018, Pakistan introduced Gilgit-Baltistan Order 2018, superseding the 2009 order, even though the Supreme Appellate Court of Gilgit-Baltistan had struck it down.[8] With the implementation of G-B Order 2018, Pakistan has converted this region in to a de-facto Pakistani province.

The mountainous landmass of slightly less than 73,000 km^2, which straddles parts of Karakoram, Hindu Kush and Himalayan ranges, is home to the longest glaciers outside the polar region and some of the tallest peaks in the world, including K2, the second highest peak in the world. Presently, the region is divided administratively, into three Divisions, namely, Gilgit, Diamer and Baltistan. These are further subdivided into ten districts. Gilgit division comprises four districts namely Gilgit, Ghizer, Hunza and Nagar, whereas Diamer Division has two districts Diamer and Astore. Baltistan Division consists of Skardu, Shigar, Kharmang and Ganche districts. GB is surrounded by Uyghur Autonomous Region of Xinjiang, Wakhan Corridor of Afghanistan, Chitral and Kohistan districts of Khyber Pakhtunkhwa (KP), and other parts of former Jammu and Kashmir State. The region is also home to the world's second highest plateau, the Deosai plains, with an area of 5000 km^2. The climate of the region is very diverse with many rain shadow areas. Gilgit and Chilas towns are hot in summers while cold in winters, while valleys of Astore, Khaplu, Yasin, Hunza and Nagar are even cold in summers. Eastern regions of Himalayas are moist but western regions of Karakoram are dry. Most valleys have desert like climate.[9]

The region has enormous ethnolinguistic diversities. In Dardistan, where people are racially Aryans, the population has traditionally been divided into four castes Shins, Yeshkuns, Kamins and Doms. Shins are the elites and Yeshkuns are landowners, Kamins on the other hand are low caste tenants and craftsmen, whereas Doms are musicians and blacksmiths.[10] They speak various Indo-Iranian languages like Shina, Khowar, Wakhi, Domaaki and Kohistani, which are interrelated and belong to Dardic group of languages. In addition Burushaski, a language isolate, is also spoken in Yasin, Hunza and Nagar Valley of Gilgit region.[11] All these languages are without standard scripts and are spoken by very small groups of people. On the other hand, people in Baltistan, who belong to Tibeto-Mongoloid stock speak Balti, a dialect of Ladakhi, a language of Tibetan group, which originally had a Tibetan script, which has since been replaced by Persian script.[12] The population is Islamic but with varying sectarian orientations which imbibe pre-Islamic customs and beliefs. In Hunza Ismaili beliefs are prevalent, in Nagar and Eastern Gilgit people follow twelver Shia Islam. Down South, near Shinkari, people follows Sunni Islam. In Baltistan, most people are Twelver Shias while a minority adhere to Nurbakshi Sect, who consider themselves distinct from both Shias and Sunnis and inhabit North and South-Eastern part of Baltistan.[13]

There has been huge discontentment in Gilgit-Baltistan against Pakistan's rule. People have accordingly been protesting against it for decades. The main cause of discontent is the absence of political rights, where the local residents for decades had no institutions of self-governance and even today the elected representatives have no real power. More significantly, for contesting the elections, one has to profess unflinching loyalty to Pakistan. To compound matters, Islamabad has been trying to change the demography of this strategic region. State Subject Rule, which was imposed by the Maharaja of Jammu and Kashmir to prevent outsiders from becoming naturalised citizens of the state, was abrogated in 1974 for Gilgit-Baltistan by Zulfiqar Ali Bhutto, which opened the floodgates for outsiders to move into this pristine region. Consequent change in demography has also affected the delicate sectarian balance as the number of Sunni members in the Legislative Assembly has increased significantly.[14]

General Zia-ul-Haq who usurped power from Bhutto, introduced and promoted Sunni Deobandi Islam in this Shia majority region, which has led to sectarian tensions. Construction of Karakoram Highway made this region accessible and brought in Sunni extremist outfits like Sipha-e-Sahaba, which tried to impose their radical ideology in the region, which was opposed by the Shias, both Twelvers and Ismailis; as well as Nurbakhshis. This culminated in Shia-Sunni and Shia-Nurbakhshi riots in Skardu, leading to grave sectarian polarisation. The realisation that the Pakistani State was supporting these Sunni outfits, led Shias to come out in large numbers to violently protest in Gilgit in May 1988. The fact that Shias celebrated Eid, while Sunnis were still fasting led to a major riot[15] In retaliation Sunni tribesmen from Khyber Pakhtunkhwa[16] and FATA descended on the region and burnt homes and crops and killed hundreds of Shias.[17] Since then sectarian riots have become a regular feature with Shias at the receiving end. Whenever the local residents demanded self-governance, the riots were engineered to divide them.[18]

During Kargil War, Lashkar-e-Taiba was given a free hand in the region by Pakistan's military establishment, which exposed the region to its rabidly anti-Shia ideology and resulted in greater polarisation and hardening of positions. In 2003-04, Shias objected to the contents of Urdu and *Islamiyat* text books as being contrary to their religious beliefs. Popular discontentment forced the authorities to close all educational institutions for one full academic year till April 2005, and open them only after all controversial portions had been removed. Imam Aga Syed Ziauddin Rizvi, the local Shia cleric, who helped the authorities to resolve the issue, was shot by Sunni extremists in Gilgit on 8 January 2005. He finally succumbed to his injuries and his death led to riots that continued for weeks and thereafter kept erupting from time to time. The riots even claimed the life of the Inspector General of Police, the senior most police officer of Gilgit-Baltistan.[19]

The sectarian violence has continued unabated since then, and buses plying on Karakoram Highway and specifically the Shia passengers in them have been attacked regularly. In September 2009 a bus carrying Shias from Baltistan was torched by Sunnis. On 28 February 2012 unidentified gunmen forced passengers to disembark from four Gilgit bound buses and killed 18 Shia passengers. In August 2012, 25 Shia passengers were pulled out from three buses and shot, with Tehrik-e-Taliban taking responsibility for the killing. In 2013 terrorists from Junood ul Haifa a new wing of Tehrik-e-Taliban Pakistan (TTP) killed 10 foreign tourists and their local Shia cook at the base camp of Nanga Parbat at an altitude of 4,200m. The growing footprint of TTP in the region has further aggravated the sectarian faultlines.[20]

The local population in Gilgit-Baltistan has been protesting against Pakistan's occupation for last few decades, however, it has failed to receive the requisite support from the Indian government or the international community. Even the Indian public is generally unaware of the sufferings of these people, who are constitutionally and legally citizens of India. The reasons for their alienation are many, which stem from lack of representation in various organs of the government, absence of self-governance, ethnic and sectarian marginalisation to economic exploitation. However, the most significant reason for their discontentment is the belief that their unique cultural and linguistic identity is getting extinguished under the sustained onslaught of radical Islamist forces. People perceive that Pakistani authorities are deliberately trying to obliterate their ethno-linguistic and cultural identity.

It is essential that Indians know about the sufferings of these people and their unique and rich pre-Islamic culture and languages, which has withstood the onslaught of time. The population of Gilgit-Baltistan looks towards the government of India and its masses to provide them moral support in their quest for political rights and freedom from Pakistan's brutal and oppressive rule.

Territory under China's Occupation

The territory of Jammu and Kashmir that has been under Chinese occupation comprises those territories that were directly controlled by Maharaja of Jammu and Kashmir in 1947, or paid taxes to him or his vassal, Mir of Hunza. These include Aksai Chin, Trans Karakoram Tracts, that comprise of Shaksgam Valley, Raskam or Yarkand River Valley and Taghdumbash Pamir, and the Principality of Minsar. There is an all-pervasive ignorance about all these regions in Indian consciousness. Unlike the territory under Pakistan's occupation it is not feasible to specify the exact area that is under Chinese control, as the Line of Control has not been exactly demarcated. As the region, with the exception of Minsar and some villages in Taghdumbash Pamir, is virtually uninhabited, there are no developments that draw media attention apart from 'military incursions' in Aksai Chin.

Minsar, a village located in a broad valley in western Tibet, 32 miles west of Mount Kailash has been part of the kingdom of Jammu and Kashmir for centuries. The revenue received from it was used to maintain Kailash Manasarovar pilgrimage and had been ceded to the king of Ladakh under a peace treaty signed between Ladakh and Tibet in Tingmosgang in 1684, which stated, "The King of Ladakh reserves to himself the village of Minsar in Ngari-Khor-sum (western Tibet)."[21] When Ladakh was incorporated in Maharaja Gulab Singh's kingdom, it became part of Jammu Kashmir State. Maharaja Hari Singh's accession made it Indian Territory. In 1865, WH Johnson, a civil servant with the Survey of India proposed the "Johnson Line," to mark India's borders with China. He talks about Minsar village in Tibet as located beyond Rudok and Gartok at Latitude 31°10' North Longitude 80°50' East. Annual revenue from Minsar was Rs 500.[22] After independence, in 1950, a special officer, N. Rigzen Ghagil Kalon, was deputed by Jammu and Kashmir State to visit Minsar. His report was forwarded by the Jammu and Kashmir Government to the Ministry of States on 13 September 1950, as 'Note on Conditions of Kashmir Village in Minsar in western Tibet,' wherein he reported that the total population of Minsar was 271. The revenue from the village was collected till 1950s. Minsar was not discussed during India China talks from 1954 to 1962, but regrettably remains under Chinese occupation.[23] At present the village is called Men-Shi and is located at the southern end of Gar (Gartok) on national highway 219 in Ngari prefecture. The nearest Indian territories are Malari and Niti Pass in Uttarakhand.

Of Trans-Karakoram tracts, Raskam Valley and Taghdumbash Pamir were the regions from where revenue was collected by the Mir of Hunza (the ruler of Hunza) and were consequently, included within the boundaries of Jammu and Kashmir as per Johnson Line. Taghdumbash lies to the north of the Hindu Kush and was connected to Hunza through Kilik and Mintaka passes.[24]

However, the status of Hunza was a complex one as it paid tribute both to Jammu and Kashmir, as well as the Chinese Emperor. In March 1899, the British through a note from Sir Claude Maxwell MacDonald, who was the British Minister to the Empire of China based in Peking (Beijing), formally proposed that China relinquishes suzerainty over Hunza and, in turn, Hunza gives up most of the Taghdumbash Pamir and Raskam Valley. Chinese silence was assumed by the British as acquiescence and consequently, Johnson-Ardagh Line, which redefined the borders of Jammu and Kashmir, did not include Raskam Valley or Taghdumbash Pamir into it. However, nomadic tribes continued to move their cattle flocks for grazing within the region and kept paying tribute to the Mir of Hunza till 1937. Only significant settlement in the region was the village of Dafdar, inhabited primarily by Wakhis at an altitude of 3400 m in the heart of the Taghdumbash Pamir.[25] It is currently part of Tashkurgan Tajik Autonomous County in Kashgar Prefecture of Xinjiang. The exact circumstances under which the people from this region stopped paying tribute to Hunza is not quite clear.

From 1899 till 1947, when India attained independence, depiction of border on various maps varied. In 1926, renowned British geographer Kenneth Mason surveyed Shaksgam Valley, which was south of MacDonald Line. Apparently, British Indian Government relinquished claims to areas north of MacDonald line in this sector in 1927, although this is not reflected in the maps published in that period. Although, the Government of India, now does not claim Raskam Valley or Taghdumbash, it is not clear as to when this position was arrived at, because Jawaharlal Nehru in a telegram to British PM Clement Attlee on 26 October 1947 stated that "Jammu and Kashmir's Northern frontiers, as you are aware, run in common with those of three countries, Afghanistan, the Union of Soviet Socialist Republics and China".[26] This implies that he considered Taghdumbash to be part of Jammu and Kashmir.

After the 1962 Sino-Indian conflict, the convergence of Chinese and Pakistani positions resulted in Pakistan handing over Shaksgam Valley to China. On 2 March 1963, Zulfiqar Ali Bhutto and Cheng Li signed a provisional agreement in Beijing to allow China to occupy Shaksgam, Raskam, Shimshal and Aghil valleys of Gilgit Baltistan.[27]China gained approximately 5309 square kilometres of territory in Shaksgam Valley, while China relinquished its claims over Hunza. The agreement was primarily an outcome of Sino-Indian conflict. The actual demarcation work was eventually completed in March 1965.[28]

Aksai Chin

The most significant part of the territory under Chinese control is Aksai Chin and most Indians consider it to be the only part of India under Chinese occupation. The area of this extremely inhospitable region is approximately 37,244 km^2. The region is separated from Tarim Basin in Xinjiang by Kunlun Mountain ranges. The elevation of this high altitude desert varies from 4,300 m at the bed of Karakash River to 7,000 m. The western part of Aksai Chin region is drained by the Tarim River. The region as a whole receives little precipitation as the Himalayas and Karakoram block the rains from the Indian monsoon. Karakash River, which originates at an altitude of over 5,800 m, northeast of Galwan Kangri peak in the Aksai Chin region, is the most significant river originating in the region. It flows northwards and then westwards to cross Indian borders South of Xaidullah. After 740 km, the river joins Yurungkash River, which also originates in Aksai Chin; and the combined river is known as Hotan River, which flows into Tarim River. Karakash and Yurungkash Rivers are also known as Black Jade and White Jade Rivers as they carry jade boulders. Karakash river bed is the only part of this region, where some vegetation appears periodically. Another river that originates in the region is Chip Chap River, which flows westward to join Shyok River in Ladakh.

The eastern part of the region contains several small endorheic basins and contains many soda and salt water lakes. The largest salt water lake is Aksai Chin Lake, which is fed by a river of the same name. Other salt water lakes in the region are Surigh yil ganning kol, Tso tang and Hongshan hu. Much of the northern part of Aksai Chin is referred to as the Soda Plains.[29] The region is covered with soda and has frequent soda dust storms, which make habitation even more difficult.[30]

Historically, the region was the eastern part of Ladakh, located in the north-western part of the Tibetan plateau and south of Kunlun Mountains. It was not part of any ancient empire, as owing to its elevation it was considered unsuitable for habitation. However, in due course the region became a transit zone for traders and hosted two flourishing trade routes connecting Lhasa (in Tibet), Leh (in India) and Kashgar (in China), through which caravans of Yaks passed in summer months. Historically, armies tend to tread the routes taken by trade caravans and consequently, the region was also transited by various armies moving to/from Xinjiang or Tibet. The growing significance of the region, due to its trade routes led to contestation between Tibet and Ladakh over this crucial region. After numerous conflicts between the two, Treaty of Tingmosang was signed, which delineated the border between the two states and placed this region, within the territory of Ladakh. However, despite being part of the territory of Ladakh's ruler, no attempt was made to occupy it, considering the hostile terrain and climatic conditions. Consequently the Dzungar Khanate used it to attack Tibet in 1717, as this was the only route from Tarim Basin to Tibet that was passable all year round.

As Ladakh came under the sway of Maharaja Gulab Singh, he inherited its boundaries with Tibet. In 1842, in a treaty signed between Gulab Singh and Tibetans, they both agreed to stick to old agreed boundaries.[31] After the East India Company defeated the Sikh empire, by Treaty of Amritsar in 1846, the British recognised Gulab Singh, as Maharaja of Jammu and Kashmir. Since Gulab Singh had already accepted British paramountcy, the border between Kashmir and Tibet became a matter of negotiation between the British and the Chinese. Within three months ofTreaty of Amritsar, British constituted a commission to delineate the eastern boundaries of Jammu and Kashmir with Tibet. The British had accordingly asked the Maharaja to depute two intelligent officers to work with the officers of the boundary commission. The two boundary commissions of 1846 and 1847 failed to get the cooperation of

Chinese officials. The commission clearly placed Chang Chenmo Valley well within Ladakh and Lanak La at the eastern extremity as part of Kashmir.[32]

The survey work in Kashmir to determine India's boundary began in 1855 and WH Johnson a civilian sub-assistant to Major Montgomery was assigned the task to survey the North Eastern Ladakh. He remained in Ladakh in 1865, at a time when Chinese rule over Xinjiang had totally collapsed and a new state of Kashgaria had emerged. However, by 1877, China had reconquered Kashgaria, which was afflicted by frequent internecine wars. Initially after the conquest of Kashgar, Chinese treated Kunlun Mountains as their southern boundary, but subsequently, moved further southward. In 1890, Captain Younghusband, who had gone to Pamirs, was told that Karakoram Mountains constituted China's southern boundary. To further assert their claim Chinese unilaterally established boundary markers at Karakoram Pass in 1892, however, it was not objected to by the British. Keith Johnston's Atlas of 1894, clearly showed Aksai Chin within India. This showed the boundary of Ladakh as running along Kunlun Mountains to a point east of 80° East and was similar to Johnson's position. However, in 1896, there were some protests from Chinese authorities about depiction of Aksai Chin as part of Kashmir.[33]

The areas up to the frontiers were regularly administered, right from the time State of Jammu and Kashmir was established. The check posts on the trade routes were marked on the maps from 1865 onwards. Till 1901, the state authorities included the territory in the Wazarat of the Frontier District. It was later divided into the wazarat of Gilgit and Ladakh. The tehsils of Skardu, Kargil and Ladakh formed the Wazarat of Ladakh and Aksai Chin and Chang Chenmo valley were parts of the ilaqa of Tankse in Ladakh tehsil.[34]

The white paper of the Ministry of External Affairs documents the revenue collection by the Maharaja's administration:

> The arrangements made by the Governments of India and Kashmir for the establishment and maintenance of trade routes across Aksai Chin, the provision of facilities such as rest houses and store houses for those using these routes and the regular use of these routes as of right by Indian trading parties—both official and unofficial—constituted powerful evidence of Indian administrative jurisdiction in the 19th century up to the traditional boundary claimed by India. The very fact that there were never any disputes about the exercise of such jurisdiction and the use of these routes by Indians as of right showed that there could have been no difference of opinion in

those times between the Ladakhis on the one hand and the authorities of Sinkiang and Tibet on the other as to where the boundary lay.

In 1866, on receipt of complaints that trade with Yarkand was suffering due to excessive duties levied by the Kashmir Government, the Government of India entered into negotiations with the Government of Kashmir for developing a new route from Chushul along the Pangong lake and across Lingzi Tang and Aksai Chin to Shahidulla, and creating other facilities. In May 1870, the two parties signed an agreement. Article 1 of this treaty stated:

"With the consent of the Maharaja, officers of the British Government will be appointed to survey the trade routes through the Maharaja's territories from the British frontier of Lahoul to the territories of the Ruler of Yarkhand, including the route via the Chang Chemoo Valley. The Maharaja will depute an officer of his Government to accompany the surveyors, and will render them all the assistance in his power. A map of the routes surveyed will be made an attested copy of which will be given to the Maharaja".[35]

Further revenue records and maps prove that the area was administered by the Maharaja of Jammu and Kashmir:

> Mangal Mehta, wazir of Ladakh during 1860-65, organized the revenue settlement of the whole area. In the regular revenue assessment reports the names of areas and villages and the amount of revenue collected from each of them, which is now claimed by China as having been under their administrative jurisdiction for centuries, were included. The report of 1908 mentioned 108 villages including Tankse, Demchok and Minsar and mentions Aksai Chin, Lingzi Tang where rights of pastures and salt collection were exercised, as parts of Tankse ilaqa. The preliminary report of Ladakh settlement outlined a revenue and political history of these areas. The boundary question found direct and indirect mention in these reports. The assessment report of Ladakh tehsil of 1909 stated, 'There have been no boundary disputes on the Lhasa frontiers and the existing boundary seems to be well understood by the subjects of both the state and the Lhasa Government'.[36]

The India–China border problem has a colonial legacy. The British drew different lines to denote the limits of the empire on various maps at different times, depending on their perception and suitability. The boundaries were never demarcated physically and remained only on the map. The three boundary lines were Johnson Line (1865), Johnson-Ardagh Line (1897), and Macartney-Macdonald Line (1899).

Johnson Line: As brought out earlier William Johnson, a civil servant with the Survey of India, proposed the "Johnson Line" in 1865, which put Aksai Chin in Kashmir. This was the time of the Dungon revolt when China did not control most of Xinxiang, so this Line was never presented to the Chinese. Johnson presented this Line to the Maharaja of Jammu and Kashmir, who then claimed the territory further north as far as Sanju Pass in the Kunlun Mountains. He had already established a fort at Shahidulla and had positioned his troops there by 1864. However, extremely inhospitable conditions forced Maharaja's troops to vacate Shahidulla by 1867. The boundary of Ladakh according to Johnson Line (boundary drawn by Johnson on map) included all the territory between Karkoram Pass and Kunlun mountains. The first edition of Survey of India Maps of Turkistan also clearly followed Johnson Line.[37] There is clear evidence to indicate that even besides the troops, civilian custom officials of Maharaja were present at Shahidulla till November 1866.[38] Even in 1889, when Russian explorer Captain Grombtchevsky visited Shahidulla, he expected it to be occupied by Kashmiri troops. He was, however, informed that Kashmiri troops had withdrawn because Chinese had prohibited export of provisions from Sanju and Kilian. After their withdrawal, Chinese came to Shahidulla and arrested 'Beg' appointed by Chinese and replaced him with a new Beg and left.[39]

Johnson-Ardagh Line: In 1897, a British military officer, Sir John Ardagh, proposed a boundary line along the crest of the Kunlun Mountains, north of the Yarkand River.[40] At the time, Britain was concerned at the prospects of Russian expansion as China weakened; Ardagh argued that this line was more defensible. The Ardagh Line was really a modification of the Johnson Line, and became known as the "Johnson-Ardagh Line."

Macartney-MacDonald Line: In 1893, Hung Ta-chen, a senior Chinese official at St. Petersburg, gave maps of the region to George Macartney, British consul general at Kashgar, which coincided in broad details with the Johnson Line. In 1899, London proposed a revised boundary, initially suggested by Macartney and developed by the Governor General of India, Lord Elgin. This boundary placed the Lingzi Tang plains which are south of the Laktsang range in India, and Aksai Chin proper which is north of the Laktsang range in China. This border, along the Karakoram Mountains, was proposed and supported by British officials primarily to create a Chinese buffer to prevent Russia's advance in Central Asia. Macartney-MacDonald Line was presented to the Chinese in Peking (Beijing) by Sir Claude MacDonald on 24 March 1899 in a note by Sir Claude MacDonald. The Qing government did not respond to the note, and the British took that as Chinese acquiescence. Although no official boundary had ever been negotiated, China believed that this had been the accepted boundary since 1949 when the People's Republic of China was established.

The Johnson-Ardagh and Macartney-MacDonald Lines were both used on British maps of India. Until at least 1908, the British took the MacDonald Line as the boundary, but in 1911, the Xinhai Revolution resulted in the collapse of central power in China and by the end of World War I, the British officially used the Johnson Line. From 1917 to 1933, the Postal Atlas of China, published by the Government of China in Peking, depicted the boundary in Aksai Chin as per the Johnson Line, which runs along the Kunlun Mountains. The Peking University Atlas, published in 1925, also put Aksai Chin in India. When British officials learned that Soviet officials were surveying Aksai Chin for Sheng Shicai, the warlord of Xinjiang in 1940–41, they again advocated the Johnson Line.

At independence, the Government of India used the Johnson-Ardagh Line as the basis for its official boundary in the west, which included Aksai Chin. From the Karakoram Pass (which is not under dispute), the Indian claim line extends northeast of the Karakoram Mountains through the salt flats of Aksai Chin to set a boundary at the Kunlun Mountains, and incorporating part of the Karakash and Yarkand River watersheds. From there, it runs east along the Kunlun Mountains before turning southwest through the Aksai Chin salt flats, through the Karakoram range, and then to Pangong Lake. On 1 July 1954, Prime Minister Jawaharlal Nehru wrote a memo directing revision of maps of India to show definite boundaries on all frontiers. Hitherto, the boundary in Aksai Chin sector, based on the Johnson Line, had been described as "undemarcated."

China occupied this region by building China Highway 219 linking Lazi in Tibet Autonomous Region to Xinxiang between 1951 and 1957. On 6 October 1957, a Chinese newspaper, *Kuang-Ming Jih Pao*, reported, "The Sinkiang-Tibet—the highest highway in the world—has been completed." The region had a flourishing trade in 1953, with Tibetan traders carrying tea, incense and veils for sale in Leh, returning with soap, cigarettes, sugar and dried fruit, while traders from Leh carried wheat, flour, barley and eggs to

Tibet and returned with wool and silver coins. The trade route ran from Khotan (Hotan) to Sugat Karaul and Shahidulla Mazar and then to Kargilik and Kashgar, while another route passed through Karakoram Pass and the Depsang plain. This is clearly a very strategic territory. Trade ended with the construction of the Aksai Chin highway.[41]

When news about China's construction of a highway (Karakoram) became public, Nehru instructed the foreign secretary to lodge an informal protest with the Chinese Embassy. On 18 October 1958, the Indian foreign secretary handed over an 'informal note' to the Chinese ambassador in New Delhi.[42] But it was only in August 1959 that Nehru dropped the bombshell in Parliament: *The 'Tibet-Sinkiang highway' had been built through Indian territory.* Sino-Indian Conflict of 1962, allowed the Chinese to advance further in the region. Consequently, today most of Aksai Chin is under Chinese occupation and is administered as part of Hotan County, which lies in the South-eastern part of Hotan Prefecture of Xinjiang Autonomous Region. The region is largely uninhabited with the exception of divided village of Demchok,[43] where Chinese have built some modern buildings to woo citizens of border villages. In addition PLA has built two military stations on Highway 219 (Aksai Chin Road) at Tianshuihai village at an elevation of 4890m and Tielongtan. At both the places some hotels and gas stations have come up and they act as transit halts for people travelling along the highway. Nomadic tribes still go graze in the region, however, the movement of graziers from Indian part has over the years stopped as Indian security forces do not allow them to cross their perceived Line of Actual Control.

Conclusion

Gilgit-Baltistan and Aksai Chin represent the most significant parts of Indian territories under foreign occupation. Both straddle significant trade routes and are strategically significant. Regrettably, despite various parliamentary resolutions, the Indian government has not taken any steps to apprise the Indian citizens about these regions, leave aside making any plans for restoring Indian sovereignty. Although the resolution of territorial disputes with China and Pakistan in the future looks unlikely, awareness about them is absolutely essential.

Indians need to be aware of developments there; institutions must be set up to study the region, so that these regions do not disappear from Indian consciousness. This chapter is an attempt to incite inquisitiveness amongst readers, as many in India appear satisfied with status quo and at times even appear willing to relinquish their claims over these significant Indian territories.

NOTES

1 BG Verghese, "A Jammu and Kashmir Primer: From Myth to Reality," Centre for Policy Research, New Delhi, Occasional Paper No. 14, p. 4.
2 Mary Anne Weaver, *Pakistan: In the Shadow of Jihad and Afghanistan*, New York: Farrar, Straus and Giroux, 2002, pp. 251–52.
3 Owen Bennett Jones, No. 11, p. 64.
4 P Stobdan, "Gilgit and Baltistan: The Historical Dimension", in Virendra Gupta and Alok Bansal (ed), *Pakistan Occupied Kashmir: The Untold Story*. New Delhi: Manas Publications, 2007, p. 30.
5 Ibid., pp. 41–43.
6 Alok Bansal, *Gilgit-Baltistan and its Saga of Unending Human Rights Violations,* New Delhi: Pentagon Press LLP, 2018, pp. 80–89.
7 Ibid., pp. 85–90.
8 Ibid., pp. 100–101.
9 Ibid., p. 103.
10 Ibid., 29–33.
11 Karl Jettmar, *Bolor & Dardistan*, Islamabad: National Institute of Folk Heritage, 1980, pp. 35–41.
12 Stephen Philip Cohen, *The Idea of Pakistan*, New Delhi: Oxford University Press, 2005, p. 209.
13 Tariq Rahman, *Languages and Politics in Pakistan*, Karachi: Oxford University Press, 1998, pp. 217–222.
14 Karl Jettmar, op.cit., pp. 55–64.
15 Senge H Sering, "Political Dynamics of Culture and Identity in Baltistan," in K Warikoo (ed), *The Other Kashmir: Society, Culture and Politics in the Karakoram Himalayas*, New Delhi: Pentagon Press, 2014, pp. 73–74.
16 Alok Bansal, "Sectarian Violence in Gilgit-Baltistan", in Mohammad Monir Alam (ed), *Pakistan Occupied Kashmir: Internal Dynamics and Externalities*, New Delhi: Academic Publications, 2015, pp. 58–59.
17 Khyber Pakhtunkhwa was then called North West Frontier Province (NWFP).
18 Akbar Hussain Akbar, "Northern Areas (1986-2000)" in Ahmad Hassan Dani, History of Northern Areas of Pakistan (Upto 2000 AD), Lahore: Sang-e-Meel Publications, 2007, p. 430.
19 Samuel Baid, "Northern Areas" in Jasjit Singh (ed.) Pakistan Occupied Kashmir: Under the Jackboot, New Delhi: Siddhi Books, 1995, p. 139.
20 Alok Bansal (2015), op. cit., pp. 60–62.
21 Alok Bansal (2018), op. cit., pp. 119–127.
22 "The Sino-Indian Boundary", New Delhi: The Indian Society of International Law, 1962, pp. 1-2.
23 Hriday Nath Kaul, *India China Boundary in Kashmir*. New Delhi: Gyan Publishing House, 2009, pp. 72–74.

24 Claude Arpi, "Indian Village in Tibet," available at https://www.rediff.com/news/special/the-indian-village-in-tibet/20180213.htm, accessed on 30 Dec 2018)

25 Hriday Nath Kaul, *India China Boundary in Kashmir*, New Delhi: Gyan Publishing House, 2009, p. 152.

26 Hermann Kreutzmann, "Ethnic minorities and marginality in the Pamirian Knot: Survival of Wakhi and Kirghiz in a harsh environment and global contexts," *The Geographical Journal*, Vol. 169, No. 3, September 2003, p. 224.

27 Excerpts of telegram from Jawaharlal Nehru to the British Prime Minister, Clement Attlee, available at https://www.mtholyoke.edu/acad/intrel/kasnehru.htm, accessed on 28 December 2018.

28 The Boundary Agreement between China and Pakistan, 1963, available at http://people.unica.it/annamariabaldussi/files/2015/04/China-Pakistan-1963.pdf, accessed on 28 December 2018.

29 M Taylor Fravel, *Strong Borders Secure Nation: Cooperation and Conflict in China's Territorial Disputes*, Princeton: Princeton University Press, 2008, pp. 116–117.

30 "Disputed Indian Borders" available at https://disputedindia.weebly.com/aksai-chin.html, accessed on 28 December 2018.

31 Hriday Nath Kaul, *op. cit.*, p. 110.

32 Ibid., pp. 37–38

33 Arun Kumar Banerji, "Borders", in Jayanta Kumar Ray (ed) *Aspects of India's International Relations 1700 to 2000: South Asia and the World*, New Delhi: Pearson Longman, 2007, pp. 186–89.

34 Ibid., pp. 190–192.

35 Virendra Sahai Verma, "Sino-Indian border dispute at Aksai Chin: A middle path for resolution", May 2010, available at https://chinaindiaborderdispute.files.wordpress.com/2010/07/virendravermapaperborderdispute.pdf, accessed on 28 December 2018.

36 Report of Officials of the Governments of India and Peoples Republic of China on Boundary issue (part 3) Ministry of External Affairs, pp. 7, 8 available at http://www.archieve.claudearpi.net/maintenance/uploaded_pics/OR_Part_3.pdf, accessed on 28 December 2018.

37 Virendra Sahai Verma, op. cit.

38 Arun Kumar Banerji, op. cit., pp. 190-191.

39 Hriday Nath Kaul, op. cit., p. 77.

40 Ibid., p. 219.

41 Woodman, Dorothy, *Himalayan Frontiers: A Political Review of British, Chinese, Indian and Russian Rivalries*, Barrie & Jenkins, 1969, pp. 101 and 360.

42 Claude Arpi, "Nehru's Aksai Chin Blunder," 3 February 2017, available at https://www.rediff.com/news/column/nehrus-aksai-chin-blunder/20170203.htm, accessed on 28 December 2018)

43 Ibid.

44 Demchok is not exactly in Aksai Chin, but for the purpose of this chapter, entire territory under Chinese occupation in Eastern Ladakh has been considered as Aksai Chin.

13

Soft Power Diplomacy: A Legacy to Explore

Sunaina Singh and Shreya Challagalla

Is it better to be feared than loved or loved than feared? This question is at the centre of most discussions on soft power and diplomacy. Niccolo Machiavelli dedicates an entire chapter in 'The Prince' on whether it is better to be feared than loved or loved than feared. He cautions that "friendships that are obtained by payments" are certainly earned but not secure and "cannot be relied upon".[1] He does however indicate a more pragmatic approach and advises that "one should wish to be both", but is careful to point out that since men in general are "ungrateful, fickle, false, cowardly, covetous" it may be "safer to be feared than loved".[2] Machiavelli concludes the chapter by stating that a prince must "endeavour only to avoid hatred".[3] Unlike Machiavelli's advice in 'The Prince', a "soft power" strategy suggests that it is better to be loved than feared.

"Soft power" is a term that entered foreign policy lexicon in 1990 when Harvard Professor Joseph Nye used the term to describe influence through "co-option". Putting it bluntly, Nye said it is soft power when "one country gets other countries to want what it wants".[4] Reflective of the time of his writing, Nye claimed technology, education and economic growth were the significant determinants of power.

Prior to the 1990s, in foreign policy at least, power was understood through a narrow framework of carrots (inducement) and sticks (coercion), excluding attraction. Nye's soft power was a fresh addition to the discourse when he claimed if one were able to attract others, one could maximise on carrots and sticks. The concept was simple: the United States of America, considered the most powerful country in the world in terms of economic and military might, had lost the war to Vietnam in 1975. In 2001, the United States, despite being a superpower, could not prevent the deadly terrorist attacks on 11 September. It was from this line of thought that Nye's concept of "soft power" emerged and then reformed over the years to reflect a more nuanced understanding and also expanded in scope. From being purely "co-optive" in nature, soft power was broadened to include values, culture, sport and information technology among others. In his later writings, Nye identified three main determinants of soft power which are widely acknowledged today. He maintained that "a country's soft power can come from three resources: its culture (in places where it is attractive to others), its political values (when it lives up to them at home and abroad), and its foreign policies (when they are seen as legitimate and having moral authority)".[5] The key to soft power he claimed lies in attraction, admiration and aspiration.

Nye's definition is, however, problematic as he varies between two accounts of soft power. On the one hand, he says that soft power can be used to change the values of others but fails to identify that values may be changed forecfully or organically.[6] In this context he discusses the example of promoting democracy and yet, if democracy is promoted through the former method, it becomes problematic. On the other hand, Nye claims that a soft power strategy becomes successful only if common and shared values exist. Again, he says a resource such as a political value, in this case democracy, can be used by countries like the United States to attract others, but will only be successful if this value is already shared by others.[7] In the Indian context, it must be stressed that its soft power has grown organically and not by force. Moreover, Indian soft power can trace its roots to its ancient civilisation.

If Nye is credited for formally introducing the term to international relations, India on its part included soft power diplomacy since its ancient civilisation. One need not look far beyond India's shores to witness the Indic civilisation's influence. From the Angkor Wat temples in Cambodia to the popularity of the Ramayana and Mahabharata in Southeast Asia, India's influence spread not by the sword but through traders and travellers, because it was attractive. Along with the Ramayana and Mahabharata, the Panchatantra was equally famous. In Mongolia for example, the Panchatantra tales were narrated for hundreds of years and slowly adapted to suit their local culture.[8] Other Indian texts like the 'Arthashastra' gave the world aphorisms such as "my enemy's enemy is my friend"[9] and scholars like Max Weber considered Machiavelli's 'The Prince', in comparison to the Arthashastra, harmless.[10] India also had an impact on English language with words like ginger, pepper and indigo entering through ancient routes. In medicine too, India's contribution can be seen in Ayurveda, Siddha and Yunani. India's contribution to mathematics cannot be overlooked. Apart from giving the world the zero, India also invented the decimal system and while "the Europeans called the numbers in the decimal system Arabic numerals", the Arabs called them Hindu numerals.[11]

Through the long corridors of over five millennia India has held the unwavering lamp of an uninterrupted civilisational philosophy of resilience, peace and harmony, through its impeccable spiritual and literary traditions. Soft power then, was an inherent part of Indian culture and permeated through all its forms—art, cuisine, dance, literature, music, folk traditions or even respect for elders and gurus, bhakti '*marga*' or '*karma yoga*'—and these expressions of life are driven by the principle of harmony within diversity. These also therefore tend to become the defining canons of 'soft power diplomacy'.

Today, India can count a rich civilisational heritage, spirituality and religion, Indian wisdom and knowledge, a thriving democracy, free media, independent judiciary, civil society, its diverse diaspora, music, dance, cinema and an impressive and influential independence movement among its long list of soft power resources. India embraces its diversity and various religions that converge to become part of Indian culture, all of which have been allowed to be nurtured and flourished, in the tradition of our vidya-gyan, our spiritual sagacity or bhakti tradition, and cultural ethos or even Natya Shastras or Indian aesthetic system, all so well amalgamated in the collective consciousness unveiling the dynamics of Indian soft power.

Bruno Latour, the French philosopher and sociologist had once maintained, "India is a reservoir of alternative interpretations of what the global is and these ways of viewing the world need to be exposed".[12] The various facets of the above illustrations can be markers of soft diplomacy that can focus both on disseminating and putting to use the unfathomable powers of soft culture in international relations. India has an advantage over other countries in terms of its rich cultural heritage but there is a need to learn to formulate a coherent structure of soft diplomacy to explicate our inherent culture, its traditions, and history of managing diversity in its varied alternative interpretations through the centuries to the world.

The general approach could be through intrinsic engagement and well informed exposition of the wealth of both our Vedantic and Buddhist teachings, which focus on harmony, peace and oneness. The art of diplomacy begins with our sages and their Vedantic and Buddhist teachings. Perhaps the best examples to cite for their extraordinary soft power skills in building an integrative, challenging and congruous ethos is the belief to embrace all—Vasudhaiva Kutumbakam—the world is one family. This then is India's candid legacy for in this we hold the ethos of "soft power" much before Nye's definition of "soft power" in 1990.

One name that shines through the Himalayan region in independent India as an example of soft power, is Kushok Bakula Rinpoche, a diplomat, widely acknowledged and admired for his wisdom and gentleness. A son of the Himalayan region, born into Ladakh's royal family, Kushok Bakula Rinpoche was declared a reincarnation of Bakula Arhat at the age of six, and was defined by his erudition, compassion and service to the growth and development of the Ladakh region. Under his vigilant and wise statesmanship, the region gained its identity and grew in stature. If the Himalayas continue to be symbolic of spiritual ascent and quest for enlightenment and peace in India, as also across Asia, it is because of the zealous protection of our sacred sites of temples and monasteries. The credit of not just reviving Buddhism in the region, but also to bind the neighbouring countries with the spread of Buddhist philosophy of 'Ananda Marga' goes entirely to Kushok Bakula Rinpoche. These mythical mountains' spiritual relevance continues to predominate the Indian-Asian psyche to a large extent due to his efforts.

The history of Ladakh transformed in the late 1940s with his policies of ensuring education, security and progress and safeguarding Buddhist monasteries.[13] He worked ceaselessly in the spirit of the Vedic dictum of *bahujana sukhaya bahujana hitaya*, a dictum that Buddha preached to his disciples—to work for the happiness and welfare of all. Bakula Rinpoche also worked towards another dictum that is reminiscent of Swami Vivekananda, a tall example of Indian soft power, through his propagation of *atmano mokshartham jagat hitaya cha*, a Rig Vedic sloka, meaning, to work towards the salvation of the self and for the well being of all on earth.

Bakula Rinpoche's earliest realisation was an understanding that politics is essential for any contribution towards welfare of his people. He showed through his statesmanship, how 'karma' could be governed by 'dharma' in day-to-day pursuit of goals. He served fervently as a parliamentarian, as a minister in the Jammu and Kashmir government and later as the longest serving Ambassador of Mongolia (1989-1999), perhaps the only monk diplomat in the world.

In his decade as a diplomat, Bakula Rinpoche established Buddhism in Mongolia and ensured peace and harmony in the region. He also propagated the rich religious and cultural heritage of Buddhism in the communist stronghold of USSR and China. He established the Asian Buddhist Conference for Peace with S Gombojac, and propagated the idea that we can overcome all challenges if we live in peace.[14] He travelled tirelessly with a focus on promoting spiritual values for the well-being of all.

When Mongolia gained independence with the fall of the Soviet Union, apart from the political, social and economic changes that took place, it also experienced a spiritual vacuum. Vesna A Wallace, an expert in Mongolia, in her writings speaks of the religious transformation and re-transformation in Mongolia. She documents the experiences of people during the re-conversation of Monoglians to Buddhism after the fall of the Soviet Union and say that the urban population, educated in Soviet schools, were especially suspicious of religion and distrusted Mongolian Buddhism.[15] It is in this context that Bakula Rinpoche, one of the most influential figures in Mongolia, worked for the revitalisation of Buddhism in Mongolia. He encouraged and regularly provided visas to Mongolians to visit India to study Buddhism, at a time when obtaining Mongolian passports was difficult.[16] Bakula Rinpoche also paid special attention to women and helped in the creation of the Lay Women Buddhist Organisation where he gave monastic ordinance to women, a first in the history of modern Mongolia.[17]

Bakula Rinpoche was known to be open and approachable. People from all over Mongolia would travel far and wide to attend the religious audiences he would hold every Saturday and seek his blessings and advice.[18] Such was the reverence for Rinpoche Bakula, that news reports at the time would often refer to him as a "living Buddha".[19] Former Mongolian President Enkhbayar once said that "a very important aspect of democratic changes in Mongolia was the revival of Buddhism. If not for Bakula Rinpoche, who else could have guided the people?".[20] It is clear that the efforts of Bakula Rinpoche were at the core of soft power diplomacy and further strengthened the bond between the two countries.

Through the work of Bakula Rinpoche in Mongolia, India's soft power grew tremendously. His activities were focused on strengthening the cultural bond between Indians and Mongolians, while also reviving Buddhism. He was instrumental in establishing the Pethub Stangey Choskor Ling Monastery in Ulaanbaatar that trained Mongolian monks in Buddhist teachings. Often, the best students would also be sent to India for further training. Kushok Bakula's single handed effort to bring about religious freedom and Buddhist revitalisation in Mongolia, a country where religion (or any form of religion) was wiped out by the Marxist regime, is phenomenal.[21]

Bakula Rinpoche was cautious of the Mongolian understanding on Buddhism in his ventures and according to G Luvsantseren, the head of the Mongolian Buddhist Studies Institute, Bakula Rinpoche's ventures were "not aimed at Indianising" the monks.[22]

During his tenure as the Indian Ambassador to Mongolia, Bakula Rinpoche ensured the viewing of the relics of the Buddha in Mongolia, which at the time were kept at the National Museum in New Delhi. The arrival of Buddha's relics in Mongolia was naturally a major event. Through these efforts he not only brought Buddhism closer to Mongolians but also enhanced the cultural understanding of Mongolians and Indians. M. Enkhbayar, the former Minister of Culture in Mongolia, had equated the "coming of the holy Buddha's relics" to "the coming of Lord Buddha to our land".[23] Through these soft gestures, India continues to hold a fond memory among Mongolians.

Bakula Rinpoche also helped setup the Indian Cultural Centre that provided a space for Mongolians to learn about Indian culture, dance and language. During his time as Ambassador, the Mongolian-Indian friendship "Nairamdal" farm was also established in the Darkhan Uul province in 1997. The Indian government supplied 1000 kilograms of "different cold resistant and early maturity wheat seeds and onion seeds" to this farm.[24] Centres like these help in promoting culture and also a better understanding of each other's countries. They act as a platform to create enthusiasm, curiosity and fondness for India's culture and way of life, thereby enabling soft power diplomacy.

Bakula Rinpoche was also credited for the peaceful transition of democracy in Mongolia. Former Mongolian President Enkhbayar, in his tribute to the Bakula Rinpoche in 2003 had praised Rinpoche for his efforts in the transition to democracy. He said that it was due to Bakula Rinpoche's presence in the country, his "advice, assistance and participation" that the transition to democracy was peaceful in Mongolia.[25]

Bakula Rinpoche's objective of centring on the Buddha's teachings at Sarnath to his five disciples' sets in motion the 'wheel of the dharma' and the 'madhyama marga', the middle path, in Ladakh and later flowed gently in the form of cultural diplomacy in Mongolia and the then stronghold of communism, USSR and China. He showed the example of how politics and spiritual values can be welded for the welfare of humanity. He also expounded the four Noble Truths and the eight-fold path of Buddha, leading to the common goals of contentment and welfare of the humanity. The four-fold path in Brahma Viharas, or virtuous life—that of benevolence, compassion, empathetic joy and equanimity—became part of Bakula Rinpoche's personality, defining the venerable Rinpoche as a symbol of soft diplomacy.

The spread of Indian influence, generally attributed to Buddhism, in Mongolia was so strong that Mongols believe the greatest river in the world to be the Ganges, and the nicest smelling wood to be sandalwood.[26] Mongol folk songs too sing praise for India. One such example is a folk song with the lines, "*Ganga l mörnii gurgaldai, Gadaa ireed dongodno*", which translates to "Only the nightingales of the Ganges, Come and sing outside". India's soft power is perhaps most visible in subtle ways and is embodied in the perceptions of people towards India. In Mongolia, it is said that a belief exists that the "sun which shines over the whole world also depends on great India".[27]

The Himalayan mountains have therefore been the foundation from where both the ancient Indian culture and Buddhism spread to different countries in Central, South East and East Asia. The influence of this spiritual confluence and reach has left its mark in the entire region and is found in art, music, literature and philosophy extending further to diplomacy. It has played an important role in the history and culture of this frontier region. This geographical location has allowed transit of cultures, trade and movement of people, assimilating religions with indigenous cultures, languages, dialects and ethnicity. India must focus on building leadership on the lines of Kushok Bakula Rinpoche, who can address the challenges of a changing geopolitical landscape and develop a synchronised common agenda on key issues of security, regional connectivity, trade, climate change, spirituality, cultural and ethnic preservation using soft power diplomacy. It is time to go back to our ancient civilisation and culture to reflect upon our collective consciousness and identity to regenerate our value systems. Soft power must not remain only in terms of rhetoric, but should translate into the domain of everyday life and academia extending to the sphere of cultural diplomacy.

NOTES

1 Niccolo Machiavelli, *The Prince: Translated by W.K Marriott* (Adelaide: eBooks@Adelaide The Univeristy of Adelaide Library, 2014), available at https://ebooks.adelaide.edu.au/m/machiavelli/niccolo/m149p/complete.html

2 Ibid.

3 Ibid.

4 Joseph S Nye, "Soft Power," *Foreign Policy,* No. 80, Twentieth Anniversary (Autumn 1990), pp. 153-171, available at https://www.jstor.org/stable/1148580, accessed on 18 September 2018).

5 Joseph S Nye, "Think Again: Soft Power", *Foreign Policy*, 23 February 2006, available at https://foreignpolicy.com/2006/02/23/think-again-soft-power/, accessed on 11 October 2018.

6 Joseph S Nye, "Notes on soft power research agenda," in Felix Berenskoetter and M. J. Williams (ed.) *Power in World Politics*, London and New York: Routlege, 2007, pp. 162-172.

7 Ibid.

8 Yu Monkh-Amgalan and G Galbayar, "Links Between Indian and Mongolian Literature: Some Perspectives" in Kulbhushan Warikoo and Sharad K. Soni (eds.) *Mongolia in the 21st Century: Society, Culture and International Relations,* New Delhi: Pentagon Press, 2010, pp. 132-138, available at https://books.google.co.in/books?id=pApejz1FQdcC&lpg=PR11&pg=PA105#v= onepage&q&f=false, accessed on 10 September 2018.

9 Daya Thussu, *Communicating India's Soft Power: Buddha to Bollywood,* New Delhi: SAGE, 2016.

10 Roger Boesche, "Moderate Machiavelli? Contrasting The Prince with Arthashastra of Kautilya", *Critical Horizons,* Vol. 3, No. 2, 2002, pp. 253-276, available at https://doi.org/10.1163/156851602760586671

11 Daya Thussu, *Communicating India's Soft Power: Buddha to Bollywood,* New Delhi: SAGE, 2016.

12 Deep K Datta-Ray, "The only shibboleth the West has is science: An interview with Bruno Latour," *Times of India*, 4 April 2011, available at https://timesofindia.indiatimes.com/interviews/The-only-shibboleth-the-West-has-is-science/articleshow/7857969.cms, accessed on 10 October 2018.

13 Martijn van Beek, "Hills Councils, Development and Democracy: Assumptions and Experiences from Ladakh", *Alternatives: Global, Local, Political,* Vol. 42, No. 4, October – December 1999, pp. 435-459, available at https://www.jstor.org/stable/40644974, accessed on 25 September 2018.

14 Vesna A Wallace, "Bakula Arhat's Journey to the North: The Life and Work of the 19th

Kushok Bakula in Russia and Mongolia," in Todd Lewis (ed.) *Buddhists: Understanding Buddhism Through the Lives of Practitioners,* Malden: John Wiley & Sons, 2004, p. 220.

15 Vesna A Wallace, "Competing Religious Conversions and Re-conversions in Contemporary Mongolia," in Arietta Papaconstantinou with Neil McLynn and Daniel L. Schwartz (eds.) *Conversion in Late Antiquity: Christianity, Islam, and Beyond. Papers from the Andrew W. Mellon Foundation Swayer Seminar, University of Oxford, 2009-2010,* Oxford: Ashgate Publishing, 2016, p. 52, available at http://www.academia.edu/30221647/Competing_Religious_ Conversions_and_Re-conversions_in_Contemporary_Mongolia. pdf

16 Ibid., p. 53

17 Vesna A Wallace, "Bakula Arhat's Journey to the North: The Life and Work of the 19th Kushok Bakula in Russia and Mongolia," in Todd Lewis (ed.) *Buddhists: Understanding Buddhism Through the Lives of Practitioners,* Malden: John Wiley & Sons, 2004, p. 223-224.

18 Nicholas D. Kristof, "Karakorum Journal; Red Tide Ebbs, Exposing Buddhism," *New York Times,* 17 July 1992, available at https://www.nytimes.com/1992/07/17/world/karakorum-journal-red-tide-ebbs-exposing-buddhism.html, accessed on 1 October 2018.

19 John Nobel Wilford, "Buddha and Genghis Khan Back in Mongolia," *New York Times,* 22 July 1991, available at https://www.nytimes.com/1991/07/22/world/buddha-and-genghis-khan-back-in-mongolia.html, accessed on 1 October 2018.

20 Vesna A Wallace, "Bakula Arhat's Journey to the North: The Life and Work of the 19th Kushok Bakula in Russia and Mongolia", in Todd Lewis (ed.) *Buddhists: Understanding Buddhism Through the Lives of Practitioners,* Malden: John Wiley & Sons, 2004, pp. 223-224.

21 Karan Singh, "Spirituality in Global Society," *India International Centre Quarterly,* Vol. 37, No. 2, Autumn 2010, pp. 26-35, available at https://www.jstor.org/stable/23006434

22 Vesna A Wallace, "Bakula Arhat's Journey to the North: The Life and Work of the 19th Kushok Bakula in Russia and Mongolia", in Todd Lewis (ed.) *Buddhists: Understanding Buddhism Through the Lives of Practitioners,* Malden: John Wiley & Sons, 2004, p. 223.

23 Ibid.

24 O Nyamdawaa, "Landlocked Mongolia and its Trade and Economic Cooperation with India" in Kulbhushan Warikoo and Sharad K. Soni (eds.) *Mongolia in the 21st Century: Society, Culture and International Relations,* New Delhi: Pentagon Press, 2010, pp. 139-153.

25 Vesna A Wallace, "Competing Religious Conversions and Re-conversions in Contemporary Mongolia," in Arietta Papaconstantinou with Neil McLynn and Daniel L. Schwartz (eds.) *Conversion in Late Antiquity: Christianity, Islam, and Beyond. Papers from the Andrew W. Mellon Foundation Swayer Seminar, University of Oxford, 2009-2010,* Oxford: Ashgate Publishing, 2016, p. 52, available at http://www.academia.edu/30221647/Competing_Religious_ Conversions_and_Re-conversions_in_Contemporary_Mongolia.pdf

26 Yu Monkh-Amgalan and G Galbayar, "Links Between Indian and Mongolian Literature: Some Perspectives" in Kulbhushan Warikoo and Sharad K. Soni (eds.) *Mongolia in the 21st Century: Society, Culture and International Relations,* New Delhi: Pentagon Press, 2010, pp. 132-138, available at https://books.google.co.in/books?id=pApejz1FQdcC&lpg= PR11& pg= PA105#v= onepage &q&f=false, accessed 10 September 2018.

27 Ibid.

14

Kushok Bakula Rinpoche: Exemplar of India's Soft Power Diplomacy

Anil Trigunayat and Shikha Aggarwal

Soft Power has gradually emerged as a dominant narrative within the discourse on International Politics. In addition, it is being increasingly recognized as a key determinant of National Power. While Soft Power is an important currency in international diplomacy, it assumes greater strategic salience for civilizational states like India and China. However, strong cultural ethos, traditions and value systems require cultural ambassadors to forge these elements into a comprehensive and articulate Soft Power strategy. In India's context one such leading personality has been Kushok Bakula Rinpoche, who is regarded as one of the finest exemplars of India's Soft Power Diplomacy. This chapter will cover this unique exposition of soft power, wherein a monk successfully carried out the diplomatic responsibilities, while transforming the society in the host country.

The usage of term 'Soft power' as a tool for influencing others is a recent phenomenon, although, history is replete with its usage. The term was first coined by Harvard University Professor Joseph Nye, who remains its most prominent proponent. He propounded it in 1990, in his book, '*Bound to Lead: Changing nature of American Power*' and further developed the concept in his 2004 book, '*Soft Power: The Means to Success in World Politics*'. The theory and its usefulness has been challenged, however, the term soft power has become immensely popular. Nye defines soft power as "the ability to get what you want through attraction rather than coercion or payments. It arises from the attractiveness of a country's culture, political ideals, and policies." He further adds that a country's soft power is enhanced when its policies are seen as legitimate by others.[1]

According to him, "Power is the ability to affect others to obtain the outcomes you want. One can affect others' behaviour in three main ways: threats of coercion ("sticks"), inducements and payments ("carrots"), and attraction that makes others want what you want."[2] He further adds that a country may elicit a favourable response in the international arena, just because others want to emulate it. This process of getting favourable outcomes co-opts others rather than coercing them and rests on a country's ability to shape other's preferences.[3] He defines co-optive power as "the ability of a country to structure a situation so that other countries develop preferences or define their interests in ways consistent with its own."[4]

Unlike hard power which is a function of countries' economic and military prowess, soft power is inherent to all national cultures. As a diplomatic tool, soft power allows nations to command international respect and authority through the attraction of their cultural systems, political ideals and policies.[5] In this sense, a meticulously crafted soft power strategy enables countries to garner international agreement for pursuing their national interests without the use of either coercion or payments. However, for soft power to be truly effective, countries' policies should be viewed as legitimate by other international actors.[6] Therefore, nations that aspire to advance their soft power potential should adopt a constructive and ideational approach in their cultural norms, domestic policies and foreign policy framework and not be governed by strict realpolitik dynamics. As such, it can be argued that soft power allows countries to shape the preferences of other countries[7] and set the agenda for international politics.

India has been the fountain of soft power for centuries and its rich heritage is what Indians are extremely proud of. Values of love, peace, tolerance, divergent schools of thought and philosophy, religious diversity and coexistence, abstemiousness and the profound thought process behind the dictum "Vasudhaiva Kutumbakam",[8] "Aham Brahmasmi"[9] and Buddhist thought have endeared India and Indians to the world while endowing it with the inimitable reverence and unconquerable spirit. Message of Lord Buddha and Indian mythological lore and philosophical treatises are explored and loved across Asia and the world. Yoga has become the preferred mode of meditation and well-being across the world which is clearly evident in the enthusiastic celebration of the International Day of Yoga on 21 June 2015 ever since it was approved by the United Nations General Assembly (UNGA) with the highest number of votes. It is also an acknowledged fact that India has been on the forefront of science, medicine, mathematics, algebra, surgery and astronomy.

Mahatma Gandhi and his non-violent and principled fight against colonialism of mind and empires ignited the spirit of freedom among large number of colonised countries. All these factors combined, give India the moral edge and inimitable soft power that it richly deserves and makes it most envied. More importantly they have become an integral part of India's soft power projection. In modern times, India has emerged as the largest producer of films and Indian films especially the acronym "Bollywood" evokes an unusual curiosity, charm and lavish expanse of rich platitudes of the stories that quickly connect people from across continents with India. In the 21st century India is acknowledged as a global power in the field of Information Technology (IT) and is looked up with respect and possibility of emulation and cooperation. This ipso-facto gives India an edge and modern area of influence as a knowledge economy.

Widely recognized for his various avatars as a great scholar, a seasoned parliamentarian, and an international diplomat, Kushok Bakula represented India's soft power credentials in all its facets. Kushok Bakula's diplomatic sojourn began in 1989, when he was appointed as India's ambassador to Mongolia. Not only was Bakula the first monk ever to have been designated as the Head of an Indian diplomatic mission, his tenure came at a crucial juncture of Mongolian history when the country was preparing for its transformation from a totalitarian communist regime to a democratic polity.[10] While the revolution of 1990 ushered in a new political environment in the country, communist legacy left a spiritual vacuum within the Mongolian society. It was under these socio-political dynamics that Rinpoche Bakula committed himself to the revival of Buddhism in Mongolia, and thereby to the rejuvenation of the civilizational and spiritual connections between India and Mongolia. His efforts were also helped by the fact that people in Mongolia believed in the prophesy that Arhat Bakula will come to revitalise Buddhism in their land. By the time Rinpoche Bakula was posted to Ulaanbaatar, this hope had turned into an ardent belief as the people had been suffering disenfranchisement of their religion since 1930s when the Communist regime had started decimating and destroying the monasteries. Most Mongolians firmly believed in the prophesy and felt that with the arrival of Rinpoche Bakula their redemption was complete.[11]

Kushok Bakula's efforts at promoting Buddhism in Mongolia entailed and represented the cardinal tenet of Indian soft power diplomacy, i.e. respect for national cultures and sensitivities. Towards this end, Bakula's ventures in Mongolia remained fully cognizant and appreciative of the Mongolian Buddhist culture and were not directed towards Indianizing or Tibetanizing the Buddhism landscape in that country.[12] Furthermore, Kushok Bakula's religious outreach in Mongolia was not informed either by rigid ritualism or an evangelical spirit. As India's ambassador plenipotentiary, Bakula devoted his religious activities to the spiritual, political and social advancement of the people. Rinpoche Bakula's mission was not limited to the revival of Buddhism in Mongolia, rather it encompassed a vision to bind the regional countries through the spread of the Buddhist philosophy of 'Ananda Marga'. It is for these reasons that he is revered as the incarnation of Bakul Arhat- one of the 16 Arhats of Thathagath Buddha in Mongolia and the entire Himalayan region.[13]

In order to revive Buddhism in Mongolia, Bakula adopted a multi-dimensional approach that involved restoration of Buddhist monasteries and temples that had been destroyed during the communist regime, facilitating institutionalized training for the Monks, establishment of new monasteries, and translation of Buddhist texts in the Mongolian language. While these initiatives remained important, it was Bakula's personal charm and integrity that earned him the revered status that he continues to hold among the Mongolian political echelons and the larger public psyche.

Ambassador Bakula was a kind man and was a source of sympathy, empathy and benediction. He was benevolence personified and became almost Godlike and was venerated as such by the Mongolians who due to providential connection with Lord Buddha always looked up to India for their religious upliftment and spiritual affiliation. Wherever Rinpoche went, large crowds followed him or stood in obeisance with folded hands for his blessings. In fact, the Indian embassy became a pilgrimage of sorts for many during his tenure. During those days, it was not uncommon to see miles long queue of people in front of the Embassy especially on the weekends to seek his blessings. As the number of followers continued to increase, the Embassy decided to install the Yurt gifted to the Ambassador by the locals at the backyard of the embassy building to receive his followers. People's faith and veneration for the Rinpoche was so deep that he was widely believed to possess magical powers that could cure any illness or ailments.

Early into his assignment, Bakula recognized the need for proper training for Mongolian monks. In order to deal with the issue, he procured Indian visas and funding for the monks who wished to study at Tibetan monasteries in India such as Gomang, Sera, the Buddhist School of Dialectics in Dharamsala, the Central Institute of Tibetan Higher Studies. This was no mean feat as during those days, it was rather difficult for the Mongolian people to acquire such visas.[14] In order to let his work and public service continue even after he was gone, Rinpoche was very keen to have his own monastery in Ulaanbatar which could be an extension of his Pethub monastery in Leh. When he broached the idea regarding a suitable piece of land in 1991, the then Mayor of Ulaanbaatar, Enebish asked him to choose any place of his liking. Today, Pethub Monastery stands as the citadel of humanity and education for the Mongolians and carries on the legacy of Rinpoche Bakula.[15] Later, Mayor Enebish turned into one of Rinpoche's disciples. Additionally, to compensate for the lack of qualified teachers in Buddhist monasteries in Mongolia, Bakula bought in highly qualified lamas from Ladakh and Sikkim to educate the students in these institutions.[16]

As a fervent advocate of human rights, Kushok Bakula fully appreciated the spiritual needs of Mongolian women. To ensure that women emerged as equal stakeholders in the spiritual narrative of the Mongolian society, Bakula started the Lay Women Buddhist Organization. In an unparalleled gesture, Kushok Bakula gave monastic ordination to women, the first ever in modern Mongolia.[17] Inspired by the endeavours of Kushok Bakula, the International Buddhist Institute was established in Mongolia. The aim of the institute is to enable international students to conduct research on Mongolian Buddhism.

In another first to the long list of his achievements as India's cultural ambassador, Rinpoche Bakula used his stature and personal initiative to bring the relics of Buddha to Ulaanbaatar in 1993. Needless to say that this gesture on the part of Indian government has become a hallmark event in the contemporary annals of Buddhism in Mongolia. More significantly, it was a momentous experience for the Mongolian people who had for long witnessed religious persecution, and were denied the practice of their faith. In fact, former Cultural Minister and President, N Enkhbayar equated the coming of holy relics to the coming of Lord Buddha to Mongolia.[18] Further, in 1991, Kushok Bakula facilitated the visit of His Holiness, the Dalai Lama to Mongolia. This visit was crucial as it re-established and celebrated the historical connect between the Mongolian people and the Sakya order of Tibetan Buddhism. However, in order to achieve this feat, Bakula had to withstand much Chinese pressure.

During his life time, both as a diplomat and before, Bakula did not restrict his soft power diplomacy to Mongolia alone. After learning about the suppression and virtual demise of Buddhism in countries ruled by communist regime, he made it his mission to revive Buddhism in these countries. He regularly travelled to Beijing, and tried his best to propagate Buddhist philosophy in both USSR and China. He was the first Buddhist monk to visit USSR in 1968 on the invitation of Soviet Ministry for Religious Affairs. During this historic visit, he was accompanied by Bato Tsybenovich Tsybenov, who was Soviet Adviser for Religious Affairs, and travelled to Leningrad (now called Saint Petersburg) and Buryatia. His visits to Ulan Ude the capital of Buryatia drew large Buddhist crowds. Thereafter, he made many other visits to USSR, despite the communist regime's suppression of Buddhism. He also appealed to the Soviet authorities to return Buddhist temple in St Petersburg, which had been constructed by Buryat Lama Agwan Dorjev and had been converted into an Institute of Zoology. During his visits, he also travelled to the regions of Buryatia and Kalmykia, which have substantive Buddhist Mongol population. He helped to revive Buddhism in these regions. In 1989, he became the first Buddhist teacher to visit Kalmykia, where Buddhist religion and Kalmyk culture had been totally destroyed by Stalin's region.[19] He established the Asian Buddhist Conference for Peace with S Gombojac and remained its President. With its international headquarters in Mongolia, it has been propagating the idea that peace is essential to overcome all challenges in life.[20]

Bakula's reputation as a monk was so strong that even the usually wary Chinese respected him a lot and even agreed to arrange his visit to Tibet in 1992. In fact, the Chinese never discounted the possibility of Rinpoche being the 19th reincarnate of one of the 16 close disciples of Lord Buddha. Ambassador during his visits to Beijing expressed his desire to meet Ngapho Nagawang Jigme who was the Vice Chairman of the Standing Committee of the National People's Congress as well as Chairman of the Standing Committee of the People's Congress of the Tibet Autonomous Region. He was also the President of the Buddhist Association of China. As such, Ngapho Jigme was well versed in Buddhist history and culture and was aware of Rinpoche Bakula's stature in the Buddhist hierarchy. Rinpoche had last visited Tibet only in 1955 and wanted to revisit the memory of his younger years there. Finally he met Ngapho Jigme who not only agreed to arrange the visit but also spoke to the Foreign Minister to facilitate Rinpoche's visa. Due to his intervention the visit was hosted by Tibet Development Fund. Rinpoche's visit to Tibet was significant in many ways as it allowed him to understand the prevailing situation in Tibet and to scout for any opportunity which could have helped resolve the impasse with regard to the Government of People's Republic of China and His Holiness Dalai Lama. In his recently released book "Kushok Bakula Rinpoche: The Architect of Modern Ladakh" Sonam Wangchuk Shakspo gives a vivid account of the visit, meetings and interactions.[21]

During the early days of democracy in Mongolia, there was a dearth of Buddhist literature in Mongolian language. To overcome this challenge, Rinpoche Bakula encouraged N. Enkhbayar to translate *The Teaching of the Buddha* from English to Mongolian. Thus, the sacred book was made accessible to ordinary Mongolian people.[22]

As India's ambassador, Kushok Bakula constantly sought ways to strengthen India's cultural relations with Mongolia. One of his primary concerns was to create better educational and professional opportunities for the young Mongolians. Towards this end, Rinpoche Bakula set up the Indian Cultural Centre to enable the Mongolian people to study Indian languages and classical dance forms. He also helped to establish the Mongolian-India Friendship Farm in the city of Darkhan, and the Training and Industrial Centre in Ulaanbaatar.[23] Moreover, Bakula secured the first ever Line of Credit for Mongolia under the Indian government's India Technical and Economic Cooperation (ITEC) programme. This was a significant achievement as Mongolia became the first country outside India's immediate neighbourhood to secure assistance under ITEC. In addition to this, Bakula facilitated open ended availability of ITEC scholarships for the Mongolian working professionals.

Rinpoche Bakula served in Mongolia for a period of ten years. During his decade long tenure, Bakula made Mongolia his home and has left a legacy of love, sympathy, empathy and compassion. In recognition for his exemplary and yeoman services to the Mongolian nation and people, the Mongolian government conferred their highest civilian honour, the "Polar Star" upon him. Bakula's contributions to Mongolia and his stature among the Mongolian people have been aptly summed up by the first President of democratic Mongolia P. Ochirbat in his words that "Ambassador Bakula Rinpoche was a statesman, diplomat and Buddhist clergy who carved out his own niche in the history of Mongolia. He recognised the historic necessity to develop Mongolia's national culture to restore the glory of Buddhism- an inseparable part of its cultural heritage. He was divine messenger at the time of peaceful transformation from communism to democracy and a source of inspiration to our people."[24]

Bakula's popularity was so extensive in Mongolia that the British and US Ambassadors often believed that by posting Ambassador Bakula -a Buddhist monk to Mongolia, Government of India had done a coup of sorts since no one could have commanded the respect and affection Rinpoche enjoyed in the host country. While there is no evidence to support such a hypothesis, Rinpoche Bakula's influence over the Mongolian people indeed remained unparalleled during this tenure and continues to remain so even today. A case in this point remains the 1992 visit by Vice President Dr Shankar Dayal Sharma. Though he was the Head of the State, Dr Sharma could not command the same popularity among the Mongols as Bakula did. In fact, this fact was mentioned by the Vice President himself during his address to the Rajya Sabha.

Kushok Bakula was the real exemplar of soft power diplomacy with a lasting impact that continues to drive the Indo-Mongolian relations into the higher orbits. As a religious leader, politically astute negotiator and a fine diplomat, Rinpoche Kushok Bakula, has left an indelible imprint on the historical landscape of our relations with Mongolia. Posterity will indeed benefit from this deep rooted synergy.[25]

NOTES

1 Joseph S Nye Jr, *Soft Power: The Means to Success in World Power*, New York: BBS Public Affairs, 2004, p. x.

2 Joseph S. Nye Jr. "Public Diplomacy and Soft Power," *The ANNALS of the American Academy of Political and Social Science,* Vol. 682, No. 1, March 2019, p. 94.

3 Joseph S Nye Jr, n.1, p.5.

4 Joseph S Nye Jr, "Soft Power", *Foreign Policy,* No 80, Twentieth Anniversary (Autumn 1990), p.168.

5 Joseph S. Nye Jr. n.2, 94.
6 Joseph S. Nye Jr., n.1, 11.
7 Ibid, p. 1.
8 Vasudhaiva Kutumbakam is a Sanskrit phrase, which means "the world is one family".
9 Aham Brahmasmi is the central essence of the Advaita philosophy founded by Adi Shankaracharya. A-dvaita means non-dualism. It says the creator and his creation are not two (dual) things, but are one.
10 For an understanding of Bakula's role in ensuring that the Democracy movement in Mongolia remains peaceful, refer to Rinchen Norbu Wangchuk, "The Extraordinary Ladakhi Monk who helped Bring Peaceful Democracy to Mongolia," *The Better India,* 26 April 2018, available at https://www.thebetterindia.com/139355/bakula-rinpoche-ladakhi-monastery-democracy-mongolia-sushma-swaraj/, accessed on 8 April 2019.
11 Vensa A. Wallace, "The Life and Work of the Nineteenth Kushok Bakula in Russia and Mongolia," *Ladakh Review,* 4, 2018, pp. 32-33
12 G. Luvsantseren quoted in Vensa A. Wallace, "The Life and Work of the Nineteenth Kushok Bakula in Russia and Mongolia," *Ladakh Review,* 4, 2018, p. 39
13 Mohan Bhagwat, "A Tribute to Kushok Bakula Rinpoche," *Ladakh Review,* 4, 2018, p. 44
14 Vensa A. Wallace, n. 11, p. 38
15 Rinchen Norbu Wangchuk, n. 10.
16 Vensa A. Wallace, n.11, p. 38
17 Ibid.
18 Sonam Wangchuk Shakspo, "Who was Bakula Rinpochee for Mongolia," *The Mongolian Observer*, Edition no.16, 10 August 2016, available at https://mongolianobserver.mn/bakula-rinpoche-mongolia/, accessed on 15 April 2019.
19 Vensa A. Wallace, n.11, pp. 35-36.
20 Daljit Sen Adel, "Kushok Bakula-The Man of the Century", *Ladakh Review*, Vol. 4, 2018, p.53.
21 Sonam Wangchuk Shakspo *KushokBakula Rinpoche: The Architect of Modern Ladakh*, Indraprastha Press, New Delhi, pp. 323-338
22 Vensa A. Wallace, n.11, p. 39
23 Sonam Wangchuk Shakspo, n.18.
24 Ochirbat, Punslamaagiin, "Bakula Rinpoche Who Left Behind a Bright Influence in Mongolia," *In Commemoration of the 91st Birth Anniversary of HH Bakula Rinpoche*, Pethub Buddhist Center, 2008, 55-56.
25 Anil Trigunayat served with Kushok Bakula Rimpoche, when he was the Indian Ambassador to Mongolia at Ulaanbaatar. The chapter primarily draws from his personal experience of serving with Kushok Bakula.

Index